Praise for *Bouncing Forward*

"*Bouncing Forward* shows us how adversity can turn us toward our deepest inner resources of trust, wisdom, and love. Through a wonderful mix of inspirational interviews, current science, Buddhist teachings, and her own deep understanding, Michaela Haas guides us in discovering the sacredness and grace that flows through these human lives."

—Tara Brach, PhD, author of *Radical Acceptance*
and *True Refuge*

"In *Bouncing Forward*, Dr. Haas weaves engaging stories of modern survival with uplifting and often surprising takeaways. Readers are given tools for not only surviving life's inevitable tough times, but consciously thriving because of them."

—Gay Hendricks, PhD, author of *The Big Leap*
and *Conscious Loving*

"Michaela Haas's latest book, *Bouncing Forward,* breaks through our great confusion around how to be happy. Full of goodness, this book shares stories, including her own, of people who have suffered in many ways and come through it into strength and love. Together these varied living examples reveal an important truth: ultimately there is no way to avoid pain in life, and turning toward our challenges, whatever they may be, *is* the way to real happiness."

—Sharon Salzberg, author of *Lovingkindness*
and *Real Happiness*

"*Bouncing Forward* propels our entire understanding of posttraumatic growth to a new level. Dr. Haas's integration of the life stories of survivors-thrivers with the latest scientific research about discovering the advantages of adversity and finding meaning in the messiness, and her very practical tools for working with difficulties, even disasters, shows the reader how to cultivate the mind-set of resilience that can catalyze healing and growth from catastrophe. Brilliant, inspiring, to be read, reread, and treasured."

—Linda Graham, MFT, author of *Bouncing Back: Rewiring
Your Brain for Maximum Resilience and Well-Being*

"This groundbreaking book offers a path to peace and contentment in the midst of life's most difficult challenges. Michaela Haas shows us how struggle and trauma can lead to wisdom, growth, and happiness. *Bouncing Forward* is a rich collection of inspiring and heartfelt interviews, personal recollections, and scientific research. We can train the mind to be resilient and to find life's blessings no matter what hardships we've faced or are facing. This is a book to treasure and to read over and over."

—Toni Bernhard, author of *How to Be Sick, How to Wake Up,*
and *How to Live Well with Chronic Pain and Illness*

"*Bouncing Forward* is a testament to the strength, resilience, and hope of the human psyche and spirit. Michaela Haas deftly weaves interviews with a dozen individuals from across the world with her experiences, ideas, and guidance, to help readers understand that 'we are stronger than we think.' *Bouncing Forward* is a wonderful and entertaining read, as well as a reasoned and reasonable guide to resilient living."

—Sam Goldstein, PhD, coauthor of *The Power of Resilience*
and *Raising Resilient Children*

"Michaela Haas has written one of the most helpful, engaging, informative nonfiction books that I've read in a long while. It will be useful for absolutely everyone. Highly recommended."

—Samantha Dunn, author of *Failing Paris*
and *Not by Accident*

"In this volume, Michaela Haas applies the wisdom of Buddhist mind training to real-life experiences in the modern world, thereby enriching the Buddhist tradition as well as our current understanding of ways to fruitfully transcend the miseries of the past, present, and future."

—B. Alan Wallace, author of *Genuine Happiness*
and *The Attention Revolution*

BOUNCING FORWARD

Transforming Bad Breaks into Breakthroughs

Michaela Haas, PhD

ENLIVEN BOOKS

—

ATRIA

NEW YORK LONDON TORONTO SYDNEY NEW DELHI

ENLIVEN

An Imprint of Simon & Schuster, Inc.
1230 Avenue of the Americas
New York, NY 10020

First Enliven Books hardcover edition October 2015

ENLIVEN BOOKS and colophon are trademarks of Simon & Schuster, Inc.

For information about special discounts for bulk purchases, please contact Simon
& Schuster Special Sales at 1-866-506-1949 or business@simonandschuster.com.

The Simon & Schuster Speakers Bureau can bring authors to your live event.
For more information or to book an event, contact the Simon & Schuster Speakers
Bureau at 1-866-248-3049 or visit our website at www.simonspeakers.com.

Jacket design by Rodrigo Corral Design Inc.
Interior design by Paul Dippolito

Manufactured in the United States of America

10 9 8 7 6 5 4 3 2 1

Library of Congress Cataloging-in-Publication Data

Haas, Michaela, 1970–
    Bouncing forward : transforming bad breaks into breakthroughs / Michaela Haas.
        pages cm
    Includes bibliographical references.
    1. Resilience (Personality trait). 2. Adjustment (Psychology).
    3. Attitude (Psychology).
    I. Title.
    BF698.35.R47H33 2015
    155.2'4—dc23
    2015019790

ISBN 978-1-5011-1512-7
ISBN 978-1-5011-1515-8 (ebook)

Contents

This one is for you, Struggling. For you, Drowning.
For you, Surviving. And for you, Rising.
You are my heroes and sheroes.

BOUNCING
FORWARD

Introduction

Crisis as a launching pad for growth

Only in darkness can you see the stars.
—MARTIN LUTHER KING JR.

The sucker that took me out does not even have a name: a teeny, untraceable virus. And yet, the invisible culprit ambushed and flattened me, whisking me away to a new benchmark of low.

I was in my twenties and had taken a sabbatical from my hectic job as a reporter to embark on a PhD and study the wise minds of the Tibetan yogis I was becoming fond of. Traveling solo through Asia was part of my grand adventure, my express ticket to Cloud Nine.

But after two semesters at preeminent Buddhist colleges in North India and Nepal, I crashed. Completely. The first blow was a fever so high and numbing that I was unable to leave my bed for two weeks. A cough and dizziness kept shaking me after the fever subsided. Then severe food poisoning gutted me. Some of the bowls of noodle soup the Tibetan grandmothers prepared in the tiny wood shacks must have contained unfiltered water, boiling with dye from the nearby carpet factories that let their toxic waste stream freely into the groundwater. The Nepalese doctors prescribed antibiotics in megadoses, three different kinds of pills so enormous I could hardly swallow them whole. They only aggravated the nausea. I am persistent, though, so I refused to give up on my quest to understand this intriguing culture and motored on. I kept breathing the diesel-filled air, feasting on the spicy chili in the cheap guesthouses, diving into the wondrous world of meditation and mantras. Until a few months later, when I reached a dead end.

No matter how much I pushed, my body just wouldn't obey. Struck by a crippling fatigue, I returned to the French countryside where my spouse lived at the time, hoping the care of friends and Western doctors would build me back up. I thought of myself as resilient and resourceful. As a TV presenter I had hosted live talk shows in large arenas and thoroughly enjoyed the adrenaline of unpredictable situations; as a reporter I loved researching tricky assignments and was used to pursuing questions until getting answers. I would figure this out, too.

But the local doctors were baffled and unable to offer a cure. The diseases they tested me for escalated in scare factor—HIV? Multiple sclerosis? Brain tumor? I grew increasingly weak, because I could hardly keep any food down. Simple tasks I'd taken for granted—such as a quick dash to the supermarket—became as daunting as my ascent toward the base camp of Mount Everest just a few months before. On some days I couldn't form a coherent sentence nor remember the names of my closest friends.

At first, everybody was very sympathetic, but when the illness dragged on for weeks and months and then for the better part of a year, most of my friends bolted, including my spouse. I watched my whole life wash away from me—my health, my career, my joy, and eventually my friendships, my marriage, and my old self as I knew it. Everything tumbled down a steep ravine.

Compared to the massive tragedies I'd witnessed as a reporter in emergency rooms and poverty-stricken countries, my suffering seemed trivial, especially since I had just spent months with Tibetan refugees who had lost everything—their homeland, their families, their health—and yet they managed to navigate their life in exile with a cheerfulness and compassion I deeply admired. I felt like my pain had no right to be so devastating, but I was overwhelmed by riptides of hopelessness that swept me away.

Ever since I watched my grandfather succeed as a businessman and father of five despite his crippling injury from polio, I'd wondered: how is it possible that some people emerge from pain fortified? Throughout my decades as a reporter, when I interviewed tsunami victims and torture survivors, these questions tugged at me: Why do some people fall apart in a crisis while others not only survive, but thrive? What makes the difference?

When I was down for the count, this quandary became deeply personal. How could I glue the smithereens of my life back together and become whole again? Had my resilience just been a mirage?

Going beyond what the naysayers say

Resilience is such a catchy concept. Estée Lauder sells "Resilience Lift Extreme" makeup, retailers market Resilience Shampoo, and Hanes produced Resilience pantyhose.[1] While I'd been pummeled by the virus, I wished getting in resilient shape was as easy as putting on the right pantyhose!

re·sil·ience

   : the ability to become strong, healthy, or successful again after something bad happens.

   : the ability of something to return to its original shape after it has been pulled, stretched, pressed, bent, etc.[2]

The everyday definition of resilience entails a sense of bouncing back from a severe crisis, but for me, the idea that we can "bounce back" from a devastating blow and "return to our original shape" falls short. We never forget the ones we've lost or the arduous struggles we've fought. The lives we lead are markedly different before and after a trauma, because these losses and struggles transform and profoundly change us.

This book is not about bouncing back, but rather about bouncing *forward*. About letting the fire of trauma temper and teach us. The title is a nod to Dr. Maya Angelou's definition of rising above hardship: "It's also a bouncing *forward*, going beyond what the naysayers said."[3]

Most people have heard of posttraumatic stress. Yet, beyond the medical community, few are aware of the evidence of posttraumatic *growth*. It may seem paradoxical to even put the words "trauma" and "growth" next to each other in one sentence. And yet, survivors and experts begin to focus increasingly on the possibility that we could use both the descent and the lessons we learn from climbing out of the ditch for a greater good in our own life and to help others. The US Army, for instance, has updated their definition of resilience to include "the mental, physical, emotional, and behavioral ability to face and cope with adversity, adapt to change, recover, *learn and grow* from setbacks."[4]

According to Richard Tedeschi, posttraumatic growth's leading researcher, as many as 90 percent of survivors report at least *one* aspect of posttraumatic growth, such as a renewed appreciation for life or a deeper connection to their heart's purpose. This does not happen immediately or easily, and rarely by itself. We need to actively work toward positive change, and we need the right tools and support in order to transform a bad break into a breakthrough.

The groundbreaking science of posttraumatic growth is still new, ever expanding and adding fresh insights. Psychologist Stephen Joseph is not the only one to regard it as "one of the most exciting of all the recent advances in clinical psychology, because it promises to radically alter our ideas about trauma—especially the notion that trauma inevitably leads to a damaged and dysfunctional life."[5]

A crisis is not a cul-de-sac, but rather a watershed moment. What we do next matters: advance or retreat, take a turn south or north, run or hide, crawl or fly. We can avert our eyes or dig deeper, try harder or grow softer, close down or break open.

Cracking the resilience code

After my own crisis, I never gained my health back fully, and my life has not been the same since. My body is an unstable companion that regularly gives out on me. My physical immune system has gone haywire, some of it beyond repair. Instead I have had to go deeper to find strategies that will strengthen the immune system of my soul.

The fundamental question is not whether we encounter suffering—because we all do. "It is how we work with suffering so that it leads to awakening the heart and going beyond the habitual views and actions that perpetuate suffering," Buddhist teacher Pema Chödrön says. "How do we actually use suffering so that it transforms our being and that of those with who we come in contact? How can we stop running from pain and reacting against it in ways that destroy us as well as others?"[6]

I didn't write this book because I have all the answers. I wrote it because I have questions. I set out to ask masters of resilience how they found strength in adversity. By researching their life stories, perhaps a bit of their magic would rub off on me. Did they have a resilience code, and could I crack it?

I interviewed civil rights icon Maya Angelou about overcoming her childhood traumas, drummed with Def Leppard star Rick Allen, fed puppies with ex-POW Rhonda Cornum on her farm in Kentucky, visited autistic animal activist Temple Grandin in Colorado, went to my first FanFest with genetic wonder woman Meggie Zahneis, and explored Berlin nightlife with famed jazz guitarist Coco Schumann, who played for his life in Auschwitz. I cheered on paralyzed surfers as they navigated eight-foot waves, learned about the power of bearing witness from Buddhist teacher Roshi Bernie Glassman, and talked with Canadian business consultant Alain Beauregard about his realization that cancer was "the greatest gift" he was ever given. I sat with Tibetan yogis in the Himalayas, attended the US Army's resilience boot camp, and spoke with pioneers of a burgeoning movement of psychotherapists, scientists, and medical professionals who are trying to pinpoint what exactly it is that makes some people grow in the midst of adversity.

It is at this interface of Western psychology, Asian wisdom, and army toughness that our journey begins. We will look at crisis from different angles: physical, mental, emotional, psychological, and spiritual. You will meet people who have approached pain from seemingly opposite perspectives—hard-bitten soldiers, soft-spoken Zen masters, creative entertainers—and yet their best strategies to tackle these pains turn out to be surprisingly similar.

My interviewees are role models for people everywhere

who are exploring their life purpose while facing challenges. One of the most insightful ways we can progress is by studying the biographies of people who have mastered the art of bouncing forward.

How did they summon such courage? Their world has shattered. Somehow, they survived.

Now, what?

The phoenix rises from the ashes

On her sixteenth birthday, Malala Yousafzai gave her first public speech since being attacked by a masked Taliban gunman who shot her in the shoulder, neck, and skull. In front of five hundred young education activists at the United Nations, Malala renewed her vow to fight for education: "The terrorists thought they would change my aims and stop my ambitions, but nothing changed in my life except this: Weakness, fear, and hopelessness died. Strength, power, and courage were born."

When Nelson Mandela was sworn in as president of post-apartheid South Africa, he invited one of his former prison guards, a man who had helped to keep him incarcerated for twenty-seven years, to witness the oath from the front row. Even while behind bars, Mandela refused to succumb to hate. He truly lived up to the words he wrote his wife Winnie from prison: "Difficulties break some men but make others."[7]

Less than a month after a tiger shark bit off her arm while she surfed off the coast of Kauai, thirteen-year-old Bethany Hamilton got back on the board, and today she continues to compete in international surfing with one arm. "You must not let disability take control of your life," she realized. "Attitude is everything. There are no limits."[8]

The phoenix had to go through the fire and be reduced to

ashes before he could rise again to new heights. There was a glimmer in the ashes that never ceased, and from this glimmer the mythical bird fanned the fire of life again.

This is a book about modern phoenixes, women and men who overcame profound trials: chronic illness, loss, cancer, accidents, war, Auschwitz. They not only rose to these challenges but they also emerged stronger, more determined, and wiser.

My hope is that these stories will resonate with fibers in your own being, and will energize and enliven you just like they have inspired me.

We are stronger than we think

Few of us will be attacked by a shark or targeted by the Taliban, but we all face profound tests. Pain comes in all patterns and proportions, stitched together in a patchwork quilt with pleasure and joy that threads through our lives.

There are the lowercase pains: the unpaid bills, the cancer scare, the worry about Johnny being bullied in school. And then there are the uppercase pains that crank up the volume until we whimper, our fist raised at life, "Why are you doing this to me?!?"

At first, I had suspected that just a few superhuman outliers, the likes of Malala and Mandela, managed to turn trials into triumphs. Though they surely exceed in courage and wisdom, they are not made of a different fabric than you and me. While caring for the very real pain of survivors who suffer from posttraumatic stress, trauma therapists tell us that most people will survive painful life events, loss, and accidents with few detectable long-term consequences. None of us floats through life on a cloud, without experiencing the loss of a loved one, without grave illness, without at least one or possibly several life-threatening events. It is normal that we struggle with what life throws at us. We're not alone in this.

When doctors and psychiatrists research loss, grief, or trauma, by default they often pay more attention to the patients who suffer the most. However, the majority of trauma survivors eventually attest to a renewed zest for life, major empathetic growth, and increased emotional maturity not despite, but *because of* their painful experiences and sometimes *simultaneously* with posttraumatic stress. We are so vulnerable, yet tenacious at the same time.

As Paralympic sprinter and double amputee Aimee Mullins says: "People have continually wanted to talk to me about overcoming adversity, and I'm going to make an admission: this phrase never sat right with me. . . . Implicit in this phrase of 'overcoming adversity' is the idea that success, or happiness, is about emerging on the other side of a challenging experience unscathed or unmarked by the experience, as if my successes in life have come about from an ability to sidestep or circumnavigate the presumed pitfalls of a life with prosthetics, or what other people perceive as my disability. But, in fact, we are changed. We are marked, of course, by a challenge, whether physically, emotionally, or both. And I'm going to suggest that this is a good thing. Adversity isn't an obstacle that we need to get around in order to resume living our life. It's part of our life. And I tend to think of it like my shadow. Sometimes I see a lot of it, sometimes there's very little, but it's always with me. . . .

There is adversity and challenge in life, and it's all very real and relative to every single person, but the question isn't whether or not you're going to meet adversity, but how you're going to meet it. So, our responsibility is not simply shielding those we care for from adversity, but preparing them to meet it well."[9]

This is the focus of *Bouncing Forward*: to open our eyes to possibilities.

My hope is that this book will offer you a new perspective on pain. A new meaning of life. A renewed sense of optimism. Because a resilient mindset not only fortifies us in challenging times, but the same qualities and skills help us in our everyday lives as well. In fact, ideally we cultivate resilience while the proverbial waters are smooth so that we have a buffer and good sailing skills when the going gets rough.

Researching these life stories has a goal: to find out what protects us and those around us from unnecessary suffering; to discover strategies to intervene when life's trajectory goes ballistic; and to help the healing. And not only to heal but also to use the crisis as a launching pad for a new beginning.

"My life is my message," Gandhi said. The life stories assembled here send a strong message: don't give up!

Over the following chapters, we will explore some of the skills we need to face life's perils and pitfalls. Our upbringing plays a role, and so do genetic factors, resources, social skills, and our purpose in life. Some of these factors are beyond our control. We cannot control the tides of life, terrorist attacks, drunk drivers, or the upstairs neighbor cranking up the volume of Metallica, but we have control over the most important ingredient: our mind.

Many think of resilience as a kind of Teflon quality, an impenetrable armor that magically wards off pain and suffering. Most likely, this magic potion exists only in Hollywood and hairspray ads.

The mavens of posttraumatic growth tell a different story: that resilience is a matter of small steps, of inching forward

one breath at a time. Only after they embraced theiɾ
ing and after they let it penetrate them to the core did things
change. As we will see, posttraumatic growth is quite the opposite of Rambo's grin-and-bear-it bravado. In fact, the lone
cowboy who thinks asking for help is a weakness is the one
most at risk. Covering up a scar with a smiley-face Band-Aid
does not lessen the pain either. Growth arises, quite to the
contrary, from acknowledging our wounds and allowing ourselves to be vulnerable. This might include recognizing the
traumas we have created ourselves.

Think of it as a grand experiment: what would happen if
we opened up instead of closing down, if we let the pain in
rather than warding it off?

Father Thomas Merton writes: "Indeed, the truth that
many people never understand, until it is too late, is that the
more you try to avoid suffering, the more you suffer, because
smaller and more insignificant things begin to torture you,
in proportion to your fear of being hurt. The one who does
most to avoid suffering is, in the end, the one who suffers
the most, and his suffering comes to him from things so little
and so trivial that one can say that it is no longer objective at
all. It is his own existence, his own being, that is at once the
subject and the source of his pain, and his very existence and
consciousness is his greatest torture."[10]

Acceptance, openness, flexibility, optimism, patience, mindfulness, empathy, compassion, resourcefulness, determination,
courage, and forgiveness are all part of a resilient mindset.
These are qualities we can train in. Maybe there is a "resilience
makeup" after all. We just can't buy it in a store.

PART I

BEYOND RESILIENCE

Strategies for strengthening our soul's immune system

Dear Pain,

I think we both underestimated each other. I underestimated your perseverance, your nuclear force to overwhelm me, and your unbroken willingness to have a place in my life. But you underestimated my tenacity, too.

Sincerely Yours,
Hanging in There

1. Survive

"Fear is not a word I even use"
Brigadier General Rhonda Cornum endured being held prisoner in the first Iraq war and now passes on her lessons in optimism to every US soldier[1]

Experience is not what happens to you; it's what you do with what happens to you.

—ALDOUS HUXLEY

When Rhonda Cornum came to, it was dark and, for a moment, absolutely still. *Am I alive?* she wondered.

Then she saw the flames.

"Fire. Fuel lines. Explosion coming."[2] Survival commands rattled through her brain, and she wiggled herself out of the tangled metal that was once a helicopter, away from smoldering debris and the five mangled bodies of her crew. On the breezy afternoon of February 27, 1991, Dr. Rhonda Cornum's Black Hawk helicopter had been shot down over the Iraqi desert. As a flight surgeon of "Operation Desert Storm," the then thirty-six-year-old medic had been on a mission to rescue an injured soldier, but her helicopter had flown into a barrage of bullets.

She looked up to see five Iraqi soldiers towering above her with pointed rifles. One of them reached down to grab her arm. The touch sparked a jolt of pain so severe that she was immediately sure of two things: she wasn't dead, but she was badly injured.

Her captors stripped off her army gear, her 9-millimeter Beretta, her survival vest, her flak jacket. They were baffled when they pulled off the helmet and long brown hair flowed down. A flurry of nervous shouts rang out. Rhonda couldn't understand what they were saying, but their surprise whirled up the desert air. They had captured a woman!

Her captors led her to a bunker and one bombarded her with questions in broken English. "Who are you? What are you doing here?" Then they dragged her back outside, next to someone she knew: Sergeant Troy Dunlap, another survivor from the helicopter. The relief she felt in reuniting with him lasted only moments: the guards motioned for both prisoners to kneel down. Rhonda felt the metal barrel of a handgun on the back of her neck and heard the command in English.

"Shoot them!"

"There are worse things than dying."

War heroes come in all shapes and sizes. This one is five feet five and weighs in at 112 pounds, a pint-sized epitome of toughness. Her blue eyes blaze with intensity when she recounts the scariest moment of her life.

What went through her head when she was kneeling there?

"Well, I just focused on the fact that it wasn't a bad way to go."

Being executed in the desert isn't a bad way to go?

"No, actually. Compared to how a lot of people go, it's pretty good," she insists with a casual smile. "I was going to be afraid for thirty seconds and then feel nothing, as opposed to being miserable and in pain for weeks and months. My thought was, I've had a great life and at least it won't hurt."

Her grandfather used to tell her, "There are worse things than dying; there is living with dishonor." She was going to die while doing something meaningful: serving her country.

But the shot was never fired, and Rhonda, now relaxing on a beige couch in her Kentucky farmhouse, tells what happened next. She was thrown in the back of a truck. Both arms, broken and useless, were dangling at odd angles. She had a bullet stuck in her shoulder and was dazed from the loss of blood. She could not see out of her left eye, which was caked shut with mud and blood, and her right knee kept buckling. Yet a few miles into the thirty-minute ride to the prison, she suddenly felt the guard's lips on her mouth and his hands unzipping her flight suit.

"I can't believe it!" She remembers being more baffled than shocked. "I mean, I'm covered in blood and dirt and probably don't smell very good. How can he possibly want to do this?" She squirmed and shook her head and protested—"No! No! No!"—but she was unable to lift her arms to push him away. She thought about biting him, but worried this would only anger him and make matters worse. So she kept still as he fingered her. But when he tried to force her head in his lap, the sudden movement caused her to scream in pain. Every time she yelled, he stopped, and Rhonda figured that he did not want his fellow Iraqis, who were riding in the front of the truck, to notice that he was molesting her. He pulled a blanket over her head to muffle her sounds.

Helpless as a fledgling bird

Over the following week, Rhonda was shuttled between bunkers and forced to do what had been most difficult for her all her life: give up control. With her arms broken she could not use her hands, much less feed herself. To use the toilet, she had to ask her captors to cut her out of her flight suit, lead her to the bathroom, and pull down her underwear. Her prison wards had to wash her, brush her teeth, and hand-feed her. For the first time in her life she experienced being utterly helpless.

Luckily, the one-hundred-hour ground offensive came to a fast end. While Rhonda counted the marks her predecessor had left on the cell wall, wondering how many marks she would add, the US government was negotiating her release. The trust in her comrades never left her. "I knew they wouldn't just leave me there."

Eight days later she stepped off the Red Cross plane in the oversized canary yellow canvas suit the Iraqis had dressed her in, her arms splinted and bandaged, carefully balancing on her healthy leg. General Norman Schwarzkopf was the first to greet her, and she tried unsuccessfully to salute with her casts. "How do you feel?" a reporter shouted out, and she yelled back the rallying cry of the air troops: "Airborne!"[3] For her, this was "the most positive, gung ho way of saying I was glad to be home but ready to go back to war if necessary."[4]

Rhonda was one of only a few women captured in the first Iraq war, and instantly celebrated as a hero. While the other twenty-three American prisoners of the Iraq war fared well, too, Rhonda particularly conquered the hearts of the public, maybe because they were touched by the discrepancy between the petite size of this wisp of woman, the extent of her injuries, and her outsized optimism.

Her experience in the desert included nearly all the elements psychiatric manuals list as likely causes for posttraumatic stress: combat exposure, sexual abuse, physical attack, and being threatened with a weapon.[5]

After her release, army psychologists, reporters, friends, and strangers cautiously started feeling her out: How damaged was she? Would she be able to overcome the trauma?

Today, Rhonda refuses to label her experience as trauma, just as she did back then. "I just call it an unfortunate accident," she explains. "We do two things that are not helpful. One is that we tell somebody they are a trauma survivor, and then we tell them to expect to be damaged by it. Well, people generally live up to your expectations."

A better doctor, a better leader, a better person

In response to the many questions about how the experience had changed her, she reflects only on the things that had improved. "I became a better doctor, a better parent, a better commander, probably a better person."

Blessed with a robust constitution, Rhonda had never before experienced being cared for. "Now I could understand my patients much better when they were infirm. I value my relationships more. I don't forget to write birthday cards, because all these things are more precious."

In particular, she is aware of a brief but deeply affecting out-of-body experience after the helicopter crash. "I think it was a decision to have life reenter that body." The doctor who had always focused on the physical aspects of existence was now opened "to at least the possibility of a spiritual life versus a physical life."

People kept asking her how damaged she was, "but I couldn't find anything wrong." Her husband, Kory, a flight surgeon with the air force, even had to undergo psychiatric evaluation, because he acted suspiciously *normal*. He says that he took one close look at his "wifelet" after she was released "and knew she was fine." Of course, the army's psychologists are aware that acting "fine" is one of the common ways we mask trauma, and that hidden, unacknowledged traumas might surface later with unexpected force.

The US government estimates that 6 to 30 percent of men and women who have spent time in war zones experience persistent posttraumatic stress.[6] The way Rhonda reads this is: the majority does well. In the early 1990s, the term "post-traumatic growth" did not yet exist. Only a decade later, when Rhonda came across an article about the research of Richard Tedeschi, was she able to name her experience. "Everybody has heard of PTSD, but nobody has heard of posttraumatic growth!"

Glad to be paralyzed

To understand the enigma of posttraumatic growth, I meet with Richard Tedeschi and Lawrence Calhoun, the scientists who coined the term. Would they have an explanation for why Rhonda Cornum described herself as "a better person" since the capture? The University of North Carolina at Charlotte is the epicenter of posttraumatic growth research. It is to posttraumatic growth what NASA is to the space shuttle. They didn't invent a new universe, but they found new ways of exploring it.

The psychology department resides in a glass and steel cube that overlooks a pond with a fountain, complete with chubby ducks that cross the university roads in slow motion, ostensibly expecting that cars will brake for them. (They do.)

When I arrive in Tedeschi and Calhoun's monthly research session on the fourth floor, team members and students grumble about a rival scientist who refutes the idea of posttraumatic growth. "You've gotta talk to the people who've experienced it!" Tedeschi exclaims passionately.

Tedeschi has done exactly that for almost three decades. He is also a clinician and for twenty-five years has guided a support group for bereaved parents. He is an attentive listener, a wiry man with salt-and-pepper hair whose calm, soothing voice captures your attention.

Tedeschi and Calhoun didn't invent a fancy theory and then try to prove it with studies; it was the other way around. They were consulting with trauma survivors, initially bereaved parents, then people who had lost the loves of their lives or were severely injured; cancer survivors; veterans; and prisoners. Again and again, people shared a perplexing insight: while they were not happy about what had happened to them, they felt they had learned valuable lessons from the experience, and these lessons eventually changed their lives for the better. They became better parents, better partners, and more compassionate friends; they discovered a new purpose in life.

One client told them, "I'm truly glad I'm paralyzed."

"Oh, really?" Tedeschi asked incredulously. He realized he was onto something significant.

One after another, patients explained that they were initially devastated, yet realized later, "Now I feel appreciation. I am a better person than I used to be. I don't think I'd be living in this better way, if this hadn't happened to me, so all things considered, this has worked for me."

How did they get to this insight?

A mental disorder or an expression of humanity?

"Trauma" literally means "wound." We have been hurt. We are hurting. The *Diagnostic and Statistical Manual of Mental Disorders* defines trauma in a way I was familiar with: involving "actual or threatened death or serious injury."[7] Potentially traumatizing events include combat, assault, kidnapping, terrorist attacks, disasters, severe accidents, sexual abuse, or life-threatening illnesses.

The *Manual* classifies PTSD as a mental disorder, but Tedeschi wonders if it might be more accurate to recognize this "disorder" as "actually just an expression of our humanity. When someone crashes their car against a wall at sixty miles per hour, they'll have many broken bones. Do we say they have a broken bone disorder? They have an *injury*. Same with trauma survivors; they have been injured. Psychologically injured, maybe morally injured. They aren't disordered; they're hurt by what has happened. That makes more sense to me."

This sympathy softens the stigma many survivors associate with the label "disorder." Trauma experts and survivors have long advocated for a change of the classification, so far to no avail.[8] Honoring and sharing the sensitivity surrounding the choice of clinical terms, I prefer to speak of "posttraumatic stress" throughout the book unless I refer to the medical diagnosis. As Holocaust survivor and psychiatrist Viktor E. Frankl famously said, "An abnormal reaction to an abnormal situation is normal behavior."[9]

After working with thousands of survivors, Tedeschi has come to an understanding that differs fundamentally from the *Manual*'s. "We define trauma not so much by the event itself but by the emotional and psychological effect an event has on people. We look especially at any event that challenges people's core belief system: people start to question how the world works, what kind of person they are, what kind of life they are living, and what future they have. So it's not necessarily something that wounds people physically, or where death is an issue. Certainly all these things *can* be traumatic, but we're looking at the effect on the individual in terms of what happens to their thinking processes and their beliefs."

The scope of this perspective readjusts and broadens my understanding of the nature of trauma. Reflecting on my own traumas, my deepest wounds have not involved death or violence, but it took an eternity for me to reel back from them. Besides the illness I mentioned in the introduction, I survived a potentially life-threatening bicycle accident with a cracked skull at age eight, and a violent attack at the Ganges River in India one night in my twenties when I was traveling alone through Asia. After both incidents, the shock gradually faded away and in the rearview mirror the events became mere blips on the road of my life. However, when I discovered that my spouse of five years, whom I trusted completely, was an accomplished liar, the news unzipped me and bruised me for years. When the stack of lies tumbled, I was not dealing with a physical death, but rather the death of trust, the death of a relationship, the death of safety.

Trauma lies in the heart of the beholder

Tedeschi tells me of one of his clients who has a serious cancer that will likely lead to his death. This client assured his doctor that he can deal with the illness, but he feels that the really traumatic event of his life is his divorce. "He almost never talks about the cancer; he always talks about the divorce," Tedeschi says. "In his world, the divorce made a huge difference and shattered his life. Trauma is in the eye of the beholder, the experiencer."

For some people, a divorce is a relief. For some, cancer is a challenge they accept to take on. For some soldiers, combat is one of the most exciting missions of their lives. However, for others, any of this could drive them over the edge. There is no universal scale for judging another's pain.

Pain is as piercing as we feel it. We never know what will etch itself indelibly into our heart.

Tedeschi uses the terms "trauma," "major stressors," and "crisis" synonymously. By framing trauma so widely, wouldn't almost anybody experience trauma at some point?[10] "Probably," he says. "Almost everybody experiences nasty events in their life, although not everybody experiences a challenge to their core belief system, and some people are not traumatized. They have, for one reason or another, ways of explaining life where these terrible things that happened don't set in motion this wholesale rethinking about their beliefs."

I understand this distinction best when Tedeschi gives the example of losing a parent. "Most people have a belief that incorporates the idea that old people die. So it's not a big surprise when your mother dies at age eighty-five. You're sad, you miss her, and it might be hard in an emotional way, but it's not like, 'I can't believe this happened! This doesn't make sense!'" Losing a grandparent and losing a child are two different kinds of grief, even though we love them both dearly, because the latter inverts the natural order we have come to expect.

Tedeschi's perspective illuminates why Rhonda was not undone by her capture though it fit the textbook description of trauma. While it was dangerous, humiliating, and ugly, it did not turn her world upside down.

Paradise in Bourbon County

I wanted to meet Rhonda Cornum because I had a keen interest in learning how she had made it through this war experience without breaking down. What has she found helpful? How did she deal with the pain? I was also a little suspicious that someone could survive such events unscarred. Could she be faking it because she thought she had to appear extra tough? Or is she one of the 70 percent of survivors who have tools to deal with trauma that the rest of us can glean advice from?

We meet in her farmhouse near Paris, Kentucky. *God's Truth Stands Any Test*, promises the billboard outside the tiny brownstone Methodist church on my way. When I arrive, she has just finished feeding her sixty-one cows. She jumps out of her truck in green Wellington boots, a scrapped army jacket, old jeans, and a bright pink sweater. Without a "hello" or a handshake she darts to the barn, yelling she needs to get a dog collar. Her ranch must have one of the most beautiful farmhouses in America. "Paradise!" I yell back instead of a more formal greeting. Overlooking an idyllic lake, the fortress-thick stone walls, built in 1810, surround a cozy kitchen and living room, where her cat Dakota purrs and rolls over for belly rubs. Her Thoroughbreds gallop across the meadows of her 690-acre property, and her exuberant Gordon setter puppies beg for attention. By the end of my visit I will be covered in mud and puppy poop, happily so.

Rhonda lives here all by herself and manages the cows, horses, dogs, cats, chickens, and turkeys with the help of only one part-time stable boy. Her husband, Kory, commands a military hospital in Mississippi, and they have not lived together since they both returned from Landstuhl, Germany, in 2005. Next to the 160-liter bourbon barrel, two guns hang above the heavy wooden doors; paintings of hunting scenes with horses and hounds are the only decoration. Even the table lamp is shaped like a setter.

Rhonda retired from the army as a brigadier general, yet she has been anything but idle. Currently the director of health strategy at the consulting company TechWerks and professor of military and emergency medicine at the Uniformed Services University of the Health Sciences, Rhonda has become an expert in resilience, first through her own experiences and then through taking the initiative to pass on her lessons in optimism to others. In the last years of her army career, she implemented the Comprehensive Soldier Fitness program, which is designed to boost the troops' resilience, hardiness, and flexibility—traits Rhonda naturally embodies. She leaves the farm a few times every month to present the resilience training curriculum she helped develop.

Core skills: Rhonda's resilience curriculum

There are several core factors Rhonda considers essential in developing resilience, based on cognitive behavioral therapy[11] skills:

- realistic optimism
- effective problem solving
- adaptability
- positive coping strategies
- the ability to self-regulate
- close relationships and social support
- physical well-being, including exercise and sleep
- the ability to remain calm, present, and engaged when under pressure
- reduced stress levels, enhanced psychological well-being, and happiness
- increased focus and engagement

We will explore these and other key factors over the course of the next chapters.

Closing the gate of pain

So, which strategies had worked for Rhonda when she was captured? "You had just survived a helicopter crash, you were shot down, you're in pain . . ." I recap, and she stops me midsentence. "Actually, I find that offensive," she says. "Not you personally, but the way we say that all the time, 'You're in pain.' Well, you are not in pain like you're dumped in a bucket. My arms hurt, my knee hurt. But globalizing it to 'How much pain are you in?'—that's just not helpful."

After the helicopter crash, pain would flare whenever her arms were moved, but when lying still, despite the torn knee and the bullet wound, she found the pain bearable. As a surgeon, she had often noticed how her patients' ability to handle pain varied greatly, and she is convinced that we can control pain impulses by various factors, including willpower.[12] "Keep control! Don't succumb!" was the mental lifeline she held on to when she was kicked around by her captors.[13]

 ### Take control

A traumatic experience hijacks our ability to control. Facing a sudden disaster or an unexpected diagnosis, we lose power over what we thought was ours: maybe our body, our freedom, or our dignity. Precisely because trauma often leaves us helpless, the antidote is taking back control. "The guiding principle of recovery is to restore power and control to the survivor," recognizes trauma expert Judith Herman.[14]

I know of POWs who rose religiously every dawn to say their prayers, Auschwitz survivors who shaved their chins meticulously in camp though they rarely used to do so at home, and multiple sclerosis patients who adhere to a daily regimen of writing or researching. Any amount of agency we can reclaim that empowers us to restore order in chaos will help, no matter how small. When no or little physical control is available, as in Rhonda's situation, we need to focus on what we *can* control: our mind. "They can control what you eat and what you do," says Rhonda, "but you can control what you think."

"A new normal"

Many scientists agree with Rhonda that our mental attitude has a decisive influence on our experience of pain. "I just set a new normal in my head," Rhonda states, "and then I don't have to think about it again until something else happens. For instance, my arms would hurt every time the truck bounced, so I just set a new baseline and move on." As a doctor she knew that concentrating on pain makes pain worse, so she distracted herself and focused on other topics. She began memorizing Arabic vocabulary, and used the endless hours in the bunker to design stables for her horses on the ranch at home.

With her ability to focus on the positive, she took stock. "I was badly injured, but I knew I'd heal eventually. The crash had been so devastating that I should have died then, and I regarded every minute alive as a gift. It was just enough good luck for me to grab on to and hold. I vowed to survive."[15] The way she describes being captured in the desert sounds unbelievably rational. "There was only one alternative, and that was being killed in the wreck like my five colleagues. I preferred being captured."

I am taken aback. If I were stuck in a hellhole in Iraq, a prisoner with broken arms, I am pretty sure I would panic. I have lost my composure over less. Way, way less. If this conversation with Rhonda was just going to be the army tune of "Suck it up, Buttercup!" I wasn't interested. When I fell apart, I had tried to whip myself into shape, and it didn't work for me. Being harsh to myself when I was vulnerable was counterproductive. On the other hand, panicking doesn't help. So there had to be more to this.

Maybe Rhonda could help me solve one of trauma's eternal riddles: when to soldier up and when to allow ourselves to fall apart.

A human shield

Rhonda Cornum's example has been frequently quoted in the debate about allowing women in combat. Rhonda has added her strong opinion to the discourse. "There is nothing hormonal about being in combat." She turns around the argument that women aren't fit for combat by pointing out that perceiving women as weak can backfire: she remembers the moments before her helicopter was shot down. As soon as they realized they had flown into hostile fire, the soldiers threw themselves on top of Rhonda, the only female officer of the battalion. "That was well intended, but counterproductive, since the bullets came from below." She smiles at the irony. "I actually protected them from the bullets with my body."

Rhonda comes across as anything but cold. She offers tea and cracks jokes, is warm and welcoming. But could anyone really be made of such tough steel? I can't help but probe for a soft spot.

In the war, Rhonda tried not to think of her daughter Regan, who was thirteen at the time, and her husband, Kory. "I put them in the family drawer," Rhonda says. "This might not be healthy, but it's helpful to be able to compartmentalize." The power to focus on the task in front of her was the emotional survival skill that served her well.

Had her husband or daughter been in danger in a foreign country, things would have been much harder for her, "because there was nothing I could have done. I would just have to sit there helplessly. But in my situation there were things I could do: stay strong, proud, and confident."

I understood. In a crisis, survival is the first priority, especially as a soldier, but the same holds true for other situations—for prisoners, accident survivors, battered spouses. We do whatever it takes to get through alive, and it serves us to have these skills.

Develop a psychological survival plan

Rhonda Cornum has been an indomitable optimist all her life. One of the sayings she lives by is, "No matter how bad it gets, it always gets better!" She calls this tactic part of her "psychological survival plan." However, this does not make her a pie-in-the-sky dreamer. Whenever she encounters a dangerous situation, she tries to imagine "the worst and the best thing that could happen." Before deploying, Rhonda consciously contemplated the worst possible outcome of her mission: death. "Then whatever does happen has to be better, or at least no worse."[16]

University of Pennsylvania psychologist Martin Seligman teaches this method to his clients: "putting it in perspective,"[17] a three-step model that evaluates the worst, best, and the most likely case. The objective is to gain perspective, so that we are neither overwhelmed by the worst-case scenario nor blind to potential risks. Many of us tend to "catastrophize" and ruminate about our worst fears come true, often unconsciously (full disclosure: guilty as charged). Naively hoping for the best is equally deceiving. We need to consciously broaden our capacity to picture a realistic and positive outcome.

Rhonda had not been taught these techniques. She had, in fact, received absolutely no psychological or practical training to prepare for her capture. As a woman, she was not even supposed to be in combat. (Technically she was a doctor on a mission to rescue a downed pilot, though she did guard six Iraqi soldiers with her Beretta during an earlier flight.) She remembered what her husband had shared with her about *his* survival training in the air force and what she had seen in movies: give only your name and rank; don't volunteer any information. With this strategy she fared better than some of her male colleagues who were tortured and beaten after giving inflammatory responses such as, "I came here to kill Saddam Hussein." She concentrated on remaining polite and upbeat. Her self-control paid off.

Master self-efficacy

Rhonda's confidence is a striking example of "self-efficacy."[18] Resilience expert Ann Masten of the University of Minnesota defines this quality as "the conviction that you could be effective, that you can master your environment and solve the problems you are facing. That motivates us to get up and take action. If we believe we can do it, we try. If we succeed, the success feeds back to our confidence: Oh, I can do it! That feedback rewards attempting. This motivation is extremely important. It is the engine that powers doing." Thus people with high self-efficacy will persist and continue to try new ways until they find a solution.

As Henry Ford said, "If you think you can or can't do a thing, you're right."

So for Rhonda, are there really no scars left from the crash in Iraq?

There are physical scars, and the arthritis in her right shoulder has worsened and is now so severe that she might have her shoulder replaced. "It is painful when I take my shirt off, and I can't do as many push-ups, but I just ran a marathon and I can still ride my horses."

The capture did not deter her from being eager to deploy again. "Whether it is combat, a divorce, cancer, a car wreck, the techniques for dealing with challenges are similar," she says. "In that sense, the event in Iraq wasn't particularly different. I just did all these things anyway, all my life. This is how I live."

She quotes a motto she remembers from a book she read in high school: "The great men in history are those that turn a disadvantage into an advantage."

Now we're talking. How exactly do you turn a disadvantage around? It took her almost two decades and meetings with renowned psychologists such as Richard Tedeschi and Martin Seligman to realize that her strategies were actual methods that people could train in.

Life as a fitness course

When Martin Seligman did his first experiments about "learned helplessness" in the 1960s, he exposed dogs to electric shocks.[19] A group of dogs could end the shocks by pressing a lever, while another group couldn't. The catch was this: when the dogs that could do nothing about the shocks were later placed in a setting where they could escape the shocks by jumping over a hurdle, most of them wouldn't. They just sat there stoically, enduring the shocks for a full fifty seconds, though they had a choice. You would think anybody who could escape pain would break away, wouldn't you? Most dogs that were put in the shock box for the first time didn't hesitate to jump out. But once dogs had learned they were helpless, even coaxing them with treats did not prompt them to move away. They had to be physically picked up, and not just once, but at least twice, to learn that they could avoid the pain.

Similar experiments were repeated with rats, mice, cockroaches, and eventually humans, and the results were perplexingly similar: after people and animals had experienced they could do nothing about an obnoxious sound or shock, most would just give up, when in fact they could have easily put an end to their distress. Suddenly psychologists had an explanation for why some survivors did not leave a damaging situation. Not only that, but the group who took the shock to be inescapable showed lower immune responses. Their perceived helplessness literally weakened their body.

However, about one third of people (and animals) were resilient, irrespective of their circumstances. They would *always* look for a way out. When the participants were interviewed, it became clear that the difference was marked by their thinking style, by how they explained the experience to themselves.

Optimistic people like Rhonda think, "I will get out, it won't last forever, and I can do my part." They focus on staying on task and search for the benefit they can derive from adversity.

On the other hand, people who tend to think, "I can't handle this, it will ruin my life forever, and nobody is there for me," remain helpless. They not only stop looking for escape routes but they also have a harder time recovering and tend to transfer unhappiness from one area of their lives into others.[20]

Rhonda looks at life like a fitness course. We strengthen ourselves by lifting heavier weights and work out on the treadmill to increase our stamina. We even seek out the machines that tax us, because we know that they are tools for building strength.

Rhonda tells me about other challenging experiences she has faced: giving birth to her daughter Regan at home, and flipping her truck over with her horse trailer after a tire blew up. Probably her biggest recent test was a morning three years ago when she went to Langley to get a regular mammogram and found out she had breast cancer. After a lumpectomy and radiation, Rhonda is now cancer-free.

An unexpected home birth, car crashes, and surviving a

cancer scare are, for Rhonda, the kind of lesser challenges that build up resilience. "Train in small steps," she advises. "We try to prepare people to face *any* challenge, not combat in particular. Those are to help you to get through big problems as much as little ones, like not getting promoted, or failing a test."

Never give up

When we take deadlocks to be transitory and workable, we overcome them much faster. This is not just wishful thinking: we literally fulfill our own prophecies. Locked in a prison cell in the desert, Rhonda had every reason to feel helpless, but she did not give up, not even for one second. Optimistic people like Rhonda look for solutions even though the situation seems grim. How motivated and positive we can remain is one of the main predictors of how well we overcome a potentially traumatic situation. Thus we remain flexible and might discover an unusual opening rather than fixating on a specific outcome. A positive mindset even has a tangible effect on cardiovascular disease, heart attacks, and mortality. However, I want to stress that the benefits of optimism derive from *realistic* optimism, not naive Pollyana-ish thinking.[21]

As Nelson Mandela said, "It always seems impossible until it's done."

Very likely, Rhonda belongs to the optimistic and congenitally resilient 30 percent Seligman's study uncovered. However, this does not mean that the rest of us need to lie down for fate to roll over us. The good news is: thinking styles can be changed. *Learned* helplessness implies that we can unlearn it. We can reassess our thinking patterns and adopt new ones.

This approach also does not suggest that anybody is invincible. Few people are resilient in *all* areas of their lives. Different things affect us differently. We are usually more resilient in some fields and less in others. There was one event Rhonda found truly traumatizing: when a litter of her puppies got parvovirus. "Most people would have put them down," Rhonda says. She tried every therapy available, and while five died, she managed to save three. "That was traumatic because I saw them suffer and was helpless."

She learned, "Do not judge other people's trauma by your own experience. There would have been plenty of people who would just have euthanized this litter and be done. Do I understand why a particular person in a particular situation is doing poorly? No, you can't judge trauma from the outside."

The growth mindset

Stanford psychologist Carol Dweck discovered a fundamental idea that turned out to be the best indicator of how successful students are at school and which managers succeed in business. Nope, it isn't intelligence, talent, or social background. These are all great starting points. However, the key is the "growth mindset," the belief that the ability to learn is not fixed, that we can expand it through effort. Simply *telling* children how their brains develop in response to challenges makes them much more likely to persevere in the face of failure. They are willing to put in the *effort*. Conversely, children and adults who believe that their intelligence or talents are fixed traits easily take failure to be permanent. They never try to go beyond their margins, much like the guinea pigs in Seligman's cage don't jump over the hurdle.

Dweck has shown again and again how the growth mindset works its magic in education, business, and relationships. But it also applies to trauma.

This is what I'm after: how to grow. No doubt that re-sources, training, intelligence, and charisma all help when it comes to navigating a crisis.[22] It is a relief not to have to fret over doctor bills when recovering from an injury. These are not necessarily factors we have a whole lot of control over, but they are actually not the *decisive* factors that predict who does well after trauma.

"How someone responds to trauma is a fork in the road," resilience expert Ann Masten acknowledges. "It is very dif-ficult as a clinician to work with someone who has given up. It is way easier to deal with someone who is acting up and giving you a hard time, because at least they are still doing something. Some people call this agency. You have to act in life, to get to things, to adapt."

Resilience is not a gift one either possesses or doesn't. It more resembles a muscle that atrophies when left idle and strengthens with exercise. Most important, even when we once learned that a shocking event was beyond our control, we can snatch back control over our lives. In fact, we must.

2. Grow

"More vulnerable, yet stronger"
How psychologist Richard Tedeschi, the
pioneer of posttraumatic growth, helps
survivors bounce forward[1]

*Out of suffering have emerged the
strongest souls; the most massive
characters are seared with scars.*

—KAHLIL GIBRAN

One of Richard Tedeschi's clients has a brain aneurysm
that may burst at any time. He had to give up pretty
much all activities he enjoyed before the diagnosis: his work,
his hobbies, his beloved sports. After a bout of depression, he
came to realize that losing some of the favorite parts of his life
meant gaining unexpected perks. He calls it the "slow life,"
analogous to the "Slow Food"[2] movement. Because he can't
be under great stress, he has no choice but to take on life in
a deliberate way, noticing things, appreciating moments, taking his time. "He says, 'Life is better than it used to be. I can
drop dead any minute, but I really appreciate the way I'm
living my life now. If this hadn't happened to me, I wouldn't
be able to see life in this way.' " Tedeschi reports, "He relates
to his kids differently, because he listens to them and spends
time with them. He's just an ordinary guy who's come to

appreciate life in an extraordinary way." This is an example of posttraumatic growth.

Five main areas of growth

Richard Tedeschi and Lawrence Calhoun have found that their clients report growth in five main areas: personal strength, deeper relationships with others, new perspectives on life, appreciation of life, and spirituality.[3] "In brief, people's sense of themselves, their relationships with others, and their philosophy of life changes," Tedeschi says. "Perhaps one of the most common growth experiences triggered by a major stressor is an increased appreciation of life."

Depending on the circumstances, Tedeschi estimates that as many as 30 to 70—in some instances even up to 90—percent of survivors generally experience at least one aspect of posttraumatic growth. I am stunned.

Contrary to popular opinion, experiencing growth after trauma is far more common than PTSD. It is vital to look closely: while most people will suffer from posttraumatic *stress* in the aftermath of trauma, few will develop full-blown PTSD, and even of those, most will heal with therapy and time.[4] "But it is important to make clear that not everybody experiences growth, and we are not implying that traumatic events are a good thing," Richard Tedeschi emphasizes. "They are not. In the wake of trauma, people become more aware of the futility in life and that unsettles some while it focuses others. This is the paradox of growth: people become more vulnerable, yet stronger."

It is crucial to distinguish between the *event* and the *outcome*. There is nothing positive about trauma itself; we wouldn't choose it, then or now. There is nothing beneficial about being captured in Iraq or being diagnosed with an aneurysm. Nevertheless, we might be able to reap something beneficial *out of the sorrow.*

The good only comes from what we decide to do with it—from our *struggle* that unveils what needs to change in us and in our society, from honing our ability to make meaning out of events that seem senseless, from not trying to rebuild an exact replica of what was lost, but to engineer a stronger, sturdier foundation for our life.

Tedeschi sees posttraumatic growth "both as a process and an outcome. The process lies in struggling with the aftermath of a traumatic event; the outcome is how people are changed as a result of struggling."

He emphasizes, "The growth does not come from the event itself as if the event itself were a great thing. It's not the death of a beloved child, but the parent's long and arduous and permanently painful struggle to cope that might produce some elements of growth.[5] Even people who have lost their children can say, 'I hate that I lost my child, but I like the person I have become in the aftermath a lot better than who I was before.' Many bereaved parents go on to be active in nonprofit work or help others in altruistic ways. It's what happens afterward, how people strive to understand and rethink what's going on. And it *is* a struggle. If it's not a struggle, nothing is really being learned."

As Maya Angelou says, "Nothing will work unless you do."

Allow yourself to struggle

Self-control is important, but struggle is inevitable. It's okay not to be okay. You don't need to hold it all together all the time. Allow yourself to be fully human, in all its beauty and ugliness.

Do we view heroes as people who don't have the same

vulnerabilities we do? But, of course, scratch beyond the surface of any hero's life story and you'll find he or she had to overcome a great deal of challenges, and sometimes they thought they weren't up to the task. It can be liberating and validating to discover this.

A devastating loss is simply this: devastating. Posttraumatic growth does not dissolve the pain. Allow the tears to flow, scream at the funeral if you must, go into the woods and curse the sky, take up boxing and beat the crap out of the punching bag. Repeat as needed.

It's from the fierce place of acknowledging the raw spots that we derive strength.

Better, stronger, tougher

On the third anniversary of Gabby Giffords's near-fatal shooting, she jumped out of an airplane. "Good stuff! Gorgeous!" Gabby yelled as she parachuted toward the mountains of Arizona. To her, this was "the most fun way" to celebrate that she was alive. And more than alive—thriving.

Exactly three years earlier, on January 8, 2011, Congresswoman Gabby Giffords had been shot in the head while greeting her constituents in front of a supermarket in her hometown of Tucson, Arizona. Six people died. Her husband, astronaut Mark Kelly, was preparing for his final flight aboard the space shuttle *Endeavour*. He immediately rushed to her bedside, where she lay in a coma, barely hanging on to life. Surgeries replaced pieces of her shattered skull. Recovering from brain trauma, Gabby had to slowly relearn the things we take for granted: walking, talking, eating. A politician once known for her rousing speeches and her indefatigable activism, she now strains to push out words and undergoes daily therapy to reclaim her body.

And yet, her husband describes her as a raging optimist who has far exceeded the physicians' expectations, with her genuine smile intact and her will to change the world unbroken. Their marriage is stronger than ever. She has found a new calling: to campaign for stricter gun laws to prevent other innocent people from being shot. She vows to come back as a "new Gabby—better, stronger, tougher."

Gabby's message of strength is truly inspirational:

"It's been a long, hard haul, but I'm getting better. I'm working hard, lots of therapy—speech therapy, physical therapy, and yoga, too. But my spirit is as strong as ever. I'm still fighting to make the world a better place, and you can, too. Get involved with your community. Be a leader. Set an example. Be passionate. Be courageous. Be your best."[6]

When Gabby Giffords is asked how the shooting has changed her life, she offers two words: "Deeper! Deeper!"

The rewards of an arduous, painful struggle

Gabby Giffords speaks frankly about the depression and despair she felt when she was wrestling with herself to utter single syllables. For weeks, this avid communicator would repeat the word "chicken" to any question. Nobody was more frustrated than she was. And yet she continued to strive until the syllables morphed into words, and then sentences, and finally her first public speech since the shooting.

Gabby Giffords's experience illustrates how not only individuals but also couples, families, and entire communities can experience this growth as a communal process, simultaneously tapping into the depth of pain and healing. "There can be a determination by communities to address tragedy by attempting to create a positive outcome," Tedeschi says. Referring to the Tucson shooting, he quotes Gabrielle Giffords's rabbi, Stephanie Aaron, who said, "Even in the midst of this troubling year, the healing, the courage that we have experienced in our community—each one of us can notice how our cups overflow with the blessings of our lives."[7] Even cities or countries can share the growth. Think of New York after 9/11 or Germany after World War II.

A catalyst for growth

Here's a caveat: posttraumatic growth does not necessarily mean people are feeling better.

"For a lot of people, a lot of distress remains," cautions Tedeschi. "Even when people are able to say they got something of value, this doesn't mean it makes everything all better, or that they no longer look at the event as traumatic. Posttraumatic growth isn't the opposite of posttraumatic stress. Posttraumatic stress is a *catalyst* for the emotional growth."

Maybe the very notion of "getting over it" is mistaken. That expectation that we could "be done," "snap out of it," and "move on" carries the hope that it has never really happened, like a horror movie that we could walk out of. But many of us, including Gabby Giffords, don't have that luxury. The worst has happened, and we are changed.

Is it not when we touch the fringe of human existence that we ask the big questions? "A little fender-bender in the parking lot doesn't make that much difference, but if an earthquake has shattered your world, why not build something better instead of the same old crappy buildings?" Tedeschi asks.

Let's face it. Few of us live our best and kindest lives. Most of us hurtle along, propelled by bills and responsibilities, somewhat impervious to our true potential. A breakdown also breaks down the musts and should-haves that ruled our daily routines, along with life as we knew it. Temporarily suspended in a vacuum, we can recalibrate, and maybe for the first time, tune into what truly matters.

Psychologist W. Keith Campbell of the University of Georgia calls this wholesale rethinking the "ego-shock."[8] Our world shatters; everything we believed about ourselves, others, and the world is no longer true. What we thought was the script of our life has been ripped up. The universe freezes. We are temporarily "scriptless," without a clue what the next act will bring.

It is when our world comes crashing down that the chance for growth occurs.

One of Tedeschi's clients was a former champion swimmer in her twenties. A brain injury left her disabled; she now needs a walker to move around, and has trouble thinking clearly. She found it hard to adjust, but eventually her struggles helped transform her into a more compassionate person, and she has developed precious friendships that run deeper than anything she has experienced before.

Open yourself to compassion

One of the side effects of suffering is that it can lead us to be more honest and more compassionate, especially toward others who suffer. We might notice for the first time the various shades of pain reflected in people around us.

That is, if we let the corrosive power of pain soften us, penetrate us.

"Grief can be the garden of compassion," the Persian poet Rumi wrote. "If you keep your heart open through everything, your pain can become your greatest ally in your life's search for love and wisdom."

However much we long to put up an invincible shield, closing ourselves off means losing out on life. The harder we are, the harder life becomes. We cannot shut out just the painful stuff and let only the pleasant stuff in. Such a BS filter for life simply has not yet been invented. Staying open and allowing ourselves to remain vulnerable is the only way to receive a precious gift: to discover what lies beyond pain, and to connect with others who have visited the places that scare us.

When Gabby Giffords got into a discussion with a colleague about the meaning of life, she settled on, "I think it comes down to this: We are here to care for each other."[9]

How the heck could they ever say anything good about their trauma?

And yet not everybody discovers the "garden of compassion" and the insight poets and psychologists promise. What makes us more likely to experience growth?

We know what's *not* helping, and it's the first aid kit most of us reach for impulsively: alcohol, drugs, tranquilizers.[10]

Every person is their own universe, or in Zen master Thich Nhat Hanh's words, "Each human being is a multiplicity of miracles." Every life is a patchwork of so many factors that make one person's experience of hardship different from another's. Tedeschi asks, "How much misery did they go through? How long did they have to go through it? Who was there to support them? How did it all turn out in the end? What changes did it produce in their life? How much did they lose?"

Statistically, women seem to be more prone to trauma; Tedeschi concludes they are also more open to the possibility of posttraumatic growth.

"And then you have these somewhat mysterious personal factors," Tedeschi continues. "Some people have just been enormously damaged by experiences, and you say, 'How the heck could they ever say anything good about what they've gone through?' Still, miraculously, it seems, they are able to say, 'I'm okay with this. In fact, I'm real good with this.' In some ways it is not the person who had the *easy* experience and often it is not the person who had the absolute hardest. Abject misery that takes virtually everything away from people is probably the hardest to find aspects of growth in, though there are exceptions; there are still people who grow. It is probably the person in the middle who is most likely to grow."[11]

"Don't assume pathology"

Surely, I thought, no one can possibly report growth after experiencing ruthless violence such as the Holocaust, right?

Whatever catastrophe I could think of, whether Auschwitz[12] or the Vietnam War,[13] 9/11[14] or the loss of a loved one, my assumption that a majority of survivors had to be severely damaged turned out to be warped. By now there have been thousands of interviews with survivors of such diverse debacles as tsunamis, rape, and kidnapping, and the majority reports growth.

When psychologist Martin Seligman added questions about "the fifteen worst things" that can happen (torture, grave illness, death of a child, etc.) to a questionnaire about authentic happiness, he learned, "To our surprise, individuals who'd experienced one awful event had more intense strengths (and therefore higher well-being) than individuals who had none. Individuals who'd been through two awful events were stronger than individuals who had one, and individuals who had three—raped, tortured, and held captive, for example—were stronger than those who had two."[15]

Tedeschi found that posttraumatic growth "commonly occurs in the short to medium term, around one to two years after an event," and it often endures. When he evaluated veterans from the Vietnam War, he discovered that they "had made significant changes that had lasted all these decades."

And it is universal: posttraumatic growth has been observed around the globe and across religions, from Chinese cancer survivors to rape survivors in the Middle East, from political prisoners to refugees from war-torn areas, in both Israelis and Palestinians, after earthquakes and shipwrecks and hunger catastrophes, in Europe, Africa, Asia, and Australia.[16] The studies not only include big Traumas with a capital *T*, but also the more common traumas that turn lives upside down: surgeries,[17] bullying, teenage pregnancies, car accidents. The similarities in our abilities to cry and grow are striking.

Even people who did not experience trauma themselves, but witnessed it closely—the children and spouses of cancer survivors, wives of combat veterans, emergency personnel, funeral directors, and trauma therapists—report growth.[18]

Speaking about growth in this context is particularly tricky, because we have a long history of *dismissing* the very real stress symptoms of Holocaust survivors, combat veterans, and victims of violence. For decades, their pain and anxiety has been minimized and ridiculed. White coats with PhDs dismissed soldiers who suffered from "soldier's heart" as "cowards" who needed to "man up," and sent them back to the front. The father of psychoanalysis, Sigmund Freud, insulted survivors of sexual abuse by calling them hysterics. Many survivors were horribly mistreated and misunderstood, even re-traumatized, by doctors, hospital staff, and therapists.[19]

"I am always afraid to whitewash the horrific effects of torture," says psychotherapist Crystal Green, who for ten years served as the associate director of Survivors of Torture, International. "Though I am moved by the posttraumatic growth I have witnessed, I don`t ever want to give torturers a carte blanche, as if to say, 'See, the victims grew from it!' Certainly not everyone comes out unscathed or somehow improved. I think every survivor wished they could have gained that growth through some lesser cost to themselves and to our society."

I am firmly convinced that the pain of trauma survivors deserves to be recognized *more*, and it cannot be emphasized enough that posttraumatic stress and growth do not rule each other out, but often appear in tandem, with posttraumatic stress acting as a catalyst for growth. However, I believe that in the last few decades, the pendulum has swung too far in the opposite direction: psychiatrists and psychologists have homed in on the negative impact of trauma, without even considering there could be a positive flip side. This is completely understandable, as these professionals are trained to focus on what's wrong—the symptoms—rather than on what works, the strengths. But this deficit model impacts survivors. Most of the trauma survivors I spoke with simply *assumed* that they would be damaged forever, or at least for a very long time.

It is worth recalling veteran Rhonda Cornum's realization: "Don't assume pathology. This is not helpful."

Extraordinary ordinary people: from victim to survivor

To communicate that experiencing trauma and posttraumatic stress does not predict doom is one of my main motives for writing this book. I want to nurture the healing and empowerment of survivors rather than stigmatize victims; to feature survivors who show us that trauma does not need to be a trap door, but can open a gate to a changed world.

What exactly trauma is and how to treat it remains hotly contested in the medical community, but by now we have a pretty good understanding of what makes trauma worse: repeated or prolonged exposure; lack of support; traumatic experiences at a young, developmental age; excessive brutality; self-blame.[20] Naturally, someone who had to relive assaults over and over, with no way out and no one to run to, might have deeper scars. For a long time, for instance, psychologists thought that children from abusive homes were sentenced to a life full of problems. But now we know that even under the direst circumstances a surprising number of neglected children become capable, happy adults who are able to hold down a steady job and build strong family relations. I believe that we belittle survivors by predicting them to fail, when in fact we are wired for survival.

Child psychologist Ann Masten, who has studied resilient children for nearly four decades, calls our ability to adapt "ordinary magic." "Our human capacity is pretty astounding. We have been naturally and culturally selected to adapt under widely varying circumstances."

The subjects in this book are no superheroes or "super-survivors." Some acted out. Some tried to douse their pain in alcohol and drugs. They all struggled, and they all had to realize: they could not outrun their woes. They found their turning point when they were willing and able to look at their experience and "integrate it into the narrative of their lives," as Tedeschi calls it.

They are extraordinary ordinary people.

The less resilient, the more growth?

Tedeschi asserts that resilient people do not typically experience tremendous growth, especially the kind of spiritual and existential growth that arises after a seismic shake-up. He likens the experience to extremely fit people for whom running a marathon is no big deal. So the less resilient you are, the more growth you have?

This sounds counterintuitive, but it is exactly what Tedeschi predicts. "Posttraumatic growth involves big change. Early on, in the immediate aftermaths of these traumas, the people who show the most growth may be the people who have the most room to grow." This is good news for chickenhearts like yours truly.

Rhonda Cornum disagrees. "Yeah, he thinks I shouldn't have experienced a lot of growth, because I am resilient. But I did." Yet she concurs with Tedeschi that posttraumatic growth results in increased resilience.

"Later as you go down that road you find that people show more strength," Tedeschi observes, "because posttraumatic growth leads to resilience and wisdom." He stresses how important it is that trauma treatment "needs to promote the development of psychological resilience that allows people to withstand the situations that remind them of past traumas, and possible future traumatic events."[21]

Because the science of posttraumatic growth is still new, the exact nature of the relationship between resilience and posttraumatic growth remains to be defined.[22] Some researchers treat them as two sides of the same coin, while others argue about the individual factors that make up good coping before and after trauma.

Do we have to fall apart in order to experience the growth? Or are there ways of learning as we go through life, to grow continuously from the small challenges so that they prepare us for the big hits? As Crystal Green pointed out earlier, even if survivors experience posttraumatic growth, everybody wishes they had experienced the growth in less brutal ways.

What is clear is that the core skills of resilience can save lives, and they serve as double agents: they fortify us for crisis, help us navigate through hardship, further the healing, and support us in finding the courage to face new challenges. So let's look further at how we can develop some of these skills.

"You can do anything"

I believe how Rhonda came to develop her resilient backbone can be a teaching for all of us in our own lives and in our roles as parents, teachers, and friends.

Rhonda was raised as a tomboy in Aurora, a suburb of Buffalo, New York. "I definitely had the firstborn son syndrome," she admits with a laugh. Her father impressed on her, "You can do *anything.*" From an early age, Rhonda was encouraged to make her own decisions. She paints the picture of an earthy, rugged childhood with adventurous playtime outdoors. Her parents weren't wealthy, so she used to clean stables in exchange for riding horses. Even as a teenager, she claims, she never threw a tantrum, screamed, or cried. "Control was always one of the greatest virtues in our family."[23]

Some researchers have gathered evidence that the reservoir for resilience lies in our genes. Rhonda agrees. Her family history suggests that fearlessness runs in the bloodline. Her grandfather was a marine and taught little Rhonda how to shoot a gun long before she joined the army. Her great-grandmother had been a pilot in the 1930s, a soul sister to Amelia Earhart, and later Rhonda and her husband continued the family tradition by building their own fiberglass aircraft.

Nature versus nurture

Just as we can now identify certain genes that increase our risk for heart disease or cancer, some genes seem to increase or lower our ability to navigate the maelstroms of life. The best-investigated culprit is the gene 5-HTT, which is critical for regulating serotonin, the "happiness hormone." A lack of serotonin can put us at greater risk for depression, especially when faced with adversity. We all inherit two versions of each gene: one from our mother, one from our father. If one or both versions of the gene 5-HTT are short, as they are in about 17 percent of the population,[24] people are more prone to depression and suicide, are easily stressed, and panic when they face a threat. Conversely, long versions of 5-HTT seem to serve as a shield against depression and anxiety, possibly making it easier to keep our cool when catastrophe strikes.

However, personality is not a case of simple arithmetic: The length of one's 5-HTT versions, by itself, does not predict depression or resilience. It's the combination with life events that activates the potential of the genes, and there is not just one gene at play in us but many. Our DNA is packed with millions of gene switches. There is no such thing as a "resilience gene" or a "helplessness gene." No genetic setup dooms us to be a wimp or fortifies us to be a warrior. Some of the genes only unleash their potential when life messes with them.[25] Researchers call this interaction GxE, the interplay of genes and environment.[26]

You could compare these genes' function to a seat belt: while you drive along you hardly notice it, but when you hit a wall, it makes all the difference.

We can see how this works in at-risk children. Joan Kaufman, a child psychiatrist at Yale, analyzed the genes of a hundred children. About half of them had been abused or maltreated. The abused children with two short 5-HTT versions had depression scores that were almost twice as high as those who had not been abused, or those with long gene versions. But the genetic effect is not inevitable: if those children with the most vulnerable genes had a supportive adult in their daily lives or if they had not been maltreated, their depression scores sank drastically.[27]

Isn't this an encouraging find? A genetic disposition might put us at a greater risk for depression, but we can counteract our disposition with the right support, much like we can offset a genetic risk for a heart attack with a healthy diet and regular exercise. Training in resilience is even more important for those of us who weren't born with the strongest genetic shield.

The extra sensitivity can even have advantages: children with the vulnerable gene might do worse in an orphanage, but benefit more from a quality foster home. Jay Belsky, a professor of human development at the University of California, Davis, compared these children to "delicate orchids; they quickly wither if exposed to stress and deprivation, but blossom if given a lot of care and support."[28]

Researchers hope that in the not-too-distant future they will invent the equivalent of a seat belt for life's ride by creating a designer drug that improves serotonin transmission and mimics the protective function of the long gene variants. But we don't need to wait for a designer drug. An even better protection is already available: a compassionate copilot who keeps us from crashing in the first place.

Stand by the one who needs you

Consulting these studies has a purpose: to find out how we can fortify ourselves and others when disaster strikes. Here is a proven plan to minimize trauma: be that one adult in that kid's (or grown-up's) life! Many say that they tried to find help, but couldn't. Be that person who does not shy away. Show up. Don't look the other direction. Listen. Trust. Believe.

"You are never afraid"

Though Rhonda's bachelor's degree is in microbiology and genetics, she never had her genes analyzed. But as a doctor she believes that the resilience factor is similar to our physical disposition: "Thirty percent is genetic, ten percent is medical care, and sixty percent are the behavior choices you make." According to Rhonda's math, our ability to boost our inner strength through our own actions outweighs the genetics or medical care that we may have little to no control over. "So we should focus on the behavioral choices. You go where you aim."

Rhonda became a urologist and surgeon, and was drawn to trauma work "because it is more fun." What on earth is fun about trauma? "The fun is to fix it. You have to make a decision and have the self-confidence to act."

A lesson in fearlessness stuck with Rhonda when she was a medical student and treated a patient with a large abdominal mass. She started to talk to the supervising doctor about the risks of the procedure. "I would like to do a percutaneous biopsy, but I am afraid that . . ." Her mentor, surgeon Dan Rosenthal, stopped her in her tracks. "Rhonda, you are a general surgeon. You may be wrong, but you are never afraid."

Rhonda laughs, remembering the moment. "That's not a bad way to live."

Anchor yourself with your breath

Humans (and animals) are hardwired to feel fear when sensing danger. The fight-or-flight response kicks in before we know it, but calming our breathing and our heart rate is an ability we can train in. Though Rhonda technically had no preparation for combat, as a trauma surgeon she was actually perfectly prepared to keep herself calm in a life-or-death situation.

She recommends breathing exercises to get rid of the physiological onslaught of panic. "Fear increases your rapid breathing; you hyperventilate. You can mentally rehearse what you are about to undergo so that you are not afraid." (Please see more information on breath-based mindfulness in the guide in the back of the book.)

The importance of not becoming overwhelmed by fear

Isn't fear sometimes useful to prevent us from taking risks? "You might be cautious, but not afraid," Rhonda differentiates. "Fear is not helpful, ever. It's not a word I even use."

Rhonda's realization meshes with the observations of emergency room doctors. When Dr. Arieh Shalev recorded the heart rate of his patients in the emergency room of his Jerusalem hospital, he found a strikingly simple predictor of PTSD: Patients whose heart rates returned to normal by the time they were discharged from the emergency room were unlikely to develop PTSD.[29] However, if their heart rate was still elevated, they would probably suffer from PTSD later.

The jolt of adrenaline might have been useful at the time of the impact, but PTSD lurks when we get stuck on high alert. Did you know wild animals rarely develop PTSD? After a close encounter with a lion, a deer might be more cautious the next time at the water hole, but it is able to discharge the rush of survival energy.[30] Animals "shake it off," and trauma therapist Peter A. Levine is convinced that we humans need to learn the same in order to return our bodies to their equilibrium.[31] However, this does not mean suppressing tension, but rather becoming aware of it, releasing it, and calming our body by refocusing ourselves in the present moment. "In order to experience this restorative faculty, we must develop the capacity to face certain uncomfortable and frightening physical sensations and feelings without becoming overwhelmed by them."[32] Naturally, this is a capacity one needs to build through practice.

"What is revealed here is the dual nature of trauma: first, its destructive ability to rob victims of their capacity to live and enjoy life. The paradox of trauma is that it has both the power to destroy and the power to transform and resurrect," writes Levine. "Whether trauma will be a cruel and punishing Gorgon, or a vehicle for soaring to the heights of transformation and mastery, depends upon how we approach it. Trauma is a fact of life. It does not, however, have to be a life sentence. It is possible to learn from mythology, from clinical observations, from neuroscience, from embracing the 'living' experiential body, and from the behavior of animals; and then, rather than brace against our instincts, embrace them."[33]

A parole date for pain?

The two questions people ask me most frequently when I tell them I write about posttraumatic growth are "What's the recipe?" and "How long does it take to get over the trauma?"

Bookstores and websites offer a wealth of manuals about the stages of grief or recovery, often with timetables, and survivors feel the pressure to fit in there. "Many people have come to me and said, 'I think there is something terribly wrong with me, because I should be in this stage by now, but I'm not!'" Tedeschi reports. "No, there's nothing wrong with you. There's something wrong with all *that*."

Many therapists have found that recovery after a crisis goes through phases, from the initial shock, terror, or numbness, through to the recovery process. Harvard psychiatrist Judith

Herman has identified three stages: "The central task of the first stage is the establishment of safety. The central task of the second stage is remembrance and mourning. The central task of the third stage is reconnection with ordinary life. Like any abstract concept, these stages of recovery are a convenient fiction, not to be taken literally. They are an attempt to impose simplicity and order upon a process that is inherently turbulent and complex."[34]

In posttraumatic growth, too, there are what "looks like steps, but I certainly wouldn't call it standardized, that's for sure," says Tedeschi. "I'm always a little wary of any concept of stages, because for most people it's a lot messier than that."

It's not just popular books that define trauma with a timeline. The *Manual of Mental Disorders* diagnoses PTSD if, metaphorically speaking, the scars aren't healing, if someone still has anxiety and flashbacks months or years after the experience, and finds themselves unable to function. But pain is a sojourn with no parole date.

"Yeah, the *Manual* says six months, which is ridiculous," Tedeschi scoffs. "Sometimes it takes years and years to deal with things that are so horrific. The one-size-fits-all idea is counterproductive. We have to look at what's going on with individuals to understand why they are still working on what happened to them two or ten or forty years ago. To call it a disorder doesn't quite fit for me. People can have all these symptoms, but at the same time they can be quite remarkable people."

When my sister-in-law Tami Carter and her husband Brett lost their three-year-old daughter, Haley, after six open-heart surgeries, they left her bedroom untouched. Haley's shoes still waited inside the hallway; Haley's petite dresses still hung in the closet. Haley's voice still greeted callers on the answering machine. It took Tami more than ten years before she was able to dismantle Haley's room.

When she broke into sobs at a therapist's office nine months after Haley's passing, the therapist told her that "other patients were further along." "You treat other bereaved parents?" Tami asked. No, he responded, he was talking about patients who had lost an uncle or another relative. "But he was still comparing me to them," Tami says, "not taking into account the complex trauma of losing your only child after several brutal surgeries." Many of her peers at the Compassionate Friends, a self-help group for bereaved parents, shared similar encounters with therapists and friends.

"People are just filled with such good advice!" Tedeschi exclaims. "Somebody is doing something in six months that takes another person ten years. So be it. You need to be very careful about claiming what's healthy and what's not in terms of time frame. People take all different periods of time. The process is not formulaic."

Resilience expert Karen Reivich told me, "There is not a correct way to grieve, just as there is not a correct way to love."

And the recipe is always and invariably the same: Show up. Stay with it. Be present.

However, we can take breaks.

Take breaks from pain

It is absolutely necessary to take a temporary leave of absence from pain. Not once, but regularly. Tedeschi even sees a place for denial and distraction. "You can't stay in the misery of this all the time. In order to cope with these things, people need to have the capability to take a dose of it, then go away from it. Some degree of comforting yourself or distracting yourself is useful. I'd call this good coping. It's smart. You have those times where you say, enough is enough, you

have to stop the bleeding, and then you come back to it
another time."

Tugging at the wounds all the time is simply too painful. But
we have to take care of the wounds.[35] We have to allow the
pain to meet us in intimate places. The raw, bloody, ugly parts
we prefer to keep hidden. The places we don't want to visit.

For growth to occur, there is no other way but to be present, to show up. We cannot avoid the pain, smile it away, juice
it away, or detour to the other side. We have to go through
the tunnel.

"Sometimes we feel that we are barely pulling ourselves
forward through a tight tunnel on badly scraped-up elbows,"
writer Anne Lamott says. "But we do come out the other side,
exhausted and changed."[36]

What would happen if we took the pain as our teacher? If
we stayed for its lecture to listen?

What's worth living?

Nothing irks trauma survivors more than platitudes such as
"You're gonna be fine" or "Maybe something good will come
of this." How is the notion of posttraumatic growth different?
"It's not," Tedeschi shoots back, "but if you're a good clinician
or a decent human, you don't say these things to people in the
immediate aftermath of trauma."

When someone is drowning, they need a lifeline, not a
swimming lesson. There are traumatic events where the mere
suggestion that growth can result from it may seem naive or
insulting. Often, time needs to pass before a survivor is open
to the idea. If you use this book as a brick to hit someone's
head with so that they grow already, I'm gonna come after
you. But at some point, the survivor might feel the urge to

learn to swim through the grief, and then these strategies become very helpful.

As a therapist, Tedeschi won't bring up the topic of growth himself. "It's all in the timing, in the way you word it, and the people who go through the aftermath of traumatic events come upon these things themselves. There's a lot of subtlety to this," Tedeschi cautions. "There are no easy answers. I'm not trying to tell survivors what to think, I'm just trying to get them thinking."

How does he respond to critics who argue that all this talk about growth is just trying to sugarcoat the shit? "There is an interesting misconception that people who report growth are in denial or naive, just putting a nice, superficial gloss on something that's really ugly," Tedeschi comes back. "I find that people who call posttraumatic growth an illusion really don't spend a lot of time with trauma survivors. Because if you do, the people who report growth do not deny that they have been through something difficult. So we can talk about both ends of this, how it's hard, and good."

 ### Dare to explore

Tedeschi finds that "the people who show this growth usually have their eyes wide open, open enough to see the difficulties along with the possibilities. They are not the people who close their eyes and say, 'I don't want to look at any of this.'"

He encourages clients to try on different perspectives, "loosening up their thinking process. Being willing to explore a possible self, the possibility for the life narrative, and me not making a judgment where a person should go with all of this, but simply accompanying them as they try to figure all this out. Many people aren't comfortable with that, so I try to

get them comfortable with ambiguity and uncertainty. The
key to this is creating an atmosphere where people feel safe
enough to consider different points of view."

Tedeschi prefers "to live in the world of ambiguity. I leave it
up to people who are going through these things to inform
me what the answers might be for them. I listen to their story,
try to put myself in their shoes, have them teach me what
it is they have gone through. They tell me a whole lot more
than the diagnostic manual. So I pay a lot more attention to
that, that teaching."

Trauma as a teaching. A therapist willing to listen. A survivor willing to explore. These could be the ingredients of growth.

Integrate the event into your life's narrative

Eventually a survivor will need to weave the traumatic event
into the narrative of their life; they will rewrite their life's
script. That process can take years, or even decades. But at
some point in our life, we need to acknowledge that what
happened has become part of our story. Quite literally rewriting our history by keeping a diary is one of the methods
many therapists recommend. However, what is important is
not what happens on paper, but its integration into our mind.

Smooth seas do not make skillful sailors

Although Tedeschi and Calhoun introduced the term "posttraumatic growth" in the nineties, they did not discover this
phenomenon. The ideas and writings of the ancient Greeks,
Hebrews, early Christians, Buddhists, Hindus, and Muslims
have all promised the possibility of finding blessings in bad
breaks.

Often they urged the *necessity* of overcoming hardships in order for the savior to return with the magic potion that would heal themselves and their people: Moses had to ascend the mountain, the Buddha left his palace, Jesus sacrificed himself.

Paul writes in the Christian New Testament, "We also rejoice in our sufferings, because we know that suffering produces perseverance; and perseverance, character; and character, hope."[37]

Roman emperor Marcus Aurelius declared, "What stands in the way becomes the way."

An African proverb tells us that, "Smooth seas do not make skillful sailors."

Even Batman only became the world's greatest crime solver after his parents were murdered.

From Buddha to Batman, from indigenous healers to the blockbuster magicians of Hollywood, the hero's emergence through trial and resurrection is among the oldest stories in history. "It is by going down into the abyss that we recover the treasures of life," renowned mythologist Joseph Campbell said. "Where you stumble, there lies your treasure."[38]

The idea that to encounter major adversity can be transformative, perhaps in radical ways, is not new. What is new is that this age-old insight is spreading into clinics, armies, and hospices.

God, how could you let this happen to me?

I am surprised to learn, though, that despite the spiritual dimension of posttraumatic growth, religious faith does not necessarily help a person's growth. In the aftermath of a traumatic event, some survivors *find* faith for the first time, and for others, faith becomes their lifeline. This is, for instance, how Gabby Giffords summons the strength to continue her struggle (her Hebrew name, "Gabriella," literally means "God is my strength"),[39] and how "soul surfer" Bethany Hamilton braves the waves again after the shark attack. Bethany takes the shark bite as God's test, and credits her survival to her prayers. "From what seems like such a horrible thing, God has just brought glory to himself," she says.[40]

But many lose faith.[41] When my sister-in-law lost her only child, she did not call for a minister. In the long hours in the intensive care unit, Tami had poured her heart into praying, but her prayers were not answered. Why miracles for some and not for others? "God, how could you let this happen to me?" is a soul-wrenching outcry.

"It depends on the degree to which people have enough flexibility in their belief system to make sense of that event within that system. So it's a big thing," Tedeschi has found. "If the system has enough breadth to it, someone might feel sad, lost, or upset, but their core beliefs don't crumble, and that's an important distinction."

Religious faith helps if survivors find a way to make sense of their trauma within this frame, but when a crisis is seen as God's punishment or instigates a wholesale questioning of one's faith, the spiritual struggle adds a deeper dimension to the distress. We will continue to explore faith in the following chapters and talk to survivors about the role it played in their healing.

Tedeschi is Christian, but he appreciates the Buddhist wisdom of change, impermanence, and mindfulness that is built into many practices and prayers. "Buddhists have this rite of not avoiding changes in life, but facing them, embracing them, actively addressing the problems."[42]

Accept the things you cannot change

If Tedeschi were to point to one single factor that he recognizes again and again in survivors who report growth, it is the willingness to "accept changes that can't be changed. People who do not avoid the fact of the change, but are able to hit it head-on, might think, 'Okay, this is the situation now, what am I going to make of it? Even if the situation is that I am probably going to be dead in one month, what am I going to make of this month?'"

Gabby Giffords, for instance, has had to accept that her existence has profoundly shifted: she lost 50 percent of her vision, her forehead and neck will forever be marked with scars, she won't be able to have the baby she so wanted. These things won't change. But she is still Gabby, the upbeat optimist who made a remarkable recovery and whose life mission is now to prevent more unstable young men from getting their hands on a gun.

Support groups have chanted the serenity prayer for decades:

> *God, grant me the serenity to accept the things I cannot change,*
> *The courage to change the things I can,*
> *And the wisdom to know the difference.*

Intellectually, this sounds somewhat straightforward, but emotionally it is not. The ability to manage emotions and distress rather than just being terrified becomes crucial for opening up the space to reflect. Tedeschi advises, "In order to move toward a growth perspective, you have to go through a phase of intense reflection. People have to figure out, 'Where does this traumatic event belong in my life story? Is this something that's central? Is it just a minor detour? Does it change my perspective and choice about how I am going through the rest of my life?'"

Shining a torch for other survivors

Which brings us to the question: Can we broaden our perspective to fortify ourselves for the maelstroms that might lie ahead? Can we equip ourselves with tools that will make the crawl through the tunnel more bearable, such as, let's say, a flashlight to illuminate the passage?

About 90 percent of us—almost everybody—will go through one or more potentially traumatic experiences in our lifetime. "We can prepare, to a degree, by just looking around us; by being willing to be up close with people who have gone through traumatic events and learning from them. They are the masters," Tedeschi advises. "So, when this terrible thing happens to you, you've seen it with other people, you talked to them and listened to them, you had some teachers, you've heard about some things you can try, you can see some possibilities. But that doesn't make it easy either. You still have to go through it, but at least you have some idea about what's happening. 'Now it's my turn. Okay. Why shouldn't it be my turn?'"

Tedeschi cites "studies that show that cancer survivors and survivors of domestic violence experience higher levels of growth when they knew somebody else who had experienced posttraumatic growth, and when they are surrounded by an environment that is supportive of and open to the idea of growth."[43]

If our environment is not supportive, and if no one offers a safe haven to speak about the unspeakable, effects of trauma go unexpressed, undiagnosed, unhealed. Many trauma survivors believe that they are the only ones the unimaginable happened to. Children, especially, respond to trauma by disassociating, and they don't have the language to talk about it. They need caring adults who can help.

"I don't think that the work of healing and posttraumatic growth can begin until trauma is named and shared with another person," says Dr. Susan Ollar, a Colorado psychotherapist who has worked with many trauma survivors in her private practice. She was trained in trauma therapy when working in the psychiatric unit at a veterans' hospital in the eighties. Without this experience, she might not have looked as closely for trauma in her civilian patients. "There are many people who have the undisclosed secret of trauma," Susan says. "Many patients will suppress their experiences and the accompanying painful feelings in the hope that if they keep the worst memory hidden from themselves, they will be better able to cope. It is not intuitively obvious to most people that going 'toward' the pain is the healing of it." Over the years of her work as a psychologist she has seen that "most everyone who carries a hidden trauma will at some point, psychologically, 'hit a wall.' They often show up in my office perplexed by the sudden onset of panic attacks, a spiral into the depths of depression, or disabling anxiety." Clients might tell her that their spouse has no idea that they are trauma survivors. "They experience panic when I suggest that sharing their experiences with their partners might be helpful. The panic is rooted in shame and fear of judgment and rejection. I often encourage patients to bring their partners in for a session, so that their partner might better understand the severity of their loved one's depression and anxiety. I have observed on several occasions that my patients' partners then divulge that they too have experienced trauma and never talked about it. The overwhelming response is relief and a deeply held wish that they had spoken together sooner."

As the saying goes, let's be kind. For everyone we meet might be fighting a battle we know nothing about.[44]

Find your tribe

Even when we are not surrounded by supportive friends and family members or can't leave the house, we can seek professional help. And we can scout for allies in books and online forums, self-help groups, and faith communities. We discover solace and companionship in connecting with others who have walked in our shoes and understand what we have gone through. "Talking to another bereaved parent was ten times more helpful than anything else," says Tami.

We all have our tribe, and we need to reach out and find it.

This is exactly what I am offering with this book. Here you are meeting people who have survived dramatic events and who now are willing to share how they went to pieces without falling apart.

Nothing is as powerful as knowing we are not alone.

3. Dig Deep

"Take out the weeds and plant flowers"
Can we prepare for trauma? A visit to the army's resilience boot camp in Philadelphia

*In the depth of winter I finally learned that
there was in me an invincible summer.*

—ALBERT CAMUS

Now, what about those of us (count me in) who didn't grow up with a "you-can-do-anything" dad, adventurous ancestors, optimal genes, and unshakeable optimism? What about those of us who aren't physically and psychologically robust enough to shut off the gate to pain at will?

More than ever before, the US Army is dealing with staggering numbers of soldiers who come back from war depressed, angry, and anxious. Every day twenty-two veterans commit suicide[1]—that's one suicide every sixty-five minutes. Does it really make sense to advocate for toughness at a time when veterans are in dire need of anything from a roof over their heads and medical care to in-depth psychological counseling, deep healing, attention, and understanding?

Before the race, not after

Rhonda believes the current state of affairs is the result of educating soldiers *after* they return from combat, instead of before they go to war. She convinced the army of a revolutionary concept. Rather than only treating people with PTSD after combat (or not treating them at all), wouldn't it make more sense to boost their resilience before they deploy? We have now lost more soldiers to suicide than to the war, and a large number of soldiers who later develop PTSD already struggle with depression, anxiety, low self-esteem, drug abuse, and lack of impulse control *before* they ever approach a war zone. With a mindset that already puts them at risk, they are under much greater danger of breaking down or acting out impulsively. Could we bolster their psyche to give them a better chance of doing their duty without paying such a high price? Are there strategies that could even "inoculate" them against the devastating effects of trauma?

"The time to train for a race is before the race, not after you've run it. You don't start learning about first aid when a person has just collapsed in front of you," Rhonda says. "You need to learn this before a challenging event, and then re-learn, and practice."

Together with an armada of resilience specialists, Rhonda started a small insurgence, aiming for a full-scale culture change in the army: shifting away from a focus on physical fitness to an emphasis on psychological resilience.[2] With pressure mounting to tackle the issue, the army rolled out Rhonda's Comprehensive Soldier Fitness program in December 2009, without even a single pilot study.

Rhonda teamed up with Martin Seligman, the guru of positive psychology at the University of Pennsylvania. She had one aha moment after another as she discovered all these principles of positive psychology she had been intuitively practicing all along: self-awareness, self-regulation, optimism, mental agility, strength of character, and connection. "The most important thing I learned is that these are trainable techniques as opposed to just luck. That was an epiphany for me, actually."

Seligman's program had already been rolled out in schools and universities, and proven to reduce depression, anxiety, and problematic behavior.[3] Just as in schools, the idea is to equip soldiers with coping strategies, resilient thinking, and antidotes to unhelpful emotional responses. "Focusing on the pathologies of depression, anxiety, suicide, and PTSD was the tail wagging the dog," Seligman writes. "What the army could do was to move the entire distribution of reaction to adversity in the direction of resilience and growth. This would not only help prevent PTSD but also increase the number of soldiers who bounce back readily from adversity. Most important, it would increase the number of our soldiers who would grow psychologically from the crucible of combat."[4] Seligman sees a clear correlation between the training and the results the army urgently needs. "As emotional fitness goes up, PTSD symptoms decline."[5]

Richard Tedeschi helped design the module on posttraumatic growth for the online ArmyFit training.[6] "After trauma, it's important to acknowledge mental suffering will happen," this module instructs. "At a certain point, and in tandem with continuing distress, a crucial foundation of posttraumatic growth is making meaning out of and reflecting about one's trauma."

Would just *telling* soldiers about posttraumatic growth enable them to accept reactions such as stress, sadness, or anxiety as growing pains, rather than trying to fight and suppress them? Trauma can cause biochemical changes in the brain that no positive thinking can easily wipe away, and some soldiers return from combat with brain damage that is not easily mended. Can we move the breaking point?

Rhonda cautions, "Not everybody who undergoes a fitness program is able to finish a marathon, but everybody will come out of it stronger and fitter. Same with resilience."

So, what does such a resilience boot camp look like?

Planting the seeds of resilience

In Philadelphia, Dr. Karen Reivich, the codirector of the Penn Resiliency Project, tries to instill some positive thinking in 178 army commanders, all garbed in camo fatigues and desert boots. When she asks them what they have learned about their thinking traps, the chorus of the commanders rings out in unison, "Diggin' deeeeeeep!"

Resilience training is now mandatory in every army leader development school in the United States. Every year each soldier answers 105 questions from the Global Assessment Tool (GAT) that has been designed to measure not only their physical but also their emotional, social, familial, and spiritual well-being.

Soldiers rate themselves on statements such as:

"When bad things happen to me, I expect more bad things to happen" (typical catastrophic thinking); and
"In uncertain times, I usually expect the best" (typical Gabby Giffords disposition).

The questions aim at identifying thinking patterns such as optimism, because we know optimism is a keen predictor of resilience.[7] In order to encourage soldiers to answer frankly, the questionnaires are taken anonymously.

Reivich, a trim, energetic mother of four, likens the process of fortifying resilience to gardening. "We try to take out all the weeds, for instance the counterproductive thinking patterns and negativity bias, and we're also planting flowers. In resilience training it's not enough to have just a plot of land without weeds, 'cause that's not a garden, so you have to plant something."

Identify unhelpful patterns

Reivich has singled out catastrophic thinking, the tendency to focus on the bad stuff, as the worst weed and a major culprit for "the self-fulfilling nature of the downward spiral that catastrophizing and believing you have PTSD engenders."[8]

If we imagine the worst, we are significantly more likely to indeed make it happen. A wise friend likes to say that worrying is like praying for what you don't want.

Reversing a downward spiral

Karen Reivich cautions that catastrophizing is *not* the same as planning for contingencies; instead, "the problem with catastrophizing is that it wastes critical energy ruminating about the irrational worst-case outcomes and prevents people from taking purposeful action."

Reivich and her team teach fourteen core skills, such as goal setting, energy management, problem solving, and assertive communication. Each psychologist might use a slightly different set of tools and terms, but we see a common thread here. "When people have mastered and used these skills in their life, they are more robust in the face of stress, they can cope more effectively with problems, they have tools to be able to maintain strong relationships, so the goal is to enhance the overall well-being and resilience of the force," explains Reivich. "The resilience myths are: never show emotion; you're always fully composed; you either have it or you don't. The resilience facts are: you learn to regulate your emotions; it's not always pretty; everyone can develop it."

She distinguishes several kinds of resilience, beyond the "bouncing back" definition I gave at the beginning of this book: overcoming negative events that may have occurred in the past, steering through everyday adversities, and dealing with major life-altering setbacks. But she also explores a kind of "resilience that transcends our desire to protect and defend ourselves. Those of you whose goal is to find renewed meaning and purpose in life and to be open to new experiences and challenges can apply resilience to reach out so that you can achieve all you are capable of."[9]

She quotes from the poem *Invictus* by the English writer William Ernest Henley (who wrote about his "unconquerable soul" while in the hospital after a foot amputation):

> "I am the master of my fate,
> I am the captain of my soul."

Be the captain of your soul

These lines of poetry articulate exactly the one core message I want to get across. No matter who or what controls our body, our food, or our freedoms, we are in charge of what matters most: our mind.

"Being a POW is the rape of your entire life," Rhonda Cornum writes. "But what I learned in those Iraqi bunkers and prison cells is that the experience doesn't have to be devastating, that it depends on you."[10]

Rhonda quotes David Jacobsen, who had been held hostage in Lebanon: "As long as you have your brain, your mind, you are free."[11]

Holocaust survivor Viktor Frankl called resilience the "result of an inner decision. . . . Fundamentally, therefore, any man can, even under such circumstances, decide what shall become of him—mentally and spiritually."[12] (Rhonda actually shared a dorm with Frankl's daughter at college, but was too young to understand the greatness of her roommate's dad.)

Most people believe that an event triggers a response. Being taken prisoner triggers helplessness, being attacked triggers fear or aggression, being praised triggers happiness. Right? But if you think about it, it's not the event itself that triggers our response, it's our mind. It's what we make of it. Otherwise, everybody everywhere on the planet would have to feel exactly the same way when they get praised, attacked, or imprisoned. Yet the reality is that there are as many nuanced responses as there are people.

You are what you think

As a practicing Buddhist, I am familiar with this idea as one of the first and most fundamental principles the Buddha ever taught, "You are what you think. All that you are arises from your thoughts. With your thoughts you make your world."[13]

Buddha's wisdom echoes what scientists call "the ABC theory."[14] "There is an activating event (A), your beliefs about the event (B), and those beliefs drive the consequences (C)," Rhonda explains. She reckons, "You have to change what you believe. Some people do that naturally, others less naturally and have to be taught the steps. The ABC theory is how I always thought; it just had never occurred to me to formulate it. It made such perfect sense."

Essentially, this stance puts all of us back in charge of our own mind and life. (And yes, it is easier said than done. The rest of the book is about how to get there.)

Communicate honestly, openly, and clearly

The army's resilience program starts with good communication—"active constructive communication skills"[15] that foster trust and positive emotions—so that soldiers learn to communicate openly and honestly.

Kinder, gentler, more effective

Rhonda gives the example of the gas chamber test every recruit has to master before graduating. "In every group there are some who are afraid to do it. Before, the drill sergeant would usually just yell at them until they either shit their pants and went home, or went in." Now the army has "a better way of doing this. You ask them, 'What are you afraid of? Think about the worst thing that can happen.' Then you can usually find some evidence to refute the worst of their fears." A recruit afraid of the gas chamber might say, "I'm afraid I won't get out." A sergeant trained in constructive communication might then say, "Okay, let's go and look: there are no locks on these doors, you cannot possibly get locked in. Two, the gas we're using is not deadly; it won't kill you. And three, you've been putting on your gas mask successfully in nine seconds for the last several weeks; what makes you think you couldn't do it today?"

Rhonda finds that "applying evidence to unreasonable fear is kinder, gentler, and much more effective than screaming at someone. We are teaching life-coping skills, and this thinking doesn't just apply to combat, but it applies to life! When something happens, many people see the aftermath as inevitable. I see it as a decision. You can control what you think."

The smile policy

Rhonda believed in the power of positivity long before she was aware of the science to back it up. We know that happiness is seriously contagious.[16] An optimistic leader can boost the morale of her entire unit. Rhonda sensed this instinctively. Early on in her career she took over a hospital department at Fort Rucker that had received "more complaints than any other." She immediately implemented what she calls her greatest innovation: a smile policy. The staff did not spend more money, but they smiled more. "We just changed the attitude." And the complaints stopped.[17]

Barbara Fredrickson at the University of North Carolina designed the emotional fitness module for the Comprehensive Soldier Fitness program. She researched the effect of positive and negative emotions and came to the conclusion that companies, relationships, and individuals thrive when positive and negative emotions strike an optimum ratio of about 3 to 1.[18] Especially when we live through hardship, inviting positivity might be the last thing on our minds, but we likely have to take active steps to counteract the bleak and bump this ratio up a notch.

 ### Invite positivity

Invite positivity into your life in whatever form it takes for you. Visit a friend, tend to your garden, take up running! After a grueling divorce from an addict, one of my friends learned deep-sea diving in her midforties. It was something she had always wanted to do but never got around to while raising her kids. She now credits it with saving her life.

Gabby Giffords's joy has become singing, and her favorite
song is U2's "Beautiful Day," a song about someone who lost
everything and yet appreciates the beauty of his surroundings.
Don't let that beautiful day get away.

Rhonda does not own a TV, "because TV bombards you with
negative images, about which you can do *nothing*. TV teaches
you learned helplessness as a by-product, which is a *really bad*
thing to learn. It is the antithesis of posttraumatic growth, self-
confidence, and self-sufficiency. So I just don't do it."

She uses a news extraction service to keep her abreast of
current events in the world, but rather than sitting in front
of a screen every evening, she spends her time playing with
her puppies, reading a good book, or paging through *Mother
Earth News*.

As a journalist, I hate to admit it, but I think it's true: the
twenty-four-hour news cycle, with its nonstop bombardment
of sensationalized stories, does damage. Of course, media in
and of itself is neither good nor bad. We can use media to
educate ourselves, to learn, and broaden our horizon. But
the average American youth spends more than seven hours
a day in front of a screen, and probably not watching the
science channel. Glaring at a screen is children's primary activity besides sleeping, and by the time they turn eighteen,
"the average adolescent will have seen an estimated 200,000
acts of violence on television alone. Much of the violence
on television and in movies is presented in a sanitized and
glamorized fashion, and in children's programming it often
is presented as humorous."[19] So it is no surprise that "recent
evidence raises concerns about media's effects on aggression,
sexual behavior, substance use, disordered eating, and aca-
demic difficulties."[20]

Choose what you feed your mind

"We choose what we put in our mouth, whether it is a cheeseburger and fries, or salmon and broccoli," Rhonda says. "In the same way, we choose what we put in our minds, whether it is puppy pictures and a good book, or watching the Twin Towers come down and a tsunami slush out a civilization over and over. It is a choice."

Resilience is an ongoing decision Rhonda makes every minute, every day.

Rhonda calls for a tectonic shift of perception—and not just in the army. "It's important that as a culture we focus more on potential positives. I really think we are massively teaching people catastrophic imprinting." Rhonda emphasizes that her approach includes assessing things honestly and dealing with them realistically. "In our society, we *encourage* people to focus on the negative. Now we have a country in which more people die of prescription drug overdoses than of illegal drug overdoses. Why do you suppose that is? Because we want to make them numb. We're afraid anybody *feels* something."

From Rhonda's perspective, resilience training should start in childhood. However, "we bubble-wrap our kids; we're afraid to let them out."

So, toughen up? "Toughen up, and rub some dirt on it!"

Always invincible and invulnerable?

But at the same time, it's important not to be *too* tough: the army has ditched much of its old Rambo rhetoric that a soldier needs to be invincible and invulnerable. In fact, the Rambo type who is prone to impulsive, lone hero acts is much more susceptible to PTSD than his or her levelheaded team workers.[21]

Soldiers who participate in the resilience boot camp tell me that the training gives them "a vocabulary to talk about mental and psychological issues before they become problematic." Part of the training is to identify dangerous "icebergs," which Reivich defines as "core beliefs and values that fuel out-of-proportion emotions." An example of an iceberg the resilience program aims to tackle is the commonly held belief that "asking for help is a sign of weakness."

Seek help

The army has recognized the dangers of projecting only strength. A disproportionate number of people who have a hard time overcoming trauma are people who struggle by themselves, who think they don't need help, or who bottle up their feelings and hide their anxiety behind an impenetrable facade. Trying desperately "to get it together" can be fatal. Now every soldier carries a phone number that he or she can call at any time, anonymously, when they need help.

For the rest of us, when things get dire and we don't know where to turn for help, the National Suicide Prevention Lifeline can be a lifesaver. Call 1-800-273-TALK (8255) in the United States.

Eradicating the stigma

Thirty-five-year-old Staff Sergeant Christian Condo-Carpio was first invited to resilience training in Philadelphia after struggling with a divorce and anxiety following his deployment at the Iraq-Kuwait border. "The program helps to eradicate the stigma of seeking help," he says, and confirms he benefited from the methods (and not just on the job). "The resiliency training works if you apply it to everyday life." Condo-Carpio takes a few minutes every morning to practice deliberate breathing before he gets out of his car at the army base. The breathing technique is known to lower the heart rate and to increase focus and self-awareness. "Let me have a few moments of calm before whatever surprise work will throw at me. The skills they teach here make you think outside the box. Sometimes there are things you can't change, but you can handle them better. You take a step back, analyze it, and it helps you solve a problem before anything gets out of hand."

The army program includes "spiritual fitness." Many of the soldiers, including Rhonda, surprise me by confessing to meditating every day. Because the Comprehensive Soldier Fitness Program recommends meditation,[22] they decided to try it and stuck with it. Maybe I shouldn't be surprised. From snipers to Google executives, Americans are discovering the benefit of mindfulness in all kinds of novel contexts. Because the most common PTSD treatments—medication and psychotherapy—work for only about half of the soldiers, the army is experimenting with alternative methods, from methamphetamine to electronic brain implants. Meditation has proven to be one of the most promising pathways. Stanford psychologist Emma Seppälä was able to show that breathing-based meditation significantly reduces PTSD symptoms, anxiety, and startle response,[23] and a new study found that US Marines with mindfulness training recover faster after combat stress.[24]

Meditation is part of a much vaster, ancient tradition, and usually coupled with training in empathy and compassion. I have been fortunate to train with some of the greatest meditation masters of our time, such as the Dalai Lama. But most scientific studies in the West employ a very basic form of focused attention meditation that anybody can learn, independent of their faith.

Train in mindfulness

We carry the most powerful tools for transformation always with us: our awareness, and our breath. The two work together as a team, with the breath nourishing us, anchoring us, and keeping us alive in this present moment. Emotions affect our breathing, but our breathing affects emotion, too, and we can use our breath to ground and calm us. As we grow older most of us unlearn what babies can do perfectly: breathing naturally and fully. The natural breath is a full-belly breath. If you put your palms on your belly, you should feel the tides of breath rise and fall in the area below your navel. In its simplest form, mindfulness meditation just means becoming aware of the breath.

Because mindfulness meditation is so helpful, I have included detailed instructions in the guide in the back of the book.

I encourage you to build a daily practice. It can be short, maybe twelve to twenty minutes, but it is better that you make it a regular habit than an occasional weekend experiment.

Mindfulness and self-awareness are essential skills in regaining mastery over our mind.

Dr. Hedy Kober, a neuroscientist at Yale University, initially started to meditate to help her heartache after a breakup, but she soon found that meditation eased not only her emotional pain and stress but also some physical discomfort. She and her colleagues designed a simple study to test this. Participants were given a painfully hot stimulus on their arms. After they were instructed to respond to the sensation with mindfulness and acceptance, they reported 27 percent less pain. They had no experience in meditation, but were simply asking themselves these questions: "Is this a tolerable pain? Can I handle it?" And they didn't just say they felt less pain to please their examiners—their nerves actually responded differently. The brain activity in the regions responsible for painful stimulus dropped more than half. "Learning to meditate can significantly alter your experience of stress," Kober concludes.[25] "It can change not only the way your brain functions during stress, but also the way that it is structured over time. A little bit of mindfulness can go a very long way."

Another extremely effective method for fostering positive emotions is keeping a journal of gratitude. Rhonda tells me that the idea of a "gratitude journal" sounded too touchy-feely for a bunch of combat guys, so the army renamed it "Hunt the Good Stuff," but the exercise is the same:

Hunt the good stuff

Find the good things that are happening and reflect on them, instead of brooding on the bad stuff. "Keeping a gratitude journal is an easy and effective method to increase positive emotions, which is really important," says Rhonda Cornum.

In the appendix, you will find guidance on how to approach this. Counting one's blessings is one of the simplest and most powerful means to throw an anchor in the midst of chaos. Especially when we are walking in the dark, we need to count every star.

"My wife just had our sixth baby!" one soldier announces in a "Hunt the Good Stuff" session. Another soldier reveals she has just been promoted to major.

During the break, Bobby McFerrin's "Don't Worry, Be Happy" fills the conference room.

The soldiers hum the melody, oblivious that only hours later, their newly acquired resilience skills will be put to the test. In the early evening, the soldiers run the two and a half miles to the Rocky statue at the Philadelphia Museum of Art, and pose victoriously with raised fists. Yet while clowning around, a few who are stationed at Fort Hood get emergency alerts: A thirty-four-year-old Iraq veteran and father of four has just shot three comrades at Fort Hood and then turned the gun on himself. The news whipsaws through the troop.

The soldiers are stunned into speechlessness. The rampage is a reminder of how fragile equilibrium is, thousands of miles away from the front. Collectively, they commemorate the victims with a minute of silence.

Michael Bourgeois, a fresh-faced twenty-five-year-old staff sergeant in the infantry who has already deployed in Iraq and Afghanistan seven times, shakes his head. "We who are here are the ones who made it," he asserts, "but we lost some people."

A petri dish for fostering resilience

The soldiers are more than happy that the issues are addressed, but they worry the efforts might not go far enough. And they have quite specific concerns about admitting to anxiety or suicidal thoughts in front of their superiors—they worry about being kicked out. "You're well taken care of as long as you are with the army," one soldier says, "but when you leave, it's an entirely different story. The American people are totally disconnected from the reality of the war and the price we pay."

I can't help but think this plays a role in the results: After a four-year run of the resilience program, the surveys show a significant decline in substance abuse, and an uptick in optimism, good coping, adaptability, and character strength. It's a success, but the correlation between resilience training and a decline in PTSD or depression has not proven solid.[26]

Psychologist Ann Masten, who grew up in an army family, cautions, "It is a problem to conceive of resilience only as fitness, analogous to physical fitness. You can go too far with that analogy. The conclusion you can also reach is, if you break down in combat, it is because you weren't fit, you weren't strong enough, there must be something wrong with you. The risk is that this approach can shift over to blaming the victim. Resilience depends on the systems we are connected to, the military as a whole, our families. A lot of what makes the difference for people is the support they are receiving, but I think the army *gets* it now." The army recognizes that resilience is a group effort. The $160 million program recently began to include army spouses, even teenage children, in an effort to boost the soldiers' overall well-being.[27]

Colonel Kenneth Riddle, the current director of the Comprehensive Soldier Fitness program, thinks that it will take about ten years before the army will see the full effect of the program.

Rhonda remains upbeat. "It is like taking aspirin. It does not prevent a heart attack in everybody, but an improvement in a small percentage is still an improvement that makes it worthwhile."

Realistically, the resilience training is but one tier in a multilayered effort to improve the army's mental and emotional fitness. Think of it as a grand experiment: More than a million soldiers have gone through resilience training, and once they have had time to put it to the test, we will have a much better understanding of which strategies in building resilience and posttraumatic growth work best. In a way, the army volunteers as a giant petri dish for fostering resilience.

The surefire way to build resilience

Tedeschi breaks the worst piece of news gently: the surefire way to build resilience is to go through hardship. Tedeschi believes that his training module "just gives people a heads-up. If you go through trauma, it doesn't mean that you're doomed to PTSD; it also doesn't mean that you'll just sail through because you're a strong guy and nothing can beat you. The most realistic alternative is: the trauma will affect you. Maybe let it change you in ways that you value."

Tedeschi differentiates, though, between learning that is intellectual and learning that comes from experience. "Resilience that comes after growth is so effective in helping people manage future traumas because they have experienced a visceral impact. It's not like, 'Okay, I read a book. When trauma comes up, I'll experience posttraumatic growth and be fine.'" Tedeschi snaps his fingers. "That's not nearly as effective as learning the hard way, through your own struggles. If we really want to implicate resilience," Tedeschi offers, "maybe we need to put all these people through some god-awful trauma and let them grow. Then they will be resilient in ways they wouldn't be otherwise."

This is what happened to Rhonda: she feels the capture only made her stronger. But at what cost? The god-awful trauma of the Iraq wars also destroyed thousands of lives.

As journalist Malcolm Gladwell asks, "The question of what any of us would wish on our children is the wrong question, isn't it? The right question is whether we as a society *need* people who have emerged from some kind of trauma—and the answer is that we plainly do. This is not a pleasant fact to contemplate. For every remote miss who becomes stronger, there are countless near misses who are crushed by what they have been through. There are times and places, however, when all of us depend on people who have been hardened by their experiences."[28]

People like Rhonda.

But there are bigger issues at play here than a boot camp can solve: Several of the soldiers I talk to signed up with the army after 9/11, motivated to defend their country, but they now find themselves in a riot of doubt. What exactly did they risk their lives for? While Rhonda Cornum was able to find meaning in her mission and trust in her superiors, soldiers returning from Iraq and Afghanistan now struggle to find purpose in their sacrifice, and they feel betrayed. Their anger is palpable. Vietnam vets suffered from similar frustration; some said getting spit at by Americans after their return was more traumatizing than being shot at in the war. Yet this "meaning-making," as Tedeschi calls it, is crucial for integrating our experiences. If our suffering makes sense, we are much more able to not only bear it but also to grow from it.

So resilience and posttraumatic growth are not just tasks for the soldier's psyche (or any survivor's, for that matter). That we, as a country, leave alone the very soldiers we sent into war makes us "complicit in a plague of American disengagement," as Jennifer Percy wrote in the *New York Times*.[29] How we, as a culture, as friends and family welcome, support, and integrate the survivors matters hugely.

This is significant: we can help our soldiers and our fellow survivors to bounce forward.

4. Play

"You can't stop me from dreaming"
Jazz legend Coco Schumann survived
Auschwitz by playing for his life[1]

> *Suffering in and of itself is meaningless;*
> *we give our suffering meaning by the*
> *way in which we respond to it.*
> —HAROLD S. KUSHNER[2]

In his tiny living room lined with yellow-brown daisy wallpaper, Coco Schumann navigates through piles of letters, photos, memories. "I need a compass!" he exclaims. His pale blue eyes sparkle with mischief that life's trials haven't managed to wipe off his round face. Looking back at a vibrant entertainment career that spans more than six decades, he proudly recounts that the hip jazz club in Munich he played just a week ago with his quartet was sold out on two consecutive evenings. Eyeing up the stash of autograph demands and invitations piled on his dinner table, Coco, now in his nineties, quips, "When I get old, I'll quit."

When I first met Coco twenty years ago, he had just begun to hesitantly unearth the most difficult years of his life after burying them in silence for five decades. "He who wants to remember has to entrust himself to forgetfulness," the French philosopher Maurice Blanchot once wrote. Coco Schumann gave himself to forgetfulness so completely that when he begins to remember, as if throwing open floodgates, images deluge him. With every word, every sentence, every flashback, Coco haltingly feels his way through unchartered territory.

A cab drive through Berlin with Coco is a trip down memory lane. He softly hums the first beats of Gershwin's "I Got Rhythm," the signature tune of the legendary Ghetto Swingers, casually flicking the beat with his fingers, his round-bellied figure swaying with the rhythm.

His index finger shoots toward the brightly lit-up Kantstraße. "There, the Delphi! They called it Europe's most pompous dance palace, and below is the Quasimodo, where I began!" Cruising through Berlin at night, the jazz legend relives his youth. Coco's hoarse bass voice resurrects the crowded ballrooms, revives the rag-doll jazz and the glitter of the nightclubs—the whole swinging Berlin of the early thirties. "The city had a jewel-like sparkle," Josephine Baker reminisced. "The vast cafés reminded me of ocean liners powered by the rhythms of their orchestras." Until Hitler sunk them.

Too short for the barstool

Coco's thoughts fly back to the summer of 1937, when the Nazis had already banned his beloved jazz. At thirteen, he was too short to fit on a barstool. But he was tall enough to climb the walls in front of the Delphi to peek into a window and catch the beats of "swing-king" Teddy Stauffer, which he found addictive. He begged his uncle for a castoff drum kit. "A wicked thing with a Charleston-machine and multicolored lights behind its skin." The whippersnapper hauled it with straps into the pubs and drummed up his first reichsmarks—enough money to buy his first guitar and to launch a short, dashing career in the flashy bars of a metropolis bent on pleasure. He fell into a passionate love affair with exactly the kind of rhythms the Nazis had just declared "degenerate nigger dance." One could never march lockstep to the blues. "And yet we played it daily," Coco triumphs. "Cronies kept watch in front of the clubs."

When the gestapo's brownshirts approached, the band switched tempi at the snap of a finger: from Tiger Rag to Rosamunde, from St. Louis Blues to the purebred kitsch the Nazis liked to hear. During daytime he fulfilled his war duties as a plumber; at night he jammed hot jazz with Bully Buhlan, Helmut Zacharias, and Ernst van t'Hoff—until 1943. Coco carried his mandatory Jewish badge in his pocket rather than on his chest.

"I had the good fortune that I didn't look the least Jewish, with my blue eyes and my strong Berlin vernacular," Coco says, giggling.

His bold banter saved his life numerous times.

"Actually, you have reason to arrest me," he once teased the SS watchdogs who regularly patrolled the Rosita Bar. "I'm Jewish, Swing, and a minor." The SS guard broke into laughter, and the whole bar roared. Coco's hiding place was the limelight. When he saw a street patrol, his strategy was to walk straight up to them and demand in his broadest Berlin dialect, "Please tell me, how can I get to such-and-such street? Isn't it just around the corner?" For a few years, he got away with this subterfuge, and his charm let the guards forget to ask for his papers.

The sweetness of oblivion

Many jazz buffs celebrate Coco Schumann as one of the world's finest jazz guitarists. His gigs after World War II with Marlene Dietrich, Ella Fitzgerald, and as sidekick of Helmut Zacharias are legendary. Stylish in his white tuxedo, Coco smiles slyly from the old record sleeves he stores away in the minuscule townhouse in Berlin-Dahlem where he's lived for fifty years. His rendering of "I Got Rhythm" recently appeared in a new edition. A musical about his life is receiving standing ovations on stages all across Germany. Coco is an entertainer through and through—ever ready to break into peals of laughter, always willing to use a silly line. I pay him a compliment about his good looks, and he breaks into a pitch-perfect traditional German folk song: "It's not Sigismund's fault that he's so gorgeous . . ."

But Coco carefully kept the years between his nineteenth birthday and his postwar career wrapped under a shroud of silence. "The sweetness of oblivion" was the Delphi Palace's slogan, written brightly above its flashing entrance, and Coco tried in vain to taste that sweetness.

He didn't speak about "it." Not for five decades. Not even his closest friends knew what had happened to him except for the barest of facts Coco volunteered.

"I was in Theresienstadt and Auschwitz," he would say and leave it at that.

But then on a visit to the Bavarian countryside in the nineties, a group of youngsters were drinking at a table next to him. The more beer they drank, the louder they declared their convictions that the Holocaust never happened, and that the stories of the concentration camps were cooked-up lies. "I'm sorry," Coco injected politely before he got up to leave. "I know better. I was there." After nearly half a century, the encounter forced him to break his silence. Now he knew he had to share his story.

A coffeehouse in the ghetto

Coco was nineteen when a snitch turned him in for being Jewish, playing jazz, and seducing German damsels. The Nazis deported him and assigned him to the next freight train to Auschwitz. His father, a decorated veteran of World War I, rushed to the train station, showed off his Aryan ID, and argued with the head of the station until he at least managed to detour his son to Theresienstadt. In its earlier years, Theresienstadt was not yet a death camp. "It was the flagship ghetto the Nazis showed the world," says Coco.

Much to his astonishment, Coco discovered a coffeehouse shortly after his arrival.

"A coffeehouse! In the ghetto! I couldn't believe my eyes."

There, Coco found the legendary Ghetto Swingers playing the music of Count Basie and Duke Ellington that the Nazis had long outlawed in the rest of Germany—a surreal, sweet background tune to the cataclysm of the war. Because the Ghetto Swingers' drummer had been deported to Auschwitz a few days before, Coco took his place. They played every day.

"We feigned a normal life. We tried to forget that there was an impenetrable fence all around."

In a propaganda film, Hitler tried to pass off Theresienstadt as a summer camp for Jewish tourists. Kids had to call the camp leaders "uncle" and grumble in front of the cameras about the rich food ("Oil sardines again, Uncle?") while the Ghetto Swingers played upbeat rhythms of "You Can't Stop Me From Dreaming" and the tango "Avant de Mourir" ("Before Dying"). In brand-new black suits (which they had to return the next day), the musicians served as extras in one of the most cynical pieces of Nazi propaganda. The camp commanders promised that they would reward all of the participants in the film by releasing them into freedom.

But every illusion of normalcy was a sham. "After the film shooting," says Coco, his voice breaking, "we were all immediately deported to Auschwitz, many of us straight into the gas chamber." Only three of the sixteen musicians survived.

Playing music in hell

"Take a good look," the commander told them upon arrival, while the emaciated prisoners lined up before him, stripped stark naked. "This is the extermination camp Auschwitz. You've already passed the entrance, and this"—he pointed to the fuming chimneys—"is the exit."

Auschwitz had all the elements of trauma in surplus: starvation, torture, random acts of cruelty, mass murder of innocent children and family members, and no escape.

Despite being surrounded by the stench of death and screams of torture, commanders competed for the best bands. The death camp was beyond reason and laws anyway, and the camp commanders cultivated their love for the jazz arrangements their propaganda minister had forbidden. Immediately upon his arrival, Coco Schumann was asked to start a band, together with two other members from the Ghetto Swingers. He spent his first evening in Auschwitz jamming popular tunes from the Hamburg red-light district. "The music," Coco keeps repeating, "saved our lives."

Coco had to play for the SS hangmen, "for hours and hours every day, especially when they tattooed the new arrivals, because they considered it such boring work."

Because he was such an outstanding musician, the commander led him to one of thirty rooms stuffed to the brim with piles of clothes, boots, glasses, and hair the dead had left behind. He allowed Coco to pick sturdy boots, an essential tool for survival in the frostbiting Polish winter. Extra portions of food saved Coco from dwindling away like so many of the withered men around him.

"The human is a peculiar creation," Coco ponders. "Unpredictable and merciless. What we saw in those days was unbearable, and yet we bore it. We played the tunes to it, for the sake of our bare survival. We played music in hell."[3]

To this day he has only shared a fraction of what he saw in Auschwitz: the charred corpses that hung from the electric fence; the spontaneous decision of his best buddy Fricek Weiss to join his parents on their way to the gas chamber; the daily onslaught of lice and fleas that spread epidemic typhus; the forlorn look of the children who stared him in the eye while they marched to the gas chamber, passing his orchestra playing uplifting folk songs. The Nazis' favorite was "La Paloma."

> *Singing joyous and free,*
> *Oh! We're going*
> *None are so gay as we!*

Coco didn't look away.

"They knew exactly that they were going into the gas chamber. Exactly!" he says, shaking his head.

"To see was terrifying, and to stop seeing tore me apart from my forehead to my throat," Maurice Blanchot writes in *The Madness of the Day*. Coco only wants to share as much as necessary to give the younger generations a sense of the regime. "I can speak about it, but I can't tell you what really happened—what we experienced was too monstrous. There are no words for it."

How does one go on living after having seen hell?

"A normal human would need five lives for all that I have lived through," he says. "To this day I don't quite know how to do this: one cannot and must not forget, and yet one cannot let one's life be dominated by that."[4]

When the Americans dismantled the camps, liberation reached Coco almost too late: Just a few days before the end of the Nazi regime, he had contracted the dreaded spotted fever that had carried off his campmates by the hundreds, and he spent weeks fighting high fevers and delirious nightmares. He and one other man were the only ones to survive the sick bay. When he was finally able to return home to Berlin, he learned that his grandparents, aunts, uncles, and cousins had perished in the camps. But he found his parents alive. Coco's father had ingeniously succeeded in keeping his Jewish wife hidden from the Nazis by declaring her dead after a disastrous fire.

Coco explored his old turf and came across a jazz bar, where some of his old band buddies were just tuning their instruments. After a stunned silence, they welcomed him back as if he had returned from the dead. Instead of discussing what happened during the years that separated them, Coco grabbed a guitar, and they jammed.

To this day he refuses to be defined by his stay in the death camps. "I am a musician who survived the concentration camp. Not a Holocaust survivor who happens to make music."

The difference matters to him.

Look forward

When I ask Coco what kept him going, he says, "I decided I could either live the rest of my life being broken by Auschwitz or be joyful that I survived." The amazement of being alive triumphs over the perils of the past. Herein lies a crucial balance we all need to strike: to make peace with our past while also looking forward.

Coco's life shows us how fragile this balance is—at times, his pain tipped into denial, and at other times, memories crushed his spirit. But eventually, there is no other way: In order to rebuild our lives, we need to acknowledge and integrate the events from the past into our personal history, while at the same time not letting them define us forever.

"Unbelievably mean and terribly beautiful"

Coco was never religious, but after the Nazis "hammered the Jewishness into me, I decided to be Jewish." When the long lines of people passed him on their way to their death, he prayed to God with all his fervor. "Do something, anything! But nobody came. No response. They all hovered above the clouds—the Christian and the Jewish God, Allah, and Buddha. When we needed them, nobody came."[5]

He still found faith, just not in a traditional idea of God.

"I know that there is 'something' that saved me," he says. "To encounter as many lucky coincidences as I have is impossible."[6]

In postwar Germany, the swing boom catapulted Coco to the zenith of his career, but he couldn't bear watching some of the old Nazis scramble back to power. "I couldn't forget the endless days in the camp. I *wanted* to forget less and less."[7]

He tried to flee from the memories by boarding a ship to Australia with his wife Gertraut, who was also a Theresienstadt survivor. There, Coco toiled in a jam factory, but not for long. A posh nightclub discovered him, and soon he rose to be a star musician, traveling around the continent.

He began a lifestyle of travels and parties, at times returning to Germany, at times seeking distance from his homeland in America, Australia, and on long cruises. A bottle of whiskey was essential to his daily diet. When jazz and swing went out of style, Coco hired himself out as a rock 'n' roll clown, played on luxury cruisers in the Caribbean and at drunken carnival parties in upscale clubs. He often asks himself, "Was my way of life right after the Holocaust? A futile question, for which there is no answer."

All the while, life kept showing its harsh face: his wife of sixty years was diagnosed with Alzheimer's and died a slow, painful death. A heart attack slowed him down; a tumor had to be cut out of his skull, leaving his bald head lopsided. And yet, Coco is one of the most joyful people you could ever meet. He is not the kind of entertainer who puts on a false smile and cracks jokes when in front of an audience, but a truly joyous person through and through. On his wall, he has pinned Charlie Chaplin's famous motto, "A day without laughter is a day wasted."

A well-known German newspaper once printed a headline above a profile of him: "Coco Schumann—the horrible life of a jazz legend."

Coco has a different perspective. "But that's not true. No, my dear, I tell myself, looking at this bright planet, it was a wild and colorful ride, at times too long, but always too short, life has shown me its unbelievably mean and terribly beautiful face. But one thing it was and is certainly not: horrible."[8]

Worthy of suffering

Coco's story illustrates a key lesson all resilience studies confirm: that the route to recovery lies neither in denial nor indulgence, but in the middle way of honest self-reflection, coupled with an inborn optimism and the determination not to give up.

Psychiatrist Viktor Frankl, whose story of survival resembles Coco's, wrote about "this spiritual freedom—which cannot be taken away—that makes life meaningful and purposeful. . . . If there is a meaning in life at all, then there must be a meaning in suffering."[9]

Even when confronted with the unimaginable horrors of Auschwitz, Frankl searched for humor in the midst of calamity, counting the smallest instances of mercy while surrounded by insanity, consciously replacing the images of typhoid-stricken corpses he had to dispose of with pictures of himself teaching his students in an imagined better future. "Here lies the chance for a man either to make use of or to forgo the opportunities of attaining the moral values that a difficult situation may afford him," Frankl concluded. "And this decides whether he is worthy of his sufferings or not."[10]

Frankl said he could always tell when someone at Auschwitz suffered from "give-up-itis." They would smoke one of their last cigarettes—important bartering assets that could be traded for a lifesaving bowl of soup—then they either killed themselves by running into the high-voltage fence that surrounded the camp, or they would simply refuse to get up at all, and a day later they'd be gone, beaten to pulp by the guards, or left outside to freeze to death. Survival in Auschwitz depended on many factors—arbitrarily lining up in the right queue not slated for execution, securing a ladleful of soup with some rice rather than just watery broth, not being assigned to the most sadistic commanders, and so on. The majority of survivors attribute their narrow escape from death to luck—to the somewhat random chance of avoiding the ubiquitous death traps.[11]

 ## Choose your attitude

Despite this element of pure luck, Frankl was convinced that survival also depended on inner strength, on the ability to forge connections, to keep a positive spirit, and to nourish resilience.

"We who lived in concentration camps can remember the men who walked through the huts comforting others, giving away their last piece of bread. They may have been few in number, but they offer sufficient proof that everything can be taken away from a man but one thing: the last of the

human freedoms—to choose one's attitude in any given set
of circumstances, to choose one's own way."[12]

If prisoners find the freedom to choose their attitude in
the midst of the agony of concentration camps, can we honor
our freedom to choose in our everyday lives?

Seven decades after World War II, researchers are still exploring the long-term effect of the Holocaust on survivors.[13] While
their pain endures and ripples through their children's and
grandchildren's lives, survivors have shown resilience that de-
fies all odds.[14]

Dr. William B. Helmreich, a sociologist at the City University of New York, interviewed hundreds of Holocaust survivors. Their moving testimonies prove that they managed to
resurrect their lives with courage, hope, and determination.
"What emerges here," writes Helmreich, "is a portrait that
is sharply divergent from the stereotyped images that many
have of the survivors as people who are chronically depressed,
anxious, and fearful. While it is true that there are survivors
who exhibit such traits, this is by no means the norm."[15]

Despite their general lack of higher education, survivors
did comparatively well economically, socially, and commu-
nally.[16] Helmreich found the crime rate among the 140,000
Jews that immigrated to the United States "almost nonexistent," their marriages (often to other survivors) more stable
than the average marriage of American Jews, and they also
had more children. "Although there was, and still is, pathology within survivor families, the overall picture is one of
great love, commitment, and caring. . . . The survivors' social
world is characterized by strong friendships and loyalties. . . .
Although they cannot forget the horrors they endured and
have been scarred by them, they function well and seem to
require less professional counseling and assistance than one

would suspect from what has been written about them to date."[17]

Ten traits of resilience

Could it be that the very factors that helped these people survive enabled them to lead meaningful lives after the war?

"Most important, perhaps, what lessons can the rest of us learn from the survivors about coping with tragedy and adversity?" Helmreich asks.[18] He identifies ten traits of resilience the survivors have in abundance: flexibility, assertiveness, tenacity, optimism, intelligence, courage, the ability to distance themselves from the past so that it did not constantly intrude on their thinking, an awareness of belonging to a particular group, assimilating the knowledge that they survived, and the ability to find meaning in their lives.[19] The more of these traits present within an individual, Helmreich found, the greater the likelihood was that the survivor would regain his or her footing.[20]

Our tremendous capacity for hope

All these survivors have one trait in common: *They never gave up.* They did not give up when they were surrounded by death and starvation, subjected to abhorrent penalties for imaginary crimes. They did not give up after the war when they discovered that many of their relatives and friends had perished. They did not give up when their relatives greeted the emaciated prisoners with a mix of angst and contempt. And as postwar refugees, they often suffered additional hardships, illnesses, and losses, and yet they were brave enough to start over, bold enough to board ships to foreign continents, tenacious enough to start new businesses, and smart enough to make their ventures successful. They were optimistic enough to bring children into a world that had shown them its harshest side. What I find most striking is that despite their ordeals they were, in fact, significantly *more optimistic* about the future than their peers.[21]

Much like Coco, many survivors refuse to let themselves be defined by the horrors of the past, and defiantly look forward.

"The story of the survivors is one of courage and strength," Helmreich concludes, "of people who are living proofs of the indomitable will to survive and of their tremendous capacity for hope."[22]

The secret of liberation lies in remembrance

For Coco, resurrecting his life was an arduous journey. "Having seen Auschwitz, one can never leave it behind, whether one wants to or not. One can't forget it; at some point one has to start integrating the memories into one's life."[23] Coco quotes the writer Armin T. Wegner: "Wanting to forget prolongs the exile. The secret of liberation lies in remembrance."[24]

He is determined to remember bravely. "To this day many people are unable to confront Auschwitz or to tell what happened there. Every day people despair because of it. With everyone this happens to, Hitler wins a victory after all. To this day I don't know how to speak appropriately about what I experienced, I only know that I have to," Coco states with determination. "The more I talked about it, the more memories came back of things that I had buried deep down. Old dreams haunted me. The remembrance didn't dispel the ghosts, but revived them. But by now I can live with them without letting them get the best of me. They never got my life, and my joy of life."[25]

Today he allows himself to indulge in his passions: jazz,

blues, some soulful salsa. He changes into his black suit, carefully places his old Gibson in his little station wagon, and then he shows up in one of the old pubs of Berlin or Munich. At five feet, he's barely taller than his guitar case. But the fans greet him like a giant. "And then we let it rip," says Coco. "Fats Waller, until they dance on the tables."

Sometimes the audience asks for "La Paloma." And Coco Schumann plays what they want to hear.

"I have at least one good reason not to play 'La Paloma,' but also a thousand reasons to play it—every single person in the audience."[26] Coco found the inner strength to speak about his life, just as he found the strength to play "La Paloma" again. After all, he says, "It's not the music that's at fault."

PART II

EMBRACING OPPORTUNITY IN ADVERSITY

Reversing the logic of good and bad

Dear Pain,

I found your hiding spot, so watch out! I know where you live! You made your home in my mind— but I'm in charge of that place.

Cheers,
In Charge

5. Accept

"Sickness as an assignment"
How I grappled with the idea that adversity
has advantages

Your enemy is your best teacher.

—THE DALAI LAMA[1]

When suffering strikes, running in the opposite direction as fast as we can seems to make so much sense, doesn't it?

After all, nobody wants suffering in their life. So we avoid it at all costs. We dodge and duck and bargain. But pushing pain away doesn't cut it, does it? It's like the three-year-old who closes her eyes and then pretends she can't be seen.

As Buddhist teacher Pema Chödrön says, "No one ever tells us to stop running away from fear. We are very rarely told to move closer, to just be there, to become familiar with fear."[2]

When I once asked Pema how she dealt with her own debilitating chronic fatigue, she said she tried to apply the advice her teacher Trungpa Rinpoche had given her. "Lean into it. Stay present. Stay curious. Go through it paying meticulous attention as if you wanted to describe it in great detail to someone who's never heard of it."[3] However, as she writes in her bestseller *When Things Fall Apart*, "The advice we usually get is to sweeten it up, smooth it over, take a pill, or distract ourselves, but by all means make it go away."[4]

I will make the case that there is something profoundly skewed about the way we approach suffering. What would happen if we stayed to pay attention?

A crash with consequences

I had no choice but to stay and pay attention when I came down with that violent illness in my late twenties. Running away was out of the question. I literally could not move. Think of the worst flu you ever had, and multiply that by eight months. When I looked in the mirror, a gaunt alien stared back. What was this stranger doing in my bathroom and in my body?

Slowly, doctors offered pieces of an explanation. A virus, plus parasites, plus prolonged exposure to toxins—this was a world-class recipe for a breakdown of my immune system. In hindsight, I had early forewarnings of allergies to chemicals even before I set out on the trip to Asia, but at the time I thought I was just overworked.

My family belongs to the do-it-yourselfers who used a very popular but toxic wood varnish in the early seventies. Shortly before my birth, my father had renovated his family's house to make space for my arrival. He treated the wood ceilings, doors, and window frames liberally with Xyladecor, a bestselling varnish. The potion worked so fabulously because it contained lindane, pentachlorophenol (PCP), and other powerful insecticides and pesticides. By the time its most dangerous ingredients were recognized as carcinogens and banned from indoor use, innumerable homes had been contaminated. So, in the first years of my life, I had breathed in a daily and dangerous dose of chemicals. Allergies, headaches, and other pains were everyday symptoms in my family, but we were unaware of the cause until much later when I worked for a science magazine, looked at the long list of symptoms of chemical poisoning an environmental specialist presented to me, and realized the connection. Though my parents immediately ripped out the contaminated wood and threw away all our furniture, blood tests still found high concentrations of the chemicals in our blood and cells two decades after the initial exposure. We all underwent professional detox treatments, but once this stuff has inserted itself into your cells, you never get it completely out of your body. No wonder a carpet laced with formaldehyde can send me to the hospital. My body had reached the limit of toxins it can absorb already in childhood.

Hindsight being 20/20, it wasn't just the Nepalese toxins and a virus, but the sum of all these attacks on my immune system that brought it down. Chronic fatigue is an inappropriate name for this monster, because every human is regularly fatigued. After a steep hike or a long day of work, fatigue can even feel blissful. An out-of-control immune system, however, sends the body into erratic physical overreactions, at times with crippling pain, and a debilitating exhaustion that neither determination nor strong espresso can overpower.

Unfortunately, some of the damage could not be undone. I just had to be patient, get acupuncture, and drink weak vegetable soup. Patient? Me? Not my forte. In the Himalayas I had met Edmund Hillary, the famous Everest pioneer, and I often think of his insight, "It's not the mountain we conquer but ourselves." I couldn't entirely conquer the illness, but I had to conquer the mountain of self-doubt and anger I felt.

At this point I had been practicing Buddhist meditation for a few years, and I wish I could tell you that I navigated the upheavals of my inflamed immune system with serenity and the poised mind of a seasoned meditator. But no: I cried and cursed and raised my fist at the sky just in case someone up there was pulling the strings. *Life, I need to speak to your supervisor!*

I was embarrassed and disheartened by how severely not only my body but also my mind swerved out of control. Why did Miss Stubborn have to roam around the Himalayas? On top of the actual physical pain, I heaped anguish, self-blame, and despair. The Buddha called this "the second arrow." We are hit by the first arrow—illness, trauma, pain—and then we stick another arrow in the open wound and churn it.

Pema Chödrön distinguishes between pain, which is somewhat inevitable, and suffering, which she defines as the mental and emotional anguish we layer on top. "Let's call pain the unavoidable, and let's call suffering what could lessen and dissolve in our lives. You could say that it isn't the things that happen to us in our lives that cause us to suffer. It's how we relate to the things that happen to us that causes us to suffer."[5]

I read such wise words, but I wouldn't stop churning the arrow. On the contrary, I used them to torture myself. I thought I should hold up better, be stronger, more patient, suffer more calmly. I tried desperately to hold it together, to be like the heroes who remain unfazed even with guns pointed at them. But the more I pushed myself, the worse it all became.

During these increasingly desperate months, I came across an eighteenth-century verse in a Buddhist prayer book:

> *The sicknesses are your teachers, pray to them.*
> *Sicknesses are your accomplishments, so worship*
> *them as the deities.*[6]

I scoffed at the absurdity of that statement. This was obviously a joke. A mean joke. Or, if not a joke, these Buddhist wisecracks must be telling this to people to make them feel better when they couldn't do anything about their misery. They certainly could not be serious!

I was so baffled by this statement I set out to prove it wrong.

Using suffering to transform our being

We can use anything, even learning about fabulous people, against ourselves if we look at them through the lens of our bruised self-esteem. Instead of being encouraged by inspiring role models, I bludgeoned myself for not being able to live up to their examples. I know I'm not the only one. This is one reason why I take great care not to gloss over the difficult passages in the stories presented here. We need to descend into the abyss with them in order to appreciate and understand how they pulled themselves out. The journey from victim to victor is hardly ever easy-breezy.

My twenty-year Buddhist training was ultimately where I found the insights that helped me deal with my persistent illness. This is because my Tibetan teachers are amazing role models in showing me how to take everything we encounter as a learning experience: the good, the bad, and especially the ugly.

The very first realization the historical Buddha Shakyamuni shared after his awakening 2,600 years ago was, "Life is unsatisfactory." He was not just talking about illness and death, but about the all-pervasive hollowness of our existence, the suffering of change, the fact that we can never get all we want and don't get to keep what we have. At first glance, his so-called First Noble Truth might sound like a depressing wakeup call. But when my friend Carol Moss, now eighty-five, came across this teaching, she felt deeply relieved. "I had just overcome cancer and was still struggling from the loss of my husband, and I was content that someone spelled out the reality of my life."

The downside of happiness

The Buddhist acknowledgment of suffering as an inevitable fact of life juxtaposes a cultural thread that runs deep: our imperative is happiness. We have a right to be happy, or so we think. Especially in America, my home for the last decade, the pursuit of happiness is seen as a birthright, a covenant we sign with life from our first cry. Happy people smile from magazine covers; merry models make even impotence and incontinence look delightful.

"To the European it is a characteristic of the American culture that, again and again, one is commanded and ordered to 'be happy,'" Viktor Frankl observed. "But happiness cannot be pursued; it must ensue."[7]

There is a counterpoint to this relentless promise of happiness: If you are suffering, something must be wrong with you. Snap out of it! Or at least take it elsewhere. Even the rally cries (for example, "God only gives you what you can handle") carry a hidden undertone of "It's your fault if you can't handle it." As if hardship was a blemish we could wipe away if only we tried hard enough.

If I had one free wish at the fairy booth, I'd use it to make the entire world happy. But the *pressure* to be happy actually makes people verifiably unhappy.[8] A society infused with the expectation to experience happiness can be quite merciless toward those who despair. Then we're not only unhappy but "also ashamed of being unhappy."[9] Viktor Frankl realized, "It is the very pursuit of happiness that thwarts happiness."

In Part I we discussed the benefits of optimism, its positive effects on health and inner strength. We presented effective methods such as the smile policy and counting your blessings. These benefits are real, these practices work, and I highly recommend you try them to see for yourself. Cracking a genuine smile can lighten up a tense situation, but beware: *Forcing* optimism on anyone, including yourself, to mask true feelings accomplishes nothing. The exuberant cries of sales personnel and well-meaning life coaches to CHEER UP! might have quite the opposite effect. I am a fan of positive thinking, but repeating affirmative phrases—"I'm happier and happier"— while refusing to deal with the mess underneath can be just another version of denial.

Before we can *overcome* suffering, we need to go through it. The way beyond suffering leads *through*, not around.

Acknowledging facts of life, being truthful about what we can handle, engaging in honest self-reflection, and asking for and accepting help are all part of developing a resilient mindset. While a positive outlook is definitely a big joker in this wild ruckus called life, glossing over difficulties is not.

This roller coaster ride

If I look around at my circle of friends at this moment, most of them are struggling: four of them are on the choppy ride of hope and fear, battling various stages of cancer; a single mother has an unstable teenage daughter who was recently busted for drugs; one is gathering her strength after a nasty divorce from a bipolar husband; another friend, formerly a lively meditation coach who loved traveling and teaching, is tied to her home, caring for her husband who was stricken with early-onset dementia. Many of the people around me are lonely or frustrated with their relationships, struggling to get ahead and dreaming of later, where they can fulfill the vision they once had for themselves. And that's not even counting the daily mess we call life, with its mortgage crunches, traffic jams, and ill-timed flu bugs.

At the same time, there are joyful things to acknowledge. Other friends have given birth to healthy babies; a friend finally found the love of her life, at age fifty, and celebrated with her dream wedding in Hawaii; a family member miraculously recovered from a stroke; and many of my buddies derive great joy from devoting every spare minute to rescuing dogs, cats, and sea lions. And the sun is shining, and the hummingbirds are nesting.

To live is to be an emotional acrobat. We have to bend, often out of shape—jump so high, fall so low. Deal with crazy madmen and then learn to walk and talk, to live and love, all over again.

"Because suffering is impermanent, that is why we can transform it," says Thich Nhat Hanh. "Because happiness is impermanent, that is why we have to nourish it."[10]

Our hurry-up-and-get-over-it society

Particularly during my travels in Asia, I witnessed unfathomable suffering. I will never forget the tender faces of the teenage girls who had contracted HIV and other life-threatening illnesses after being sold to a brothel by their parents; I visited the slums of Bangkok and Delhi; I saw the grinding poverty and violence of dirt-poor rural areas. Compared to the abject poverty and utter lack of health care I observed in Asia, many quagmires we have are first-world problems. We fall ill, but at least we have clean hospitals. We might lose our home, but few of us are in danger of starving on the streets.

But that I kept telling myself my suffering was minuscule

compared to others' did not alleviate the pain. We have no universal yardstick to measure the *size* of suffering. When I visited the army boot camp, one sergeant hissed under his breath that Rhonda Cornum *hadn't even been tortured!* But then, Sergeant, in order for you to accept Rhonda as an authority on resilience, how long does she need to be tortured? And how severely? It never ends. Suffering is not a competition. Viktor Frankl likens suffering to the behavior of gas: any quantity of it fills an empty chamber entirely. "Thus suffering completely fills the human soul and conscious mind, no matter whether the suffering is great or little. Therefore the 'size' of human suffering is absolutely relative."[11]

And yet it is striking how few of us feel we can easily share our load with even close friends and family, especially if our problems are not dissolving fast. "They listen once or twice, but as the issues are long-term, I am somehow expected to deal with it and move on," one of my neighbors confided. "I had no idea how fast my friends could run." The phenomenon of deteriorating support is well-known in both individual and communal tragedies.[12]

People simply often don't know what to say after they have expressed their condolences and brought chicken soup. If your crisis drags on, if you don't get better, if you can't participate in the fun outings you enjoyed before, if you continue to be a "buzzkill," if, worst of all, the doctors can't prescribe a cure that promises an expiration date, well, good luck.

"Our culture is grief illiterate," my sister-in-law Tami realized. "In other cultures there are rituals; you are allowed to cry and scream and wail. But in our hurry-up-and-get-over-it society, you get three days of bereavement leave when anyone dies. *Three days!* Then you are supposed to get on with it." She longed to speak about her daughter, but people would avoid the topic. "You're crying inside all the time anyway.

You might look fine, but you're not. People don't want to disturb that and think you might have forgotten for a few minutes, but a mother never forgets." When the silence became too deafening, Tami would go to her local Starbucks and give her name as "Haley," just for the brief moment of the barista shouting out her daughter's name aloud: "Haley! Latte for Haley!"

The isolation I observe here is markedly different from my experience in Asia and Africa, where an ongoing relationship with suffering is commonplace, and suffering there is often a shared experience. Solidarity carries the community. And though the family networks have holes and the social hierarchy in developing countries can be infinitely cruel, especially to women, there is an underpinning of connectedness that Western culture, with its emphasis on the individual ego, does not share.

It seems to me that there really is no place for suffering in our society outside of the designated zones we have specifically marked for it: hospitals, hospices, homeless shelters. How we, as a society, deal with suffering tells us at least as much about ourselves as the myriad ways we promote to achieve success.

Is it coincidence that America has the world's highest documented incarceration rate? Case in point: In 2014, the city of Fort Lauderdale passed a law that bans feeding the homeless in public, and sheriffs there arrested the ninety-year-old war veteran Arnold Abbott, who runs weekly feedings with his organization Love Thy Neighbor. He could feed the homeless *indoors*, just not, for Christ's sake, outside his church on a Sunday in plain daylight where we could see them. We live in a world where you can shoot a young unarmed black man and walk free, but face jail time for handing a plate of vegetables to a vagrant.

We go out of our way so that we do not have to stare suffering in the face. We lock people up, make them go away. Out of sight, out of heart.

We need to find ways of weaving our suffering into the tapestry of our lives, individually and as a community. We need to bravely explore a new relationship with pain and sorrow and ask where it fits in. We need to *make room* for it to fit in. Because it is already here.

Shutting it out just means shutting ourselves in.

Finding our life's purpose

There is a difference between happiness (temporarily having our needs and goals satisfied), and meaning—finding and fulfilling our life's purpose.[13] Forty percent of Americans say they do not have a purpose in life.[14] I find this number startling. Not having a purpose in life has a direct impact on our well-being, our health, even our life expectancy.[15] If we don't know what we're here for, what are we doing here?

This is one of the avenues of posttraumatic growth: suffering reduces our happiness, at least temporarily, but it often sets us on the path to finding meaning, and thus ultimately, a different, deeper kind of well-being.

Discover meaning

We obviously don't *need* suffering to find our calling, but it happens to be where we often discover it.[16] It was only through her capture that Rhonda felt a vocation to teach resilience. After her daughter's passing, Tami found meaning in volunteering for Compassionate Friends and rescuing animals. Coco's courage to share his story is fueled by his passion not to let history be retold by right-wing fanatics.

Everybody in this book found or deepened their life's purpose after they were challenged to the core.

"In some way, suffering ceases to be suffering at the moment it finds a meaning, such as the meaning of a sacrifice,"[17] Viktor Frankl realized. "Those who have a 'why' to live, can bear with almost any 'how.'"

A student once asked Frankl to express the meaning of his own life in one sentence. Frankl wrote down his response and asked his students to guess what he had written. After some moments of quiet reflection, a student surprised Frankl by saying, "The meaning of life is to help others find the meaning of theirs."

"That was it, exactly," Frankl said. "Those are the very words I had written."[18]

"It's all good"

I have my personal hero of posttraumatic success—my grandfather.

Born just before the beginning of World War I in Germany, he contracted polio at six months old. The virus paralyzed his right side, but at least he lived—his brother, a year older, didn't survive. Grandpa walked with the help of a crutch and a cumbersome metal apparatus that helped him thrust his right leg forward in a lopsided motion. He always listed a little, like a ship tilting dangerously close to its tipping point.

You might say his handicap should have been obvious. But to me it was glaringly irrelevant.

Grandpa was constantly in motion, always out and about in his baby-blue Volkswagen Beetle, selling insurance policies and his custom-tailored suits to his many buddies. A wheeler-dealer kind of guy, ready to crack a joke, forever willing to engage in a chat or a game of cards. In my favorite memory of him, he opens his arms sky-wide, his blue eyes flashing love and excitement, and I'm thrusting myself at full speed into his warm, all-embracing hug.

He and Grandma lived with my parents and me in the small Bavarian village where he was born. I can't remember ever seeing him grumpy, angry, bitter, or complaining, and while I took this for granted as a kid, in hindsight I consider his upbeat spirit a remarkable achievement. I have never met anyone as sunny, and because I lived with him, I know it wasn't a mask.

Much later I pieced together the jigsaw puzzle of his childhood. After he contracted polio, he had to spend the next years crawling. This particular image has always stuck with me: I picture his village friends playing soccer and running after kites, and him crawling on the sidelines. I imagine him being taunted and called names. It wasn't until after he turned six that a compassionate carpenter crafted him a makeshift wooden splint so he could start walking.

Being crippled in Nazi Germany, with all its fanaticism about the ideal of strong, healthy youth, couldn't have been easy. I can only guess—he never opened up about his childhood, or the war. I had to pry the bare facts out of my father and Grandma.

As a teenager, my grandfather modified a simple bicycle for himself. He could tie his lame leg on one pedal and push with his good one, conquering the hills of the nearby villages as he hustled his father's milk and meat, and then later his hand-sewn suits and aprons.

With the help of a matchmaker just before the start of World War II, he managed to find himself a hardworking wife—my grandmother—and they had five children together: four girls plus the youngest, my father. Hans and Maria were such an odd pair—she always stern and reprimanding, he soft and smiling. She was tall and attractive, he round and short, but he made up for his stature with an abundance of energy and enthusiasm. She shooed the village cats with her broom; he took them on his lap and comforted them. I was afraid of my grandma and her quick slaps, while I loved and idolized him.

He was simultaneously strong and soft, an intriguing combination I have encountered in many successful survivors. He reminded me of Zen teacher Roshi Joan Halifax's core message of "strong back, soft front," which, she explains, "is about the relationship between equanimity and compassion. 'Strong back' is equanimity and your capacity to really uphold yourself. 'Soft front' is opening to things as they are."[19] Halifax spoke about it in the context of caring for the ill, but the description fits so well with many of the heroes in this book, as they, too, are tough and tender. It also points to one of the questions I have been wrestling with: when to push and when to surrender?

I can't remember my grandpa ever being ill. Independence was his main concern, possibly a leftover from his childhood years when he was so dependent on others. He never complained about pain, and when my grandmother or his children managed to force a physician's visit on him, his nightstand filled up with prescription pills in their plastic wrappers. Shortly after he turned seventy-five, the doctors deemed it necessary to perform what they called a small, routine stomach surgery; none of us expected what happened next. Or did he know? When they cut open his abdomen, they realized cancer had already conquered his intestines and spread to his bones. The doctors were in disbelief—with terminal cancer, he had to have been in excruciating pain for many months. Yet he had never said a word. The surgeon quickly sewed him back up, and my grandpa died within a week.

I wish I could ask him now all the many questions he left unanswered: Had he swallowed the pain and let it poison him? Or did he choose this ending with his eyes open, busy living life and convinced death would catch him when his time was up?

My grandpa played a final joke on us after his passing. When my grandmother went through the dozens of sample suits he left behind in his tailor's room, she noticed that one suit was considerably heavier than the others. She carefully unraveled the seam, only to pull out banknote after banknote. When they counted the huge stash of small notes, the tally ran more than $100,000—a fortune for a village tailor.

My grandmother was more stunned than anyone. He had never told her he was saving for rough times. Throughout their five decades together, she always had to argue with him for little luxuries: thrifty senior bus tours to the nearby countryside for a holiday, a new pair of shoes every two years or so when the old ones wore out. They had lived a frugal life, and unbeknownst to her, he had stashed away a treasure.

My grandfather was loved dearly by his five children and six grandchildren; he lived for his family, and they would have done anything for him—but he stemmed from a war-torn generation that did not allow itself to share a whole lot of doubts and emotions. Maybe he had been tormented by the fear he might become a burden? Was the treasure some kind of insurance, an unresolved shadow from the years of humiliation? I wish I could ask him now, but in a way he has given me his answer:

During his final week in the hospital, he was dizzy with drugs. Yet in his waking moments he was his old smiling self, joyfully receiving a steady stream of concerned visitors. Up until his last breath he taught me how to live. "It's all good," I remember him repeating as he neared the end.

Whenever the going gets rough in my life, I can count on his voice in my ear, whispering, "It's all good."

Neither suppressing nor indulging

Some of us—like my grandpa—seem to deal with suffering better than others, and this is what this book is about. In Buddhism, to "deal with it" means something specific: it means to go toward the places we are afraid of, to embrace the pain and be present with it. This is the middle way the Buddha eventually discovered: neither to suppress nor to indulge, neither to shun nor to fight.

Before he became Buddha, the "Awakened One," young Prince Gautama Siddhartha started out as a superior denier. His father, a wealthy clan chief in North India, ensured that his son only experienced happiness. The chief lavished the most coveted foods and fun, sights and sounds, pleasures and playmates on him, all with the firm intent to prevent his son from being bruised by any suffering, because he did not want his firstborn to abandon the home turf and look for happiness elsewhere. But on his outings into town, Siddhartha came across a leper, an old man on crutches, and a corpse. He inquired how this abject suffering could possibly be halted, and he was told the truth: there is no way out; we cannot escape old age, sickness, loss, and death.

Siddhartha was aghast. He realized that no quantity of food, women, or other pleasures could halt, let alone erase, the reality of our finite existence.

Siddhartha left the palace on a journey to discover the origin of suffering, and a path beyond it. Because outward efforts to curb illness and death are so obviously thwarted, he realized the universal cure had to be found inside. While we could not expect to master illness and suffering, we could learn to master the mind that experiences them. "Mind is the creator of happiness and suffering," he concluded. Liberation from suffering, a promise of the Buddhist path, is primarily a matter of the mind—an internal revolution and shift of perspective.

There is no way out, but there is a way in.

"When you learn *how* to suffer," says Zen master Thich Nhat Hanh, "you suffer much less."[20]

This is exactly what trauma therapists recommend. Plunging head-on into confronting the trauma experience is likely too overwhelming, but eventually we have to acknowledge and meet it. "In order to experience this restorative faculty, we must develop the capacity to face certain uncomfortable and frightening physical sensations and feelings without becoming overwhelmed by them," advises Peter Levine.[21]

As I found out the hard way, my fair-weather meditation as a newly minted Buddhist calmed me in happy times, but it was not holding up in the storm. I realized that I had fallen into the common trap of using meditation as a relaxing feel-good activity, rather than the powerful ally in facing the fullness of life it actually was. I needed to go deeper in this journey of getting to know myself and my mind.

Meet pain with mindfulness

Many methods of meditation are being promoted these days, and you will find suggestions in the guide in the back of the book. Focusing on our breath or on a positive image is among the easiest, most widely taught methods. Generally, mindfulness has two elements: being present in the moment, and meeting whatever is happening with an attitude of acceptance. Can I be present with how things are right now? Can I breathe spaciousness and awareness into the tight places? Can I accept myself lovingly while writhing in all the snares in which I am caught?

I discovered that I am not in pain when I am fully present. I had read about meditation masters who were able to undergo surgery without pain medication and I wrote it off as fairy tales, but I eventually made the discovery for myself. I can never sustain it for long, but when I am truly, truly aware in the present moment, pain finds no hooks to latch onto.

Both emotional and physical pain can become a fascinating journey if we watch it like a scientist through a microscope. We have to become students of our own pain. Where is the pain pointing? The magic of meditation is that it simultaneously detaches and immerses us in experience. Being fully present unhitches us from the story line and alerts us to what is really going on underneath.

One of my Buddhist teachers has a bright yellow sign on the entrance door to his meditation cabin that reads, _Don't believe everything you think_. Don't buy the story line, the "poor me" and the "damn them," but become aware of the true colors that wove the story's fabric. Meditation opens up a space between us and our thoughts, an opening _to be_ the experience. Less plot, more adventure.

Meditation better than morphine

Mindfulness and self-awareness are essential skills in regaining mastery over our mind.

Results can be swift: Dr. Fadel Zeidan from the Wake Forest Baptist Medical Center in North Carolina tested people with no previous experience in meditation. They were instructed to practice twenty minutes of focused attention meditation every day. They focused on their breathing and letting go of distracting thoughts in the presence of an unpleasant hot stimulus. After just four days of meditation training, Zeidan's subjects experienced a 40 percent reduction in pain intensity and 57 percent reduction in pain unpleasantness. "Meditation produced a greater reduction in pain than even morphine or other pain-relieving drugs, which typically reduce pain ratings by about 25 percent," says Zeidan. "One of the reasons that meditation may have been so effective in blocking pain was that it did not work at just one place in the brain, but instead reduced pain at multiple levels of processing."[22]

Zeidan and his colleagues believe that meditation has great potential for clinical use because so little training was required to produce such dramatic pain-relieving effects. "This study shows that meditation substantially reduced their pain without medications," Zeidan asserts. When the heat stimulus study was repeated with experienced meditators, their reaction to pain was directly related to how many hours of meditation they had practiced.[23] The more we train our mindfulness muscle, the stronger, more flexible, and supple it becomes.

"It has taken us a century and a half to rediscover the fact that the mind has something to do with pain and can be a powerful tool in controlling it . . . It is now abundantly clear that we can retrain the brain to reduce pain: 'float rather than fight,'" Stanford psychiatrist David Spiegel says.[24] If you need more proof about the power of the mind, think about patients who choose to undergo major surgery, even amputations, with only a small amount of anesthesia (or with none at all), just with the help of an experienced hypnotist.[25]

"It is entirely possible to substantially alter pain perception during surgical procedures by inducing hypnotic relaxation," says David Spiegel. "Hypnotic analgesia is real, no less palpable an analgesic than medication."[26] Hypnotic relaxation also has been shown to reduce anxiety and pain and ease recovery.[27]

Meditators have known the power of the mind for a long time: when His Holiness the Sixteenth Karmapa, a highly trained Tibetan monk, was dying of metastatic stomach cancer in a hospital in Chicago, the staff was amazed that he never asked for pain medication. "Most people in this situation would be in a fair amount of pain, and yet you could never tell it from his confidence," his doctor, Mitchell Levy, told me. "He was always cheerful, always asking more about other people, and did you sleep last night? What struck people the most was his beaming smile throughout the last days of his life." Because of his kind demeanor, the nursing staff in the ICU came to call him "grandfather."

My own grandfather, who also died of stomach cancer, comes to mind. I ask Mitchell Levy if he has witnessed this power of the mind in the face of severe illness with other patients who are not rock star meditators.

"Yes, we see it all the time. The Karmapa just did it on a more comprehensive level, but the experience is available to all of us," Dr. Levy is convinced. "Two people might have the same level of illness, but one could be struggling with it much more. I have seen many times where people during the dying process handle it in a joyful and open way that is pretty breathtaking. They might be afraid, but they embrace the dying process and their illness with tenderness." He cautions, though, that he does not promote a simple mind-over-matter approach that ends up blaming the patient for the suffering.

Maybe the most encouraging takeaway is that one doesn't need to practice meditation for decades to experience how the mind influences our perception of pain. Anybody can do it. We, too, can be our own mind whisperers. We might have no control over life, but we have the power to decide how we deal with it.

I don't want to make it sound as if it were easy, though.

To this day, after almost twenty years of meditating, I still find this the most challenging: to stay present when pain strikes. Roshi Bernie Glassman compassionately jokes that the whole notion of escaping is ridiculous: We cannot ever be *not* present. We *cannot* escape. And yet, the longing to reach for a drink, for the remote, for sex, for revenge, for *anything* that just promises a relief, no matter how temporary, is irresistible.

The lotus turning mud into fertilizer

I have come to meet and grown to love many people who have overcome adversity with astonishing grace. Meeting the subjects of this book changed me. They have been assaulted with sufferings that seem too big to bear, yet they bore them. They could have been crushed, yet they grew. They could have broken down, yet they broke through.

We learn resilience not in isolation, but only from other people, by interacting, connecting, and observing. I recommend that you don't undertake this journey alone, but instead find a skilled guide. A conversation with a wise man is worth more than ten years of reading books, my grandpa used to say. I sought out people who could show me how to stay open when I was aching to close down: teachers like Pema Chödrön, Bernie Glassman, and meditation masters in the Himalayas.

I had to change my whole attitude toward suffering. When I hit the roof after receiving a letter that outed my partner as a serial cheater while I was bedridden, a Buddhist teacher advised me, "Well, he can only hurt you as much as you allow him to hurt you. He can cheat, but he does not have any influence over your mind, you know?" Somehow he got through to me: *I* was inflicting jealousy and disappointment on myself; anybody else could only hurt me as much as I let them. It was actually better to find out now that our relationship was not what I thought it was before we built more of a life together.

Before things got better, though, they got worse. For about two years I could get nothing right. As soon I had somewhat recovered from the illness, I moved back to Germany. There, my beloved grandmother (my mother's mother) fell ill, had her leg amputated, and then passed away after an infernal year in the hospital. Not long after I moved, I got word that my ex-partner (whom I had just left) was diagnosed with a lung disease; doctors gave him only one or two years to live. He had health problems before, but we hadn't thought they were so serious. He passed away four years later in a hospital bed in Versailles, after organs for a heart-lung transplantation could not be found fast enough. How could I have left a dying man? My own body was still feeble and would give out on me at the worst times. Whenever things looked up—I landed a new job presenting a prestigious TV show—they turned into traps. The TV station was engulfed in a bitter fight over leadership that spared no innocent bystanders. Screaming matches, door slamming, and slandering were daily occurrences. Then they relocated to a new office with carpets so toxic I literally could not breathe. For the job, I had moved to a new city where I had no friends, when friends were what I needed most. My cat Tiger died. I tried to recharge my batteries by treating myself to a detox at an ayurvedic clinic, only to get fish poisoning so severe I lost all the weight I had just barely put on. The manager of the clinic took me hostage and threatened me until I paid him off. You wouldn't believe all the plot twists that went haywire. I was perpetually in the wrong place at the wrong time. Whenever I thought I had found firm ground to stand on, it turned out to be quicksand. I spent my evenings alone in the City of Pity, taking refuge in whiskey and repeating Buddhist mantras. Yep, I'm aware booze and Buddhism contradict each other, but Johnnie Walker and Buddha seemed to be the only buddies willing to stay by my side. Eventually, I was able to ease up on the malt and focus more on the mantras.

When I look back now, I can see how I could have coped with each of the events individually, if life had been kind enough to space them out over several years. But losing all sources of support at once (my health, my partner, my community, my grandmother, my pet, a sane work environment), the onslaught was so overwhelming that I lost sight of the shore. I only had myself to lean on, and I was not holding up. Sometimes you just have to let go of everything.

Much later, when I moved to California, I learned what to do when caught in a riptide: Instead of struggling against the current with all my might until exhausted, as I had done, you swim parallel to the shore until you're out of the current. Then you relax, and wait for a wave that carries you back to safe land.

Even better, meditation is like going deeper, diving into the big blue. I'm a scuba diver, and if you have ever been in stormy seas, you know you get bopped around the most when you stay stagnant on the surface; but when you dive down, oftentimes you can float in a panorama of calm.

The still-revolutionary insight of the Buddha is that we are what we think—that our reality is what we create in our minds, and that there really is no limit to the depth of the mind's potential. That's not carte blanche to let people trample over us as if we're doormats, but ultimately our minds are the creators of our happiness and suffering, independent of the outer events we encounter. What this meant for me is that I had to look at my underlying attachments to a certain life I had envisioned and an image of myself I could no longer hold up. I had to let go.

The lotus, a symbol of Buddhism, represents exactly this

capacity for transformation: the pristine flower emerges from the mud, using the muck as a fertilizer for growth.

Turning suffering and happiness into liberation

One of the most poignant teachings in Tibetan Buddhism is called *Turning Suffering and Happiness into Enlightenment.* It refers to taking any and every circumstance, whether beautiful or ugly, as an opportunity for waking up.

"We need: first, to get rid of the attitude of being entirely unwilling to face any suffering ourselves and, second, to cultivate the attitude of actually being joyful when suffering arises," the author, nineteenth-century Tibetan teacher Dodrupchen Jigme Tenpa Nyima, writes in a commentary widely taught today.[28] "Think about all the depression, anxiety and irritation we put ourselves through by always seeing suffering as unfavorable, something to be avoided at all costs. Now, think about two things: how useless this is, and how much trouble it causes. Go on reflecting on this repeatedly, until you are absolutely convinced."

Seriously?

I know, I know. I wasn't convinced either.

The text then goes on to produce a long list that tallies the advantages of "seeing suffering as an ally to help us on the path" and "cultivating the attitude of being joyful when suffering arises." The listed benefits are suspiciously similar to the findings of Richard Tedeschi's twenty-first-century post-traumatic growth inventory. Suffering readjusts our priorities, eradicates arrogance, encourages us to reach for a purpose larger than ourselves, nudges us to help others who are worse off, and helps us find joy in positive action.

If pain is not an assignment, what else could it be?

The compelling logic of embracing adversity

First of all, it is simply not possible to run away from the bad stuff, so instead of exhausting ourselves, we might as well use our energy to meet it at the finish line. Second, a lot of the stuff we call "bad" may not actually be that bad. For instance, we need bacteria to develop a healthy immune system. Children growing up playing in the dirt at a farm are often healthier than city children who are scrubbed daily with disinfectant. Or pain; as you will see in the next chapter, pain can be a close ally.

Third, "bad" is only a category in your mind. What we call "bad" now might turn out to be a blessing in the long run.

Consider this tale, one I have come across in Taoist and Buddhist writings.[29] A family has one son they love more than anything, and one horse upon which they depend for their farm work. The horse runs away, and all their neighbors pity them. "Oh, you've only had one, and now it's gone. What misery!" A year later the horse comes back and brings with it a foal. "Oh," the neighbors cheer, "Lucky you! First you only had one horse, and now you have two!" Then their only son tries to ride the foal, falls off, and breaks a leg so hopelessly he is permanently crippled. Again, the neighbors' pity sweeps in. "What calamity! You have only one son and now he is useless!" Two years later a war starts; the army soldiers go from door to door and draft all the able-bodied men. Now it's the family's turn to feel lucky. They get to keep their son.

It's hard to know what's "bad." We really can't know until time unveils its meaning.

Maybe it was "bad" that my grandfather contracted polio, but because of his "bad" leg the Nazis couldn't draft him to World War II, where he might have joined the millions of war casualties or, like my other grandfather, returned from Russian imprisonment as a hardened, broken man. Maybe it was "bad" that Maya Angelou's dream of becoming a dancer was crushed by an accident, but had she succeeded as a dancer, we might have never been transformed by her poems. I found it unbearable that my partner cheated on me after I fell ill, but if he hadn't, I wouldn't have found the love of my life. What we call "misfortune" might just be a fortune that will come around in a different shape.

I often reflect on how different my life would be if I didn't have chronic fatigue. I find it intensely frightening that I never know if I can rely on my body to accomplish everyday activities other people my age find utterly unchallenging. When I guide a workshop at a company that's been recently remodeled and painted, I risk having an allergic response and am forced to move the workshop to another venue. To this day I have unexpected attacks of fatigue and fainting spells, and often wonder whether I will make it through an assignment in one piece. If I weren't sick, I'd probably have accepted a tempting job offer to run a magazine. I'd have more energy, I'd get more work done. But would I use my energy for the right things? Would I get *good* work done? Is it my life's purpose to run a magazine?

Instead I took a year off to go into solitary retreat at the ocean. I turned down a magnificent job offer in Germany to move to California and marry the partner of my dreams. I had to slow down, take time off, and think deeply about how I could find a new purpose in my altered existence. This is what led me to spend two years of my life researching *Bouncing Forward*, and in the process met amazing people I now call my friends. I doubt I would have done any of these things if I had continued the healthy, active life I led in my twenties. I would probably have been too consumed with my ambitions and travels. I am certain I would be less compassionate and much less able to empathize with—let alone notice—the facets of suffering around me. The experience of being helpless and weak has erased much of my judgment about people who need help and appear weak.

Today, I find deep meaning working for nonprofits, especially for the rescue of trafficked women and abandoned animals. When you don't have a lot of energy to spend, you don't waste it on stuff you don't consider meaningful. My experience also profoundly changed the way I work with my coaching clients and managers at my communciation and mindfulness workshops. Before, I tended to focus on helping them achieve their career goals. Now I look at the whole person, and we explore what they *really* want for themselves.

I have found most of the advantages listed in *Turning Happiness and Suffering into Enlightenment* to be true: Suffering readjusted my priorities, eradicated the arrogance I had as a successful career woman, and encouraged me to reach for a purpose larger than myself. It nudged me to help others, and to find joy in positive action.

What about you?

Reflect on the benefit

Is there a gift hidden in the mistake or the pain? Is there a silver lining in the suffering? Is there anything you learned, even if it might be a difficult lesson?

These questions might be too provocative when the wounds are fresh. Being able to reflect on them honestly is a sign that we are well on our way to becoming trauma alumni.

I hesitantly put these questions to my sister-in-law Tami, whose despair I had witnessed so closely. How could I even ask her if there was a hidden gift in her grief? Even though

I had already done research on posttraumatic growth, I still didn't expect her to exclaim, without the slightest hesitation, "Yes! Any trauma, there is growth too! But unfortunately it takes years. I would have slapped someone in the face if they had told me that earlier. People say all these clichés such as 'It's gonna get better' or 'Things happen for a reason,' and I was very offended. I used to envy people who led a sheltered life, but now I don't. What we went through was horrific and awful. But trauma is an opportunity to more deeply know yourself and others. It's not what happens to you, it's how you handle it that defines who you are. It's empowering, because you're growing."

One woman at a trauma workshop shared that the most traumatic thing that happened to her was a violent rape when she was a teenager. She felt it ruined her life. The assault resulted in a pregnancy and PTSD. As a teenage mom in the sixties, she decided to keep the baby, with all the accompanying shame and poverty and conflicting emotions she faced. But now she considers her daughter and her three grandkids the greatest joy in her life. This is not an excuse for the rapist, but a testimony of her character and strength.

We are in charge of our life. Something "bad" might happen, but it is up to us if we let it be bad forever.

I would strongly argue that accepting suffering is not a passive stance and is very different from fatalism. Quite the contrary: accepting suffering as an assignment is active, disciplined, and involved.

The concept of the "wounded healer" is central to many indigenous cultures. Daniel Gray Bear, a Native American elder and Vietnam veteran, was only able to emerge as a leader of his community after he had worked through his trauma from the war and from growing up with an alcoholic mother and various stepdads. "You need to know both sides to understand; you have to know the darkness to understand what the light is," Gray Bear sums it up. "Sometimes you need to have a breakdown before you can have a breakthrough."

The advantage of disadvantages

Buddhists, Taoists, stoics, and indigenous leaders are by no means the only ones who teach that obstacles are the path. Science also supports this notion.

In his popular book *David and Goliath*, journalist Malcolm Gladwell points out that an unusually large number of successful innovators, prime ministers, and US presidents had lost a parent in childhood. "Too often, we make the mistake . . . and jump to the conclusion that there is only one kind of response to something terrible and traumatic. There isn't."[30]

Gladwell quotes the psychologist Dean Simonton, who tried to find out "why so many gifted children fail to live up to their promise" while some disadvantaged children thrive.[31] "Geniuses have a perverse tendency of growing up in more adverse conditions."[32]

Let's look at a few startling experiments:

UCLA psychologist Robert A. Bjork introduced the theme of "desirable difficulties." We greatly underestimate the value of hardships. For instance, when undergraduates at Princeton received a Cognitive Reflection Test in difficult-to-read *10 percent gray, ten-point italics Myriad web font,* they were suddenly doing significantly better (64 percent correct answers) than their counterparts who got the test in normal font (43 percent correct).[33] They paid *more attention,* and I think this is one of hardship's greatest virtues: it forces us to pay attention.

The first time pianist Glenn Gould's maid turned on the vacuum while he was playing Mozart's Fugue, he got angry, but then he realized his sensitivity was in fact keener when the vacuum tuned out the music; he could give himself over to the feel of his fingers on the keys. After that, he purposefully turned on noisy machines to figure out difficult passages.[34]

My point is: we often react too quickly in wanting to erase the "obstacle" or trying to swipe away the sadness. Instead, I suggest that we see what it has to teach us. When people watch depressing movies or listen to heart-wrenching music, they not only become sad, but they are suddenly able to pay closer attention to detail.[35] Exposing people to the somber Adagietto by Gustav Mahler enables them to remember more accurately.[36]

Compared to angry people, sad people are less inclined to judge others by stereotypes, and they observe their surroundings more thoughtfully, with less bias.[37] "Sadness slows us down, and, by doing so, seems to slow the world down,"[38] concludes psychologist George A. Bonanno. "In general, then, sadness helps us focus and promotes deeper and more effective reflection."[39]

In Part II we will meet people who turn the conventional idea of good and bad upside down: wonder woman Meggie Zahneis who can't feel pain; business consultant Alain Beauregard who calls terminal cancer the best thing that ever happened to him; autistic savant Temple Grandin who would not give up her autism even if doctors found a cure; and Zen master Roshi Bernie Glassman who spends his retreats in Rwanda and Auschwitz.

Wisely selfish

I only began to grasp the possibilities of this vast attitude of finding the opportunity in adversity after studying with Tibetans who had spent years (some of them even decades) in prison. They looked at their time under the rule of a cruel regime as a perfect opportunity to practice compassion, and they actually *meant* it. "My biggest fear in prison," the late Tibetan master Tulku Pegyal told me in Kathmandu, "was not to die, but to lose my compassion for the Chinese guards."

Tulku Pegyal was one of the first Tibetans I made friends with when I studied Buddhist philosophy in Nepal. He is the reason I immersed myself in the study of Buddhism, because I was so intrigued by his gentle fierceness that I felt I needed to know what he knew. When I met him, he was well into his seventies, his wrinkled face covered in a blanket of kindness.

He had spent fifteen years in Chinese labor camps, imprisoned for teaching Buddhism. Twenty years after he had been released from prison and fled the Chinese regime, he still moved with a slow gait that disclosed the aching of tortured and fractured limbs. His body had not been able to withstand the hard labor, the paltry food, and the sadistic abuse. Yet it's hard to imagine a face that could look softer, warmer, more loving. It never fails to impress me how true practitioners come out of devastating events with even more compassion and empathy. He was one of the kindest people on the planet. Tulku Pegyal would always try to give me cookies, chocolate, food, and even money, though as a refugee he had very little himself. I wouldn't take anything beyond a cookie, and our meetings usually ended in a hilarious standoff where he would try to stuff presents in my pockets and I would try to outdo him by putting more in his drawers.

Whenever I get really upset about someone who has hurt me, like the chemical companies that destroyed my health, I try to remember Tulku Pegyal's face. He endured the harshest of treatments by people who even killed his own mother, and yet he managed to harbor no hate. He explained to me that anger is like picking up hot coal to throw it at the object of your hate: you might manage to hurt him, but you're sure to get burned yourself.

The Dalai Lama calls a compassionate attitude "wise self-ishness." He famously advises:

"If you want others to be happy, practice compassion.
If you want to be happy, practice compassion."

This kind of attitude does not come from naive idealism, but from working, daily, each minute, at training the mind. The Buddhist mind training starts with recognizing that we are all not that different. We all want happiness and we want to avoid suffering.

"If we could read the secret history of our enemies," American poet Henry Wadsworth Longfellow wrote, "we should find in each man's life sorrow and suffering enough to disarm all hostility."

I have seen this compassion in action, but was still astounded to find proof that this mind training actually *prevents* trauma. Maybe the Tibetan meditators have found the formula the army is looking for.

Tortured, but not traumatized

Fordham University psychologist Emily Sachs and her colleagues interviewed 767 Tibetan refugees in North India. Like Tulku Pegyal, many of the refugees had experienced imprisonment, harassment, and torture at the hands of the Chinese regime before making the life-threatening escape, often on foot, through inhospitable mountain ranges, to North India. Many suffered from physical consequences, and some torture survivors reported depression and anxiety, but the researchers were stunned that only one torture survivor

(0.1 percent!) had clinically significant PTSD symptoms.[40] (I am focusing on Tibetans because I have studied with them the most, but such findings are not limited by nationality: when a British psychiatrist explored the Buddhist response to the 2004 tsunami in Sri Lanka, he concluded that survivors did not suffer from PTSD when they perceived the deluge as not traumatic.[41])

How did they do it?

Most scientists believe that the severity of the torture is the determining factor for the severity of the PTSD, yet the Tibetans defy the classification of Western doctors. When the researchers probed about how the Tibetans dealt with the hardships they had encountered, torture survivors emphasized their kinship with their people and insisted that other Tibetans had "suffered worse." For many, seeing their religious monuments desecrated and their beloved teachers humiliated was more upsetting than the actual torture.[42]

This resonates with Richard Tedeschi's finding that trauma comes with a rattling of one's core beliefs. Tibetans speak about the "vast mind" that is infinite enough to even meet atrocities. Their life perspective was so spacious and flexible they were able to accept the Buddha's discoveries: that suffering is part of human existence, and that liberation from suffering lies in the mind. Even while they were in the midst of agony, they recognized the hardship as fleeting, ephemeral, and ultimately not affecting their true nature.

In this space, healing arises.

Perhaps most important, the Tibetans strive to find meaning in their hardship. The philosophy of posttraumatic growth, the conviction that suffering can carry great opportunity, has been hardwired into their beliefs for thousands of years.

Counterintuitive to our normal thinking, the Tibetans let themselves be guided by wisdom slogans like this one:

"When misfortune fills the world and its inhabitants,
Make adversity the path of awakening."[43]

Many, many times I have seen students lay out their problems to their Buddhist teachers, anything from getting their car stolen to serious illness, and the teacher would clap his hands and exclaim, "Oh good! You're being purified! Rejoice!"

One Tibetan Buddhist teacher, Garchen Rinpoche, was imprisoned at the age of twenty-two during the Cultural Revolution, when Mao Zedong cracked down on the spiritually devoted. He arrived in prison irate, bitter about the many horrors and losses he had already observed. Friends, family, and fellow monks had perished at the hand of the Chinese soldiers, his monastery had been desecrated, and he spent his next twenty years in labor camps.

Now Garchen Rinpoche half jokingly calls the massive prison complexes built by the Chinese government an act of kindness: "How kind of them to build all these retreat centers for us so that we can deepen our practices." He met his teacher, Khenpo Munsel, in prison, and received his most important meditation instruction: to practice compassion for everybody, including the guards. In his first weeks in prison, Garchen Rinpoche tried to provoke one of the meanest guards to get himself killed. But under Khenpo Munsel's guidance he realized that his guards, too, were trapped under a cruel regime, and suffering. Some of the Chinese guards were so moved by his kind spirit that they secretly became his students.

I met Garchen Rinpoche in the South of France. Incredibly, he stated that he did "not suffer *at all*" in the labor camp. He did say, though, that he was unable to save his best friend who had been imprisoned alongside him. They were of the same age, ate the same rotten food, endured the same beatings, and carried the same heavy loads of stones for roadwork. There was only one difference: their minds. They chose a different attitude. His friend got so overwhelmed by the atrocious prison that he committed suicide after a few months.

Garchen Rinpoche and Tulku Pegyal knew what Viktor Frankl understood, what Roshi Bernie Glassman teaches, what Rhonda Cornum practiced, what saved Coco Schumann: The inner freedom to choose their attitude under any given circumstances.

6. Thrive

"The luckiest girl on earth"
Meggie Zahneis lives a life that is pain-free,
but not painless

> *For there is nothing either good or
> bad, but thinking makes it so.*
> —SHAKESPEARE, *HAMLET*,
> ACT 2, SCENE 2

Meggie Zahneis's body harbors a secret that scientists all over the world are eager to decode. Just last week it happened again: she picked up a baking sheet that her mom had just taken out of the oven. Three hundred degrees Fahrenheit with her bare hands. She dropped it after five or six seconds not because she felt the burn, but because she heard her mom scream. "You can't look away for two seconds," her mother Cindy says with a sigh. "Meggie just turned eighteen; we have to let her be more independent. It's just so hard."

At their quiet family home in a suburb of West Chester, Ohio, a snowstorm softly etches out the meadows in front of their living room windows, while Cindy, Meggie, and her father, Bob, toss memories back and forth. Remember the supermarket parking lot when a screw drilled itself through Meggie's sneaker into her foot? Anybody else would have gasped in agony, but Meggie was oblivious until she later sensed blood soaking her shoe. The visit to the public pool, when Meggie was five? Suddenly people started screaming— Meggie had scratched her legs so badly on the rough pool floor that her blood was clouding the water. Or her cousin's wedding four years ago when she bounced on the dance floor for two hours? The party was joyous, except that her parents discovered the next day that her right ankle had swollen to double its size. The emergency room doctor diagnosed a stress fracture. Ever since, a daily "joint checkup" has become part of their routine. Her legs are strewn with scars and old cuts. While recounting the events, Meggie pauses, surprised to find a fresh cut on her right palm. "Honestly, I have no idea how that got there just now."

The world record in avoiding pain

I promised you I would challenge your assumptions about what's good and what's bad. Pain is bad, right? Right.

It must be! Why else would we be waging a war on pain?

Americans consume 80 percent of the world's supply of painkillers,[1] including more than 108 tons of the highly addictive Vicodin each year—enough to numb every American around the clock for a month. That's a lot of pain we're trying to get rid of. Is it working?

In the last fifteen years, overdose deaths from painkillers have *quadrupled* and, for the first time in history, even surpassed traffic accidents as the leading cause of preventable deaths. The Centers for Disease Control and Prevention calls this an "epidemic." Every day, painkillers kill forty people and send more than a thousand to emergency rooms.[2]

Our society is so obsessed with avoiding pain that we'd rather kill ourselves than hurt. More people die from overdosing on prescription painkillers than from cocaine and heroin. We are literally numbing ourselves into unconsciousness. Unfortunately, we cannot numb the pain selectively: we cannot shut out the dark without also dimming the light.[3]

The sheer amount of painkillers we ingest makes it obvious that we are not using them just to sensibly manage unbearable physical pain. You may take painkillers, but no amount kills the pain in your soul.

"Numbing the pain for a while will make it worse when you finally feel it," says headmaster Albus Dumbledore in J. K. Rowling's *Harry Potter and the Goblet of Fire*.

Have you ever asked yourself what it would be like not to feel any pain? The answer may surprise you.

Four life-changing letters

Let's start at the beginning, Meggie suggests. A long-awaited Christmas present, she arrived as a breech baby on December 25, 1996. The doctors immediately sensed something wrong. Though she was full-term, she was listless, pale, without reflexes. They rushed her to the intensive care unit of the Cincinnati Children's Hospital, the best clinic in the area. "I'm basically a medical catastrophe," Meggie volunteers.

Those first thirty-eight days in the ICU launched a long and taxing search. What was the matter with her? Her voice crowed loud and strong, yet she had no reflexes. She could not suck, so the doctors had to insert a feeding tube. She had no gag reflex either. "This really worried the doctors, because if something got into the wrong pipe, she could die," her father explains, anguished; this could still happen today. For the first months, Meggie was fed with a G-tube that bypassed her mouth and went directly into her stomach.

Six months after Meggie's birth, the Zahneises heard for

the first time the four letters that would change their world: HSAN II, short for Hereditary Sensory and Autonomic Neuropathy Type II, a rare genetic disorder. Meggie could live to a hundred, but she wouldn't feel pain. Sounds awesome, right?

Slowly, over the years to come, Meggie and her parents would have to figure out what this meant. Bob is a warm, round-faced IT engineer, and Cindy an energetic, earthy media strategist (who returned to her job after staying at home with Meggie and her brother Nick for sixteen years).

Many mistakenly believe Meggie's diagnosis means that she is numb. She can feel pressure and touch, but the sensors for pain and for pressure are different. Every one of us has nerve channels that report temperature and pressure, and so does Meggie. She feels my handshake, and can lower her foot accurately on the gas pedal when she drives. But when our bodies encounter extreme temperatures or pain, they turn the task over to finer, more delicate channels that shrill 911 to the command center of the brain. However, Meggie's internal alarm system has been disconnected by her genetic coding. She is also deaf (she wears cochlear implants), prone to losing her balance, and sometimes slurs her speech. Scientists are still trying to explain how the loss of balance or the lack of finer sensations in her mouth relates to the gene modification.

When I ask her what exactly she feels when things should be painful, like her hip surgery, she hesitates, unsure what to say. It's like asking a color-blind person to describe deep purple. "Before the surgery, her hips would pop out of their sockets, and she would simply lift her knees and pop them back in," her mother chimes in. Cindy imitates the dismissive voice of the doctors talking to a young child: "No, your hip can't really be out, this would be excruciatingly painful." And then they were stunned when they saw the X-rays.

Pain as a friend, a guide, a protector

One only realizes what an important guide pain is when it is absent. "Pain is truly a friend, a precious protector, an alarm system," says Dr. Roland Staud, a German-born rheumatologist at the University of Florida in Gainesville. "The richness of life includes pain."

HSAN patients often don't live long, because they don't note a burst appendix or a heart attack.[4] When Cambridge geneticist Geoff Woods went to see a ten-year-old boy in Lahore who reportedly didn't feel pain and had earned a living by walking over burning coals and running knives through his limbs, he arrived too late. "For his birthday, he'd wanted . . . to jump off the first-floor roof of his house," Woods told the *New York Times*,[5] "and he did. And he got up and said he was fine and died a day later because of hemorrhage. I realized that pain had a different meaning than I had thought. He didn't have pain behavior to restrain him."

We need pain as a guide to alert us to danger and protect us from injury. Maybe it also serves as a reminder of our evanescence and vulnerability in a way that transcends our physicality. I am making the case that pain is not all bad, whether it be physical or emotional.

Pain is a strange animal. On some days, it charges in roaring, loud and boastful. On other days, it quietly eats you up from inside. Pain can be overwhelming, all consuming, so thought-stopping that there seems no space for anything else. It leaves scars in tender places.

"Pain insists upon being attended to," the author C. S. Lewis wrote. "God whispers to us in our pleasures, speaks in our consciences, but shouts in our pains. It is his megaphone to rouse a deaf world."

Pain does more than claw at our attention. Pain breaks through our shell of oblivious living. Pain pierces our cocoon of comfort. Pain puts a question mark to many of our endeavors. Pain adds a depth to our life that we cannot negate. "I wonder sometimes . . ." says Dr. Staud, "the people I treat who don't feel pain—do they feel the same empathy? Something has been taken from them."

The International Association for the Study of Pain defines pain as "an unpleasant sensory and emotional experience associated with actual or potential tissue damage."[6]

That's right: "sensory *and emotional* experience." Pain has many dimensions, and scientists have recognized that the magnitude of pain is not only related to the severity of the physical impact, but to a multitude of social, cultural, and emotional factors as well. Experts call it the "pain landscape."

The quandary is: How to navigate this landscape? If pain is a kind of interface that gives us information about our world, how should we work with it? We don't want to shut it down completely, because then we could miss out on crucial intel. But we also don't want to be incapacitated by our fear of it or plowed under when it's hitting us hard.

This is a query we'll continue to explore in the following chapters, as people offer different insights into how they approach their physical and emotional pain panorama.

Lucky to feel pain

Steve Gingras, the father of fourteen-year-old Minnesota HSAN patient Gabby, let out a sigh of relief when he first heard the diagnosis that his daughter feels no pain. "I thought, wow, that's easy, that's something we can deal with. Then I started thinking about it." Gabby's mother Trish offers, "People always think of the pain, pain, pain, how they can get rid of the pain. I always say, you don't know how lucky you are that you can feel it."[7]

There are probably fewer than a hundred people in the world with the gene mutation like Meggie's. "We have sensory channels that identify hot and cold. They work until something turns painful or too hot, and then they turn over to the pain channel," explains Dr. Staud. When he examined one of his HSAN patients with a brain scanner, he realized: "She could feel warmth, but when we turned the temperature over 112 degrees Fahrenheit, the channels simply shut down." Meggie merely senses that a 300-degree baking sheet is warm.

Her parents recognized for the first time that her sense of temperature was off when she was four and Bob took her to a public swimming pool. She had fun playing in the water, but suddenly, "curled up in a fetal position and wouldn't stir, like a corpse." He didn't know what was wrong, holding her and frantically rubbing her, until fifteen minutes later she sprung to life again and told him how much she loved him.

"She had hypothermia," Bob realized, "but by the time she notices that something is too cold or too hot, it is basically too late." Tests revealed that she detects no difference between 80 and 104 degrees Fahrenheit. "If my parents weren't so dogged, persistent, and smart, and didn't care so much," Meggie acknowledges, "who knows if I would even be here?"

Short of dramatic events, everyday tasks are an adventure. During the first years of her life, her parents hovered over her with eagle eyes, in an ever-futile attempt to replace their daughter's pain sensors with their own senses—rushing into her bedroom at every cooing, trying to get to her before she could injure herself. "There were many nights Bob didn't get any sleep," Cindy says. Often they came too late. Sometimes Meggie would chew her tongue to pieces in her sleep, and they would find her chin and chest covered in her own blood. Some children with HSAN have their teeth pulled out to protect their mouths, wear goggles to prevent them from clawing their own eyes, or have lost their eyesight due to injury. Have you ever had a tiny splinter in your eye? If so, you know how agonizing the sensation is. HSAN kids can scratch up their corneas irreparably and never know it until they go blind. Meggie's eyes are scarred, but intact. Because she lacks reflexes, she doesn't blink, and her eyes have been sewn half-shut at the corners to protect them from drying out. "She loves reading and writing so much," Cindy says. "We do absolutely everything we can to save her eyes."

The multibillion-dollar pain industry

HSAN is probably not a new disorder, but before advanced genetic testing, people who displayed the symptoms were likely misdiagnosed and died early. Roland Staud mentions tribes in Africa and Pakistan with significant numbers of HSAN kids, "but because these are poor countries where modern medical care is the exception, the children don't live long." Until recently, little effort was devoted to HSAN, because the number of patients is so small. But this is changing. Fast. Pain is a multibillion-dollar industry. Finding the key to switching off pain channels would be like hitting the jackpot. "The pharma industry is really working on this," Roland Staud says. He cautiously expresses optimism that a medication to disable the pain channels could be developed in the foreseeable future.[8] "But it's a Manhattan-type project," he warns, likening its brisance to the endeavor that developed the atomic bomb. "I greatly worry about its potential for abuse. Just think of football. Who do you think would want to take this medication?"

Already, athletes tolerate physical pain significantly better than nonactive people.⁹ They *feel* the same amount of pain, but they respond to it differently. Who doesn't remember gymnastic legend Kerri Strug's famous second vault in the 1996 Olympics on a sprained ankle with two torn ligaments, thus winning her team the gold medal before she broke down on her knees? Or Hanley Ramirez, who wanted to beat the Cardinals badly enough to play shortstop despite a broken rib?

Scientists don't have a precise answer yet about what exactly is different in athletes, but the combination of adrenaline, habituation, and willpower probably beats the pain. Simply popping a pill to eliminate the pain response would be a lucrative temptation.

The love of her life

The love of Meggie's life is baseball. "It's America's pastime," she beams. "Baseball is more than a spectator sport. You can have a deeper meaning and understanding; the layers of history are so deep." Since age four, Meggie has hardly ever missed a game of her beloved Cincinnati Reds.

"I'm fiercely competitive," she asserts. She tried to play soccer and baseball, but after a two-hundred-pound boy collided with her eighty-pound frame at a tournament, "I've had to channel my love of baseball a little differently. The next best thing to playing is being one of my Cincinnati Reds' most diehard fans, and becoming a walking baseball history encyclopedia."

Focus on the things you *can* do

Meggie tries to "focus on the things I *can* do. Instead of saying, 'Why me?' I changed it to 'Why not me?' Yes, I have this disorder, and it might inhibit me in some minor ways, but look at what I get to do because of it. I got this fabulous opportunity to write about and interview my heroes."

Breaking barriers

These opportunities were offered to her when she opened up about her vulnerability. Meggie entered a writing contest called "Breaking Barriers," initiated by the daughter of baseball legend (and MLB's first black player) Jackie Robinson. "I know what it's like to be different from everyone else around you, to overcome obstacles, to confront adversity," Meggie wrote in her essay entry. "It may not be on the baseball field, but I face many of the same social and emotional barriers that Jackie Robinson did. Because of my disability, many kids I know have judged this book by its cover, without taking the time to look a little closer and see that I'm just like them inside. This is where I personally identify with Mr. Robinson, as he dealt with the same issue."

Find your inspiration

Research the lives of people you admire. Find your heroes. Learn from them. How did they overcome what they were struggling with?

Meggie won the essay contest, and Major League Baseball's commissioner, Bud Selig, was so impressed with Meggie's wit and dedication that he offered her a paid position. Since 2011, Meggie has been working as the youth correspondent for MLB.com, regularly interviewing players, tweeting, and blogging about games. "Your knowledge and passion rivals that of many longtime reporters," Bud Selig wrote in his job offer. Her boss at MLB.com, Jim Banks, cites working with Meggie as "the highlight of my professional career. Her zest for life, her intelligence, how she overcomes obstacles, that's simply inspiring to watch."

She is a truly talented writer. "Writing is a path for me to make a difference," Meggie says. "I want to leave my mark on the world. If something I do can bring a smile to someone's face or inspire someone, make their life a little better, change their outlook on things—that's what makes me happy."

Write the best script for your life

Many psychologists emphasize the importance of developing "positive scripts" for one's life, and the benefits of expressive writing have been proven in numerous studies.[10] We are often unaware of negative scripts that trap us in a downward spiral, such as blaming others, projecting thoughts of unworthiness, and focusing on what goes wrong. These are roadblocks on our path toward growth. A trauma or handicap might destroy the old script with its more conventional story line, forcing a new plot upon us. Rewriting the story line fires up our imagination to perceive a struggle differently. In this sense, Meggie is literally writing the plot for a happy, fulfilled life, focusing on her many strengths and qualities, such as projecting realistic career goals, successful interviews with star athletes, and the joyful expectation to start a family.

In their book *The Power of Resilience*, psychologists Robert Brooks and Sam Goldstein describe the main features of a resilient mindset:

"Feeling in control of one's life, knowing how to fortify one's 'stress hardiness,' being empathetic, display-
ing effective communication and other interpersonal
capabilities, possessing solid problem-solving and
decision-making skills, establishing realistic goals and
expectations, learning from both success and failure,
being a compassionate and contributing member of society, living a responsible life based on a set of thoughtful values, feeling special (not self-centered) while
helping others to feel the same. Possessing a resilient
mindset does not imply that one is free from stress,
pressure, and conflict, but rather that one can successfully cope with problems as they arise. We also use the
word *mindset* to capture an important premise of this
book: *mindsets can be changed.*"[11]

Keep this in mind as we spend a weekend with Meggie
Zahneis.

At the yearly FanFest in Cincinnati, Rod Stewart's voice
crows from the loudspeaker, "Wake up, Maggie." Meggie
storms the stage like a pro, raising her arms high to wave
to the crowd that greets her with familiar cheers. "If you
have any questions or feedback that you don't get to tell the
players tonight, tweet me, and I will ask the questions for
you!" she offers, and spells out her Twitter account: @meggie
zahneis.

Take that in for a moment. Most people say that public
speaking scares them more than death. Would you volunteer
to walk onstage and speak in front of four thousand people if
you had walking and speaking impediments? But this is Meggie, a girl who dreams of a career in public speaking, writing,
and psychology.

Be an inspiration to others

"I believe the only way to help oneself is through helping others," Meggie says. "I want to inspire other kids with special needs, not to give up. If just one person says, 'I didn't give up because of you,' my life has had a purpose."

Meggie reels through the crowded convention center in Cincinnati like a sailboat in rough sea, her gamine figure swaying from side to side, occasionally toppling over. But her balance issues don't slow her down much. Smartphone and recorder in hand, she barrages the players with questions. "Hey, Meggie, when are we going to do that interview?" they beckon. Third baseman Todd Frazier high-fives her and raves, "I prefer Meggie to any other reporter. She knows every game, every score, the history of baseball, you name it. She is asking really good questions." Her colleagues nicknamed her "Scoop," because she often disarms the players until they open up to talk about more personal issues they would not share with other reporters. The players treat her with respect and courtesy. As top athletes in their field, they intimately understand physical injury. Outfielder Ryan Ludwick can rattle out his surgeries ("Shoulder, hip, knee . . .") just like Meggie. She only slightly supersedes him in the surgery department.

Baseball is a team sport, and she is one of the team. On her sixteenth birthday she was stuck in the hospital after spinal surgery. The best birthday surprise was that her team appointed her "Most Valuable Player" and sent her a special jersey with her name and all their signatures.

The Reds are more than a hobby for Meggie; she calls them her family, and the stadium her second home.

Having the team's support is all the more crucial for her,

as she has hardly any friends her age. "They simply don't understand," she says. "I am different, and people perceive that as negative. But hey, what does normal mean anyway? There is no sense in being normal, because everybody is different." She does not play the games the other teenagers like to play. "I'm just not interested in Justin Bieber, fashion, or makeup. I'm into baseball and books."

Poems of battle scars

The poems and diary entries she writes after the stage lights in the convention center have dimmed reveal her true struggles with loneliness and despair. In her poem "Battle Scars" she writes:

> *Every day I fight a civil war*
> *Heart and mind and battle scars*
> *A cross to bear; guilt and shame*
> *Why couldn't I just hold it together?*
> *What's the point? What's the hope?*
> *How am I expected to cope?*

When I asked Richard Tedeschi about the possibility of growth arising from a struggle with chronic illness like Meggie's, I learned that there is precious little scientific information about the link between the two. I regard chronic illness as an ongoing crisis, a small death we die each time our body gives out on us, every time a doctor misdiagnoses us, every time someone regards us as worth less (or even worthless). Equally, each of these moments of defeat is a challenge to grow, to overcome, to rise above. To defy the naysayers with a strength that builds over time.

One of the unsolved problems of flying into space is that astronauts lose a significant percentage of their bone mass. Their bones weaken because there is *too little* resistance. We need resistance to stay strong.

In this sense, the school of hard knocks provides us with ongoing resistance we can use to fortify our soul.

The mantra of hope

From that initial moment when Cindy and Bob saw their first-born in the ICU, they decided to focus on the positive. "PMA!" Cindy yells, when Meggie hesitates to approach a famous baseball icon for an autograph. It's the family's shorthand for *positive mental attitude*. "It could be worse," has become Bob's mantra that he repeats frequently over the three days we spend together. "It could be worse," echoes Meggie, and then tells me of her thirty-one-year-old friend Kim who also has HSAN II, but to a more severe degree. Kim can't even feel the sensation of her feet touching the ground when she walks, and thus must use a wheelchair.

Meggie is determined to leave home for college in Miami, to live independently without an aide, and she is longing to have children, a family of her own. She is certain she would welcome her babies, whether they have HSAN or not. "I wouldn't wish it on my worst enemy," she says. "On the other hand, I've been there, done that, so I could help them through it." HSAN is a recessive condition; the father of her child would have to carry this rare gene as well in order to pass the condition onto the baby.

Childbirth could carry its own risks for Meggie. Another HSAN patient in her midthirties, Karen Cann, bore two healthy children in New York.[12] But for several weeks she felt an uncomfortable stiffness in her hip after her first child was born. The doctors told her to relax, but she insisted. Finally, X-rays revealed she was walking around on a pelvis that she had shattered during childbirth. Though they knew of her genetic disposition, the doctors still couldn't believe the woman wasn't screaming in pain with an injury this severe. They had to commit her to bed rest for six months.

Cindy and Bob already had Meggie's diagnosis when they decided to have another child, fully aware the baby would have a 25 percent chance of also being born with HSAN. "Well, we figured, if they both have HSAN, they at least have each other. And if he didn't have HSAN, they'd still have each other. We wouldn't let it deter us." Nick, Meggie's brother, is twenty-one months younger and healthy. While Meggie is wise beyond her years, physically her body is about three years behind. She is five foot one and weighs only ninety-five pounds; Nick is six foot three and outweighs her twice. Meggie's face crumbles when people mistake her for Nick's younger sister.

Aside from Jackie Robinson and Mahatma Gandhi, she lists Lou Gehrig as her role model, the iconic New York Yankees first baseman and six-time World Series champion who had to cut short his illustrious career on the field due to his struggle with amyotrophic lateral sclerosis (ALS). The condition slowly stole away all his bodily functions. "Not only was he a great athlete, a tremendous physical specimen," Meggie raves, "I just so admire the grace and the poise he had in dealing with an illness so debilitating. Of course Gehrig's disease is infinitely worse than my disorder, but I think I have that personal connection, because he had physical challenges to deal with like me." Two baby-blue chairs from the original Yankee Stadium grace a special room already filled to the brim with baseball paraphernalia of bobbleheads, autographs, and posters. Meggie has watched the famous retirement speech Gehrig gave at Yankee Stadium over and over.

"I consider myself the luckiest man on the face of the earth," Gehrig said, two years before his death. "I might have been given a bad break, but I have an awful lot to live for."

In honor of Gehrig, Meggie describes herself in her Twitter bio as the "luckiest girl on earth." Yes, she affirms enthusiastically, "Because I *am*. I mean, look at what I get to do! I feel very blessed, very grateful."

7. Pray

"Let go, but don't give up"
Why Alain Beauregard calls terminal cancer
the "greatest gift" of his life

*If you can solve your problem, then
what is the need of worrying?
If you cannot solve it, then what
is the use of worrying?*

—SHANTIDEVA[1]

Alain Beauregard's story perplexes his doctors, his family, and even himself. "I am the victim of a miracle," he states proudly. "A very willing victim."

The Canadian business consultant has led an extraordinarily successful life. On his "shopping list of life," as he jokingly calls his goals, he's already ticked off most of the hot items: Starting a successful tech company at age twenty-seven? Check. Selling the company for millions of dollars a few years later? Check. Taking vows with his college sweetheart? Fathering two children he adores? A huge villa on the Saint Lawrence River in Montreal? Luxurious vacations in the Caribbean? Check, check, and check. Then—checkmate!

At age forty-five, when Alain detected blood in his urine, he brushed off any sense of urgency. Alain describes his urologist as a gruff, bearded man who sent him for tests after telling him bluntly, "Well, this could mean anything, from nothing at all to you're gonna die in two weeks." Since the first three tests revealed nothing, Alain decided to forget about the fourth. In hindsight, the fourth test would have exposed that Alain was harboring a malignant tumor. "I will always remember this. Here I was, trying to just get on with my life, looking normal, and yet death was so close. I told myself I'd have decades to live."

As the president of his own tech companies, Alain speaks with the calm authority of a man who has always been his own boss. He exudes the air of someone in charge, albeit in a pleasantly quiet, unassuming manner. A physicist by training, he grounds himself in facts and figures, softening the intensity of his words with his charming French accent. We meet at the beach near Los Angeles, where the Canadian is on a consulting trip. He specializes in building three-dimensional laser eyesight for robots, and he chuckles at the irony of the shortsighted way he approached his own life.

After the visit to the urologist, a year and a half passed. Alain felt weak, constantly plagued by pain in his lower back around his kidneys, but he convinced himself he had just pulled a muscle and kept heating up beanbags to soothe the ache. "Basically I was pushing it away." Denial became increasingly difficult. On some days he was "just peeing blood." In June 2006, his ex-spouse Nadia Capolla finally insisted on driving him to the emergency room. "The pain that I had tried so hard to suppress all of a sudden seemed to have multiplied by ten. I was crying, screaming, and begging for help."[2] He suspected kidney stones, but instead, the doctors discovered a massive tumor in his bladder. Eight centimeters, the size of a big grapefruit, and it was blocking his kidneys.

In the following weeks at the hospital, the doctors ran

more tests, and every time they came back with results, their faces grew grimmer. After a biopsy of the cancer cells, Alain's kidneys shut down. "The level of toxins in my blood shot up to the point where the doctors told me I would only have forty-eight hours to live."

Only a few specialists in Montreal could perform the emergency surgery, and they were all already overbooked. It was Thursday evening when the doctors realized the life-threatening nature of the emergency, yet the earliest surgery date they could secure was Monday. Alain wouldn't make it through the weekend.

Suddenly, death became real.

"Before that, I have to admit I really didn't take it so seriously. Death was something that happened to others or maybe to me in thirty years. But that night and that morning, I felt my body slipping away from me, being poisoned by my own blood. I was terrified," Alain relates.

Alain had met a Tibetan Buddhist teacher ten years earlier, but he hadn't taken the Buddhist teachings about impermanence to heart. With death approaching, "I prayed like I never prayed before, with all my cells in my body screaming for help, 'Please don't let me down! Help me!'"

The final verdict

And help came. Early Friday afternoon, Alain's urologist rushed in. One surgeon had a cancellation. "Today at four o'clock. You have to go right now. He won't wait too long." The doctors put Alain in an ambulance, which sped across town. When he arrived, the surgeon and his team were already waiting. "They barely said hello, turned me over on my belly. There was no time to put me to sleep, I was on morphine anyway. They started surgery to unblock the kidneys right away. I could feel them sticking needles in my kidneys, but by this point I was quite used to pain."

Alain's life was saved, at least for that weekend—"a huge relief, and a really big lesson: death is real. This determination to live stayed with me."

But the reprieve was temporary. A few weeks later his oncologist sat down by his bedside while Alain was receiving his first intravenous chemotherapy. Alain describes her as a compassionate, caring doctor in her midthirties. Before telling Alain the final verdict, she wanted to be a hundred percent certain and had sent his file to the so-called tumor board of five cancer experts for review. The sarcoma had spread into the bones, the rib cage, the left lung, the hip, and the spine. The chemotherapy might slow the growth and possibly prolong his life a few months, but all experts unanimously agreed: his cancer was inoperable and incurable. Stage IV, terminal, this was it. The doctor's eyes welled up as she told him, "There is no hope. Taking out your bladder will only weaken you further and probably kill you faster. There is nothing we can do for you. You'll have six months to live, at best."

Without hesitation, Alain blurted out, *"Je ne vous crois pas, je vais vivre!"*—I don't believe you, I will live!

The words flew out of his mouth. "The next moment I was thinking, 'Huh, how can you say this?'" He had just contradicted seven experts in the field. "In fact, I was not denying those facts, though it looked like this to my family and friends. I am a scientist myself; this wasn't an airy-fairy response of, 'Oh, cancer is just an illusion.'" And yet he discovered "a deep, fundamental core of resilience. In me there was this scream, 'No, I'm going to live!'"

His ex-spouse Nadia, a nanophysicist, thought, "He doesn't get it!"

Over the following weeks, two voices battled within Alain. "There was the fearful Alain who was scared shitless and could only panic, 'I'm gonna die! I need help!' And there is a very stable, subconscious base underneath from which resilience comes. There was a greater power, a strength in me that I could count on."

When to fight and when to let go

Alain was too weak to take care of himself. Nadia compassionately welcomed him into her home for hospice care. She had left him six years earlier, but they had remained friends and she was willing to create a family environment so that he could pass away surrounded by their two children. Their understanding was that Alain would only live for a few more months. Nadia had a new partner who at first generously agreed. However, after caring for Alain became her first priority, her boyfriend left her.

"Chemo was a horrible experience," Alain says. Because it was not expected to help much anyway, he had asked for the strongest possible dose. "I did not know what I got myself into. If I had to do it again, I would hesitate to ask for the strongest dose. Chemo kills you." The tests had shown that the cisplatin could only kill 20 percent of his cancer cells. "The other eighty percent were on me," Alain says.

Weakened from the chemo, "I could maybe walk twenty meters. Going to the bathroom seemed as daunting as crossing the North Pole. I became useless." Alain had to "let go of everything: my home, my car, my clothes. There was no point in putting on nice clothes anyway, because I was lying down all day. Initially, I wasn't able to let go. Slowly, slowly I was *forced* to let go."

Alain defines letting go as "very active. It does not mean

giving up or being resigned. I was fighting for my life, but I had to let go of all the things I held on to."

A line from a prayer he had read years earlier now kept coming back to his mind: "May your will be accomplished!" He wasn't exactly sure to whom he was addressing this prayer, but he repeated it over and over.

Unexpectedly, he found happiness in this process. "I lived through much pain and anxiety, but at times there were moments when I was very happy, happier than I had ever been. I just surrendered." He would look out the window and contemplate, "This is the last summer," drinking in every second of it. Knowing his life was slipping away from them, he especially cherished every instant he spent with his kids. "I won't see them grow up," he grieved. More than anything, he longed to be able to accompany his children on their journey through life.

Winning or losing

With his body forcing his life to an abrupt halt, now he had time to reflect. Why did he, a fit man in his forties who went jogging regularly, ate healthily, and had never smoked, develop cancer? The doctors told him that his cancer probably had taken five to ten years to develop. "It is not something that happens in an instant or within a year," says Alain, snapping his fingers. There were likely physical reasons for his sarcoma. The doctors called his type of cancer "old man's cancer"; younger men rarely get it unless they have been exposed to chemicals. As a graduate student of physics, Alain had spent many hours in the lab. When he started his own company producing vision for robots, he also had a lab, and, for a decade, handled many of the industrial-grade chemicals himself—"the bottles with the skulls and the crosses on it." He had protected himself with gloves and masks, but this exposure probably had done some damage.

Alain could think of other risk factors as well. After selling his first firm he became the president of a NASDAQ company. When the dot-com bubble burst, the board held him responsible for the stock crash. "I got blamed and felt I was used as a scapegoat. I was powerless. Those factors are all well-known in scientific research as great conditions for cancer to flourish."

Alain and the board hunkered down in a legal showdown. The board declined to offer a "golden parachute," and Alain refused to resign. The company took away his assistant and his authority, yet Alain "couldn't stay home, because then they would have had grounds for termination." For a year and a half Alain still showed up at the company every day. "It might not sound so bad to go to the office and not have anything to do, but this was a form of psychological torture. It was so humiliating, seeing my former assistant and managers across the hallway, and people looking at me with a shy kind of embarrassment, their eyes full of pity. It drained me totally."

Eventually he won the war. "I thought I was winning, because they paid me every cent, but maybe only my wallet was winning. I hurt myself." The golden parachute didn't save him from crashing.

A year earlier, Nadia had left him. "Although it was very much my fault, I couldn't stand that she left," Alain admits. Nadia had wanted him to focus less on work. "Money doesn't bring happiness," Nadia kept repeating. Alain knew this to be true, yet "the urge was too strong. I went full throttle." Alain knows he is a man with strong determination, at times stubborn. "I had set myself certain goals for financial security, and once I have an objective, I get it done. I was stuck." When he now shares his experiences, "A lot of men recognize themselves in this kind of suffering when you know you need to change, and you try to mimic change as much as you can, but eventually the whole thing cracks."

Up to this crisis he had reached all his objectives. "I should have been happy, but inside I was empty. I found myself with no more dreams, no more goals." After the company paid him off, he could barely muster the motivation to get out of bed in the morning. "Nothing seemed interesting anymore. In hindsight, I would say I was depressed." Alain self-deprecatingly coins this a "man-depression." "You tell everybody, including yourself, you're fine, but in actuality, you're not fine at all."

Letting go is active

The cancer diagnosis was a mortal alarm signal, forcing Alain to take a candid look at himself. "Only the threat of imminent death was strong enough to outsmart me. When the doctors tell you there is nothing they can do for you, then there is really no place to go."

Stuck in bed, he had all the time in the world to turn his thoughts inward. "I am not generalizing for anyone, but for me, I was so deadlocked in my ways that cancer was necessary to break through that shell, that really tough shell around my heart. And it had to be a really strong and aggressive one at that."

The shell was made of all the myriad ways he had defined who he was, "as a businessman, a physicist, a father, a husband, as Alain; there are many identities we hold on to. Letting go happened by force. I was basically cracked open, systematically losing bit by bit the things I hung on to."

Let the pain crack you open

It is all too easy to let a shock like this harden us, close us down, make us more anxious and uptight. Yet, we could use it the opposite way, like Alain: to let it crack us open. This hurts like hell, but it is the only way to reveal the hidden treasures inside. Holding on tight does not prevent the pain anyway. As spiritual teacher Ram Dass says, "The cost of armoring your heart against reality is more costly than you may appreciate."[3]

Alain remembers sitting in a doctor's waiting room, flipping through a magazine. A full-page advertisement by a drug company sprung out at him with a slogan that screamed, "Hate cancer back!" Alain was stunned. "With this attitude, you cannot win. It's like fighting fire with fire. Yes, cancer is the enemy, but you have to work with this enemy. For me, cancer was self-hatred, or a rejection of a part of myself." Thus, the antidote became apparent: "The only weapon I had against cancer was love. There is no other weapon."

 ## Be kind to yourself

The self-hate and guilt Alain reveals are among the most common feelings after a trauma. They are also among the most damaging.[4]

Psychotherapist Susan Ollar acknowledges, "We desperately don't want to feel shame, but we also shame ourselves on a regular basis. It's in our culture. There is absolutely nothing beneficial to be gained by shame. It's a soul killer."

Sometimes Susan asks her clients to bring in pictures of themselves when they were a baby or a toddler, so that they can see themselves how they really are: fundamentally good, worthy, and deserving.

Be kind to yourself. Getting sleep, physical exercise, and eating healthily are basic steps toward sanity. Show some respect for your own good heart. Rather than hating the parts of yourself you reject, actively take steps to nurture yourself.

In the guide in the back of the book, you will find a simple loving-kindness meditation to connect with your basic goodness.

A blockage of energy

Alain had never been particularly religious. Growing up Catholic, he had a connection with Jesus, but hadn't lived it. At a visit with his mother-in-law a decade before he was diagnosed with cancer, Alain had picked up a Buddhist bestseller from her coffee table—*The Tibetan Book of Living and Dying*, by the Tibetan master Sogyal Rinpoche. Alain was intrigued, and even attended courses with the author, but describes himself more as a leisurely Buddhist.

Tibetans have a fundamentally different understanding of the body than Western physicians. Tibetan doctors consider any illness the product of mental and emotional poisons, such as anger, passion, and ignorance. When Alain asked Sogyal Rinpoche what the reason for his cancer was, Rinpoche said, "Cancer is a blockage of energy." Emphasizing that he can only speak for himself, Alain acknowledges that this diagnosis rang true. "In retrospect I was really blocked. My cancer was composed of shame, guilt, and self-hatred." Shame of what? "All the aspects of myself that I rejected. I was not following the flow of my own life." He realized that bladder cancer was a fitting metaphor for the state of his life, "because the bladder is associated with flow, and I could not pee anymore. Literally, the flow in me was blocked."

Unblock the blockages

Are there aspects of yourself that you have suppressed or not paid enough attention to? Are you honoring your soul? Is this crisis an opportunity to do something you have always wanted to do but never found the space? Trust your intuition. Spend more time in your heart. Find something, anything, that brings you joy and that connects you with your creative energy.

For Alain, there were entire aspects of himself that he had not honored in decades—for instance, his creative, artistic ability. "In business I thought I had to show my tough side and I could deal very successfully in that environment without letting things get to me. But I wasn't happy. I actually hated myself, and I wanted this guy to disappear. Unconsciously. If you had asked me at the time, I would have said, 'No, I'm fine, I like myself,' but underneath were all these layers of self-hatred and lack of self-esteem." As a young man he had wanted to study philosophy, but had succumbed to the wish of his father, an engineer, to dive into physics instead. "There was this whole sensitive side in me that I had suppressed." The businessman had convinced himself not to show emotions, not to appear "soft."

"I began to love my cancer and see the benefit of it," Alain shares. "I know it sounds crazy. My body was destroyed, but my mind opened up more and more." Instead of being his enemy, cancer became his guide. Alain started to listen what cancer had to say. "It was one of my specialties to suppress emotion. Finding a way to heal is to follow the guidance of cancer and allow the walls, even the fake identities one has built up, to let go and to open to love. Therein lays the true fight."

Brutally honest

Alain asked Nadia and his children if they would allow him the space to be "brutally honest." He realized that "if I wanted to heal I needed to connect with my own reality of what I was *really* feeling, deep down underneath." He needed to vent his thoughts and emotions, say them out loud. His son Olivier, twelve years old, couldn't bear to watch his father wither away, and instead retreated into video games and rather excelled at *World of Warcraft*.

Nadia and their fifteen-year-old daughter Alexandrine, however, made a commitment to be there for him even when things got tough. "When you see me crying," Alain told them, "don't try to console me. Don't! The most precious gift is just to give me that space to go through whatever I have to go through, without trying to change my mind or my situation." Whether it was "I am suffering so much, I am afraid of dying," whether it was sobbing uncontrollably, "most of what you voice in such a situation is not very pleasant. But it was part of my healing, a way of reconciliation. I had to express it, accept it, and say yes to it."

Psychiatrist David Spiegel, the director of Stanford's Center on Stress and Health, is internationally renowned for his pioneering research into the mind's effect on physical health. He encourages supportive-expressive group therapy, which supports cancer patients to confront their illness honestly. Whether the therapy prolongs patients' lives, as some studies have shown, is a matter of debate,[5] but Spiegel could prove that the therapy led to less pain, depression, and anxiety.[6]

Not everybody wishes to express his or her deepest emotions. Some find it counterproductive, as they don't want to dwell on the negative. But many feel it is helpful or even indispensable.[7] No method is universal, yet Richard Tedeschi thinks that "expressing emotions is helpful for *most* people—because trying to constrain yourself and not express how you feel takes a lot of effort, too. When we ask people about their trauma, they usually thank us and say they don't talk about this nearly enough." Tedeschi stresses that for "constructive self-disclosure, the telling of the story is not just about the trauma, but living life in the aftermath of the trauma. This is often even more important, because that is the current struggle."

Express your emotions

Are there supportive family members, friends, a therapist, or a support group with whom you feel comfortable sharing your feelings?

End-of-life conversations can be harrowing to hear. They might be unfair, not polite, raging with anger and frustration, or full of contradictions. Very, very few close family members will be equipped to listen with an open heart. The same can hold true for discussions about deep trauma.

"The responses to disclosure are crucial and can further a healing and growth process or impede it," cautions Tedeschi.[8] There is a danger that listeners will take things personally, hold a grudge, aggravate bad emotions by arguing their side, or try to convince patients that they should feel differently. That's why professionally guided therapy groups, support groups, and therapists are a safer alternative. It is important that trauma survivors learn how to find people with whom they can have these bare-heart conversations. Tedeschi calls them "expert companions."

If you can't or don't want to talk, try expressive writing, disclosing your true feelings on paper. Later, you can decide when and with whom to share these pages.

Like many people in a severe crisis, Alain noted that "because people feel uncomfortable they start saying things that are really unhelpful such as, 'You're gonna be fine, things are gonna be okay . . .' These are the worst things to say. It provoked anger and all sorts of emotions in me. But if someone can stay with it, that means you are also able to look at yourself at that time, so maybe some spiritual practice could be helpful to observe how you are going through this emotional process with the other person."

Alain had the great fortune to be able to surround himself in his illness by very loving, capable people. Remember that Alain was actually single when he fell ill. One crucial skill of resilient people is that they *reach out* for support and cultivate nourishing relationships.

"Every day was a roller-coaster ride," Nadia remembers. "We laughed together, cried together; there were no masks anymore."

Researcher Tzipi Weiss has documented that the loving support of a spouse contributed significantly to the experience of posttraumatic growth in cancer survivors. She found that supportive spouses often shared the growth experience. Though her study focused on female breast cancer patients and their husbands, her findings suggest that this shared growth could occur among other cancer survivors and their spouses as well.[9]

Nadia confirmed this experience for herself. While Alain was going through the process of working through unfinished emotional business, she realized that the honest communication had cleared away pent-up anger about the end of their union and brought them closer together.

Setting boundaries

But Alain also had to make the heart-wrenching discovery that some of the people he felt closest to weren't able to support him in his illness. This, too, is a common experience. After a few weeks he asked his mother, gently, to visit him less. Why? "Because her own way of taking that illness was to treat me like a baby, and give me all kinds of advice, which doctor to see and what to eat and what to do and what not to do." At one point, she said to him, "I am losing my baby."

Alain was her beloved firstborn, and the sorrow of watching him die was overwhelming. Yet Alain was in no position to console her; he needed every iota of energy to deal with his own pain. He told her, "You know, cancer is a *physical* illness, so while my body looks very weak, my mind and my intelligence are intact. I am forty-six years old and have lots of life experience. The doctor I chose is my doctor. Yes, we can discuss it, but in the end, decisions are *mine*."

Feeling divine love

His daughter Alexandrine, though, was able to support him lovingly. One afternoon, while Alain was lounging on the couch, she asked him if he wanted to go for a stroll to the historic Catholic church that was only a few hundred feet away. An easy walk, but in Alain's condition he struggled with all his might to get there, leaning on his daughter the whole way. He reflected on how their roles had reversed. "I am the father, but now I am being helped by this teenager who is greater than me. I need her help, I cannot help her."

Alexandrine, educated in a private school run by Catholic nuns, shared with him Christ's story at each of the twelve stations of the cross. Alain couldn't help but think about his own suffering and contemplate, "Christ went through all this to change, to purify his sins, and to take upon himself the sins of everyone. Not to compare myself, but what if I could find meaning in all the suffering?"

Alain lay down on a bench in the churchyard by the river. Looking up at the sky and the trees, "everything seemed so divine. I had an experience of divine love. Just pure love. My heart completely opened. This happened many times during this period of healing where I would go from the extreme of pain, discouragement, and suffering, to these divine experiences of complete openness. I couldn't call it meeting God, but it was a pure experience of happiness and such joy that it didn't matter if I was dying."

Tibetan healing meditation

Alain started to practice meditation every second he was awake.

We have seen in the previous chapters that mindfulness has proven to lessen physical pain, anxiety, stress, and other symptoms of posttraumatic stress.

In particular, Alain immersed himself in a healing meditation Sogyal Rinpoche taught him. Tibetan Buddhists employ a great variety of methods, often including visualization and mantras. As instructed by his teacher, Alain visualized the eighth-century pioneer of Tibetan Buddhism in Tibet, Guru Rinpoche, a mystical, larger-than-life figure. In his right hand, Guru Rinpoche held a thunderbolt, and Alain visualized thousands and millions of sparks of wisdom fire flooding him from that thunderbolt, attacking his cancer vigorously, burning it away. In the second phase of this practice, Alain visualized a cup of nectar in Guru Rinpoche's left hand. He pictured the healing nectar flooding his body through his fontanel, flushing away all the cancer cells, and purifying all illness with a powerful, steady stream. Alain immersed himself in this practice with all the vivacity he could muster.

He also learned the Tibetan practice of "giving and taking" (in Tibetan, *tonglen*).[10] His Holiness the Dalai Lama practices it every day, and it might just be the most stunning reversal of the conventional logic of avoiding suffering that we discussed earlier. Instead of getting rid of pain, we open our heart to welcome it. We breathe in our suffering, the suffering around us, and then the world's. Pema Chödrön instructs, "Every time you breathe in, the heart gets bigger and bigger, so that no matter how bad it feels, you just give it more space. So when you breathe in, you're open to it. And then when you breathe out, you just send out a lot of space."[11]

We break down the walls that enclose our hearts. We breathe out healing, joy, and love—for us, for those close to us, for the world, even our enemies. Alain's teacher Sogyal Rinpoche calls it "Buddhist air-conditioning." We make the world a bit more tender with each breath, but mostly we gentle our own hearts.

Alain started with his children, wishing, "May I be able to take on all their illnesses, so that they never get cancer. Then I extended the circle further and further. This gave my suffering meaning, a purpose."

All these years he thought he had no faith. He had actually been quite critical of the mystical aspects of Tibetan Buddhism that did not easily fit with his physicist's understanding of the material world. "Then cancer happened and it turned out, I had tremendous faith; I just didn't know it until it was tested."

Coincidentally, at the same day Alain was diagnosed with cancer, Sogyal Rinpoche's Buddhist community was starting a meditation retreat in the South of France. Six hundred people had gathered in the temple and began praying for Alain. This show of support reinforced the self-love Alain was starting to connect with: "If hundreds of people feel enough love to pray for me, how could I possibly hate myself?"

Alain believes that the power of prayer is universal. He shared his healing practice with a good friend, a Moroccan Muslim who had cancer. She wanted to pray to Allah, but she found it difficult to find healing practices in her faith. Alain advised her to keep praying to Allah, and practice the healing meditation using her own faith. "Because the worst thing when you want to heal is to have *no* faith. Yes, doctors and treatments can help, but on the spiritual level it is *so* helpful to believe in *something*. Which could be just a cosmic principle, Virgin Mary for my mother, Christ, Allah, light, whatever. If you have no faith in something greater than yourself, your prayer lacks power."

Align with the divine

Strong faith can influence the positive outcome of an illness. For instance, in a four-year study with HIV patients, 45 percent showed an increase of spirituality after the diagnosis, while 13 percent decreased.[12] The striking conclusion of the study is that increased spirituality predicted a measurably slower disease progression, and the religious patients had a significantly greater preservation of healthy blood cells. The HIV patients who lost faith or experienced their God as punishing stunted their recovery. In other words, faith can have a tremendous impact on our health if the faith carries us through the crisis. However, we cannot force nor forge such a connection.

If we *can* connect with a compassionate force greater than ourselves, we have found a powerful ally in healing. Alain is convinced: "Faith can move mountains."

In the Buddhist faith, the notion of karma simply means "cause and effect." Anything we think or do has an effect, and anything that happens has a cause, even if we can't see it. Alain understood the Buddhist faith to say, "You are very much responsible for yourself. The past is the past, you will reap what you have sown, but you are entirely responsible for what you do now." When he mentioned this at a workshop, a woman raised her hand and shouted angrily, "So, you're saying it's my own fault that I have cancer?" Alain was taken aback. "I can only speak about myself. How astonishing that we can use absolutely anything to make ourselves feel bad. What I am talking about is an empowering message of responsibility, not blaming anyone or anything."

Surrender, but do your part

The prayer that spoke to Alain so intensely—"May your will be accomplished"—meant that he was striking a balance: "I recognize I have no control and need to surrender, but I am still being responsible; that's the key. This is a lesson I learned early on in my illness. I prayed and I asked for help, but at the same time I made a commitment to also do *my* part."

When the doctors had first told Alain that he had cancer, his immediate reaction was to grant all authority to the doctors. "Okay, heal me, cut it, whatever you have to do." After the doctors conceded that they could do nothing to cure him, "they gave me back my power. There is something unconscious here that I think everyone who suffers should look at: Am I really taking responsibility or am I secretly hoping an outside force will do it for me?"

Alain tried a few more times to hand over the responsibility. When he heard a miracle healer was guiding a weekend outside Montreal, he made his way to the gathering. He quickly realized that the savior was just a quack, but he was stuck at the remote location. "This was quite funky. But the weekend ended up being very helpful because I realized, I had done it again—hoping someone would save me. I have to take healing in my hands, not what a lot of cancer patients do: running from one attempt to get help to the next. That was a strong lesson for me."

Take charge

It has been well recognized that feeling helpless is a strong intensifier for pain, and one of the most effective ways doctors and hospitals could reduce pain and the intensity of an illness is to empower their patients.[13]

Alain put himself back in charge. He explained to his doctors that he would listen to their expert opinions, but he would make the decisions. "Ugh, that didn't sit well with them." He even fired a doctor who was unwilling to take the time to explain his findings to Alain. "In my position, firing a doctor could be an extraordinarily stupid thing to do. I needed all the help I could get. But while I showed respect to the doctors, they also needed to show respect for me and treat me as a grown-up who was capable of making decisions. Hospitals are not set up for this, and so I had to have this conversation several times."

Alain's decision reminds me of Norman Cousins, the late journalist and UCLA professor, who resolved to fight against his "pain intensifiers" with a creative program that inspired patients around the world. Stricken with painful arthritis, he was way ahead of his time when he set out to prove that positive emotions—"purpose, determination, love, hope, faith, will to live"—could activate healing forces.[14] For instance, he enjoyed watching the Marx Brothers and Charlie Chaplin and discovered that he could laugh away the pain for up to an hour. He took charge of his hospital regimen by posting a sign on his door that limited the nurses to take only one blood sample every third day.[15] Despite various ailments, he lived to a happy seventy-five.

Don't believe everything the experts say

Do your own research. Become your own expert. You have to manage your condition, and therefore you have to get to know yourself intimately. This is *your* life, nobody else's.

This might sound obvious, but several people in this book would be in a nursing home or dead by now had they followed the advice of their doctors and insurance specialists blindly. If you have doubt, get a second opinion, maybe even a third or a fourth.[16]

Research all your options. Read up. Exercise discernment. Stay open-minded.

The sheriff next door

While Alain had given up the search for miracle healers, he recognized that he needed to keep an open mind about receiving unconventional help. "Help came in some strange ways that I had to open up to accept."

A new neighbor moved in, a tough-looking, burly, gun-carrying sheriff who had retired early at age fifty-five. He told Alain that he had the ability to see emotions and illness in people. Rather than appreciating this as a gift, the sheriff's sensitivity had made his working life hell for him. Alain was skeptical of this New Agey neighbor, but curiosity got the better of him. He invited him over for tea and found that the ex-cop was indeed able to guide him to sense blockages and help him through it. "He didn't touch me physically. He would just invite me to scan my body mentally and sense where I was blocked." They did regular energy work parallel to Alain's chemotherapy. "I was not anti-medical," explains Alain. "I did all the medical treatments, but I also kept my openness about alternative forms of treatment. The right people appeared at the right time; small miracles happened every day.

"I was ready to explore *anything*. I used to say, if I need to run naked in the main street of Montreal to heal, I will do that."

Stay flexible

Alain's "whatever it takes" approach is remarkable. Flexibility can hardly be overrated as a crucial asset when we face difficulties. It means to be tough and unyielding at times or soft and adaptive at others; to express our emotions honestly when surrounded by people who can hear us, or to stay quiet and just listen. It means to keep searching for options, but to settle when decisions need to be made. Diverse dilemmas demand diverse strategies. Alain demonstrated a rare flexibility: for instance, he stayed open to alternative as well as traditional medical treatments, he shared his honest feelings with those who found it beneficial and cut off others, and he accepted advice from a wide range of people while staying in charge.

"By and large, the people who deal best with these different situations are those who can do what it takes to get through the event,"[17] psychologist George A. Bonanno noted. When he observed students after 9/11 he found that "the students who were flexible—that is, who could either express or suppress emotion as needed—were markedly less distressed two years later. . . . Flexibility is adaptive because different kinds of adversity create different kinds of demands. The better able we are to adapt ourselves to those demands, the more likely we are to survive. An intriguing implication of this idea is that in some circumstances, it is adaptive to think or behave in ways that we would normally think of as inappropriate or even unhealthy."[18]

Relax. Nothing is under control

Alain didn't have to turn into a streaker, but things started to improve. Over the following few months, Alain discovered he was able to urinate again. "Something was changing. I could start peeing again normally, and would find brownish-black clusters of cancer cells in the urinal."

Whatever the result of his prayers, his emotional healing, and the chemotherapy would be, Alain valued the process. Alain felt that he had to do this work of healing *anyway, whatever the outcome.* If the result was death, he feels it would have been even more important.

Value the process, not the outcome

"The healing process is important in itself, not as a goal," Alain recognizes. "If you go through a healing process expecting to heal, not only do you have no guarantee that your wish will come true, but you might miss the most important parts. Whether you live or whether you die, going through a healing process is extremely helpful. If you are going to die, it is probably even *more* helpful because it prepares you for life *and* death."

Nadia seconds, "He was prepared to die. The real healing is the healing of the heart, and if you die that way, you're okay. If you live, it's a bonus, but the real goal is not to survive, it's to heal the heart, and that's what happened to him."

Alain lists what he believes he accomplished through this healing process: "reconciliation with myself, with others, opening my heart, really surrendering. Normally we have this illusion that we are in control, and this illness shows that we have no control whatsoever." At first he found this insight debilitating, but eventually he came to see it as liberating. Alain laughs, "Once you let go of all these pretensions and the need to control, what you find is extraordinary freedom. Illness showed me that. When you let go, then you can die successfully." He even speculates, "If I had been able to let go, I might not have had cancer to begin with."

Norman Cousins wrote, "Hope, faith, love, and a strong will to live offer no promise of immortality, only proof of our uniqueness as human beings and the opportunity to experience full growth even under the grimmest circumstances. . . . Far more real than the ticking clock is the way we open to the minutes and invest them with meaning. Death is not the ultimate tragedy in life. The ultimate tragedy is to die without discovering the possibilities of full growth. The approach of death need not be denial of that growth."[19]

Alain now calls cancer "the greatest gift of my life. All these great sufferings . . . I'm convinced there is a great blessing underneath." He pauses. "Of course, if anyone had told me in the midst of this, 'Oh, one day you'll be so happy you've had this,' I'd have punched them in the face."

Cancer had become a messenger, and Alain got to "thank the cancer, how fortunate I am the cancer came to show me this lesson, because the message was clear: I had to change. Change or die. And not just a change of clothes, but change deeply. Open up, stop thinking too much, become a more loving person."

Nadia describes the change like this: "His good heart was always there, but it was buried underneath all kinds of stuff. Now he is still Alain, but his best version of Alain, without the shell."

The final scan

On October 26, 2006, Alain finished three months of chemotherapy. He had lost twenty-five pounds and his legs had become so atrophied he could barely walk. Alain describes himself as "a zombie; I hardly recognized myself." His oncologist conducted the final PET scan to reveal the spread of the cancer. Alain waited nervously to hear the results before she called him into her office. "I can't explain it," she said, "but the cancer is gone. We cannot find any trace of it, not even in the bladder or the bones."

Alain's heart jumped. Usually even in the rare cases of complete remission, a massive tumor leaves a scar, but his urologist could find no evidence at all cancer had ever been there. "If I hadn't seen the tumor with my own eyes," said the doctor, "I wouldn't believe there ever was one."

When Alain's oncologist had told him only three months earlier that his cancer was incurable, she had said so with tears in her eyes, but Alain had remained optimistic. Now her face was lit up by a bright smile, but Alain burst into tears. He couldn't believe it. "Are you sure?" he kept asking. "Yes," she repeated, "I'm sure. Maybe it is the power of the prayer."

Alain asked for a copy of the paperwork; he wanted proof. "I stared at the documents and couldn't understand a single thing, the terms are so technical. But at the end it said,

'Patient—excellent response to treatment.' I knew it was the power of prayer; she was right."

Nadia thinks that Alain had optimal help on three levels: "the physical level, the emotional level, and the spiritual level. That's what was really powerful, all three together." He sometimes speaks at healing workshops now, and people are eager to hear his advice.

"My recipe was surrender, prayer, and love," he says, "but I don't have a recipe for you. If I gave you my recipe, it probably won't work for you. You have to find *your own* recipe."

After what Alain has lived, life appears fragile, and intensely precious. When asked what has changed for him, he says that he lives much more love in his life, pays attention, and goes with the flow.

Alain has remained cancer-free.

8. Evolve

"How much *does your pain hurt?"*
How Temple Grandin, the world's most
successful autistic animal behaviorist, deals
with pain and panic attacks[1]

> *Therefore I take great pleasure in my*
> *infirmities, in insults, in hardships, in*
> *persecutions, in difficulties. For when*
> *I am weak, then I am strong.*
> —2 CORINTHIANS 12:10

Temple Grandin's love for animals is visible from afar: horses gallop across the brush-painted prairie on her blouse, and several cow brooches are pinned to her black tie.

Temple is one of the most brilliant people I have ever met. She is a professor at Colorado State University, has written multiple bestsellers, and, as an animal behaviorist, runs her own thriving company. She has designed more than half of the cattle stations and slaughterhouses in the United States, with the goal of making the brutal business of killing animals for food more humane. She is also an autistic savant[2] who possesses a profound ability to understand animals.

Though we meet in a café in downtown Boulder, Colorado, Temple moves with the stiff gait of a cowgirl who just dismounted her horse. She looks older than her sixty-seven years. Her wavy gray hair is pulled back tight; her face is without makeup, but covered in a mask of worry. Her voice sounds harsh and impatient. No niceties, no small talk. With the disregard for social conventions that's characteristic for many in the autistic community, she cuts straight to the chase: "What do you want to know from me?"

I want to ask her how she has learned to deal with pain and fear, because Temple knows both intimately. With puberty she experienced an onset of anxiety, a near-constant state of terror. "See, I found out that my amygdala, the center for fear activity, was much bigger than the normal size," she explains. "Fear is the main emotion in autistic people and also in animals." How did she transform herself from a juvenile outcast to one of the most successful autistic people on the planet? Though she has learned to navigate an impressive speaking circuit, a nervous skittishness has stayed with her. She startles when the man at the next table erupts in a sudden peal of laughter, and asks to change seats. "I'm always vigilant." So the fear has not left her, but she has learned to deal with it, and this holds interesting lessons for the rest of us who deal with fear.

What makes Temple unique is that she is the very first person who was able to successfully articulate what happens in the autistic mind. Before she wrote her memoirs, *Emergence: Labeled Autistic* and *Thinking in Pictures*, nobody had yet described what the world looks like from an autistic perspective. People on the autism spectrum were routinely labeled as idiots (literally!). Temple Grandin shifted the notion of autism as a dreaded, bewildering diagnosis to a fascinating glimpse into the workings of a brilliant mind. "I knew I was different, but for a long time I didn't really know why. Think of the brain as an enormous office complex," she suggests. "Usually there's a CEO with his team sitting on the top; below him are the departments for finance, human resources, law, acquisition, and so on, the geeks. All the departments constantly communicate with each other through e-mail, phone, meetings, etc. In my head some of these wires are not connected. The white matter in the autistic cerebral cortex is often overgrown, comparable to cable clutter, which leads to frequent short circuits. The vast diversity in autistic behavior depends on which departments are wired."[3]

In Temple's case, the graphics department is overdeveloped, her social department stunted. "My brain works like Google Images." She has a dozen brain scans to prove it. When she first looked at an MRI of her brain, it immediately struck her how asymmetrical it looked.

"I probably wouldn't be alive"

Temple is a shining example of a supremely resilient person, especially considering how her life started out. As a severely autistic child, she screamed for hours, refused to be cradled, and violently attacked herself and others "like a wild animal." She didn't speak until she was three and a half years old. Very few doctors knew about autism in the early fifties, and so they simply told her parents that their baby was brain damaged and needed to be relinquished to a mental institution. Her father wanted to do just that, and we might never have heard of Temple had her mother not refused to give her up. "If they had locked me up, I wouldn't be sitting here today," Temple says. "I probably wouldn't be alive. The worst you can do to an autistic child is to leave her to herself. My mother was lucky to find a good neurologist who referred me to speech therapy school."

Her mother, Eustacia Cutler, noticed how musical Temple was; the toddler hummed along when she played Bach on the piano. Eustacia hired nannies and speech therapists who sang to Temple, played with her, and patiently repeated words such as "ball" ad infinitum until Temple echoed them. What Eustacia instinctively did with Temple has now been recognized as the recommended therapy for autistic children. Temple was extremely fortunate that her mother's intuition was decades ahead of her time.

Temple's life story highlights a number of the factors that are crucial for building resilience: a loving relative who believed in her, a highly developed gift for empathy, and a stunning resourcefulness in a world that ostracized her.

Temple's classmates bullied her mercilessly.[4] "It was horrible, truly horrible," Temple says. "I didn't know why I was such a social idiot. They called me 'tape recorder' or 'retard' because I kept repeating the same phrases over and over. I got kicked out of school, because I hit a girl."

She had to create her own map for how to live her life. She observed social scenes and replayed them in her mind in order to learn social codes. "My brain works like a computer that is constantly updating its software." Direct eye contact, hello, how are you? None of these everyday social interactions came naturally to Temple. Why the other teenagers got hysterical over the Beatles or were consumed by their awe for a cute boy escaped her grasp. She detachedly calls these things "ISP, interesting social phenomena." She taught herself how to decode humans like a tourist would study the vocabulary and rhythm of a foreign language. She played examples from the vast video library she stores in her head and reenacted the appropriate social gestures. While falling in love might forever elude her, she is happy. She has taught herself to function in a highly complex world, to become an engaging, witty public speaker, and she has found her mission: to help animals and autistic children.

Embrace your uniqueness

Temple is a beacon of hope for people with a so-called handicap, because she turns it into an advantage. She found a powerful gift in her ability to think differently, and it changed her life in ways nobody could have imagined. Thinking in pictures made social life difficult for Temple, "but it made animals easy, because animals think in pictures, too. Animals are like autistic savants. I would go as far as saying that animals *are* autistic savants." With her supersharp focus on details, she often notices pertinent details that other people simply overlook, for instance a metal object in a pathway that reflects the sun and thus scares cattle. "Why can't the designers see that? It's not stupidity, they just simply don't notice." This makes her consulting business different from any other, because, as she adds proudly, "*I* am different."

Despite having being taunted as an outcast, Temple grew up believing in herself. At the tender age of eighteen, she found the courage to cold-call the most famous psychology professor at Harvard to present to him a novel machine she had invented to calm her anxiety. She felt so in awe as if visiting the Pope at the Vatican.[5]

However, the meeting didn't go as planned. Not only did the professor try to touch her legs, but he also dismissed Temple's interest in how the brain works. He told her we did not need to know about the brain in order to understand behavior. Temple disagreed. "I don't think I believe that."

Later, when she was hired to design slaughterhouses, she was the only woman in the cattle yards. Ranchers bullied and harassed her; once she found her truck entirely covered with bulls' testicles. Temple just shrugged her shoulders and drove away. "They almost couldn't bear it," she says. "Here comes this idiot, and a woman, and then she designs slaughterhouses that work so much better than theirs!"

Temple was hurt by the hostility, but not broken. She knew better than to take the assaults to heart. And that, she says, is also a positive side effect of autism: "I have an iron will."

Stand up for yourself

Coco Schumann walked straight up to the SS patrol and challenged them to arrest him for being Jewish and a minor. Alain Beauregard told his doctor with firm conviction, "I am going to live." Temple Grandin stood up to one of the most famous Harvard professors of her time and to her colleagues in a male-dominated business.

While they risked their livelihoods or even their lives with their defiance, I believe that few of the subjects in this book would have survived had they not shown this tenacity. Their spirited determination aided their survival and success in an uncertain and sometimes hostile world. For resilience not only includes the ability to adapt to one's environment when necessary but also the courage to challenge it to change.

"I'm here to improve the world," Temple says, "so I can't let any of that nonsense get to me."

We are all dandelions

The perception of autism and other changes in brain function has shifted dramatically since Temple was a child. Temple has been a pioneer in exploring the advantages that accompany overstimulation of certain brain regions. Aren't we often too quick in condemning people who process the world differently?

One of Temple's greatest worries is that people like her are excluded from the places that matter: colleges, universities, workplaces. "Where is the next Einstein? Were he alive today, he would drive a FedEx truck, because he could not pass his graduation. Einstein did not speak until he was older and he was kicked out of school, but he still managed to get a Nobel Prize!"

Temple may be an outlier in that only 10 percent of autistics are savants (meaning they possess outstanding mental capabilities), but psychologists have come to admit that they severely underestimated the general intelligence of people on the spectrum.[6] These abilities don't just characterize an outstanding savant such as Temple, but many others as well who are too easily labeled as "crazy."[7] If by crazy we mean people who perceive the world profoundly differently than "neurotypicals," we need more crazies in the world! "Don't get me wrong," Temple cautions. "I'm not saying that autism is a great thing and all people with autism should just sit down and celebrate our strengths. Instead, I'm suggesting that if we can recognize, realistically and on a case-by-case basis, what an individual's strengths are, we can better determine the future of the individual."[8]

Thorkil Sonne, a Danish father of an autistic boy, was so encouraged by his son's ability to play speed chess that he started a company exclusively designed to hire autistic consultants. Specialisterne, Danish for "the specialists,"[9] banks on the fact that people on the autism spectrum have specialized skills such as photographic memory, sensory hypersensitivity, and the ability to detect patterns. "That's great for quality control or the IT industry. It's hard to find people who pay this much attention to detail," Thorkil told me. About a third of autistic people have exceptional cognitive skills,[10] but more than two-thirds of them do not attend college and do not find jobs.

Thorkil calls his approach the "dandelion model." "We call dandelions weed when they pop up in our lawn, but the spring greens can make a tasty salad if we nourish them." Similarly, the apparent shortcomings of autistic people (for instance, their attention to detail, and their directness) can become sought-after strengths.

"It is up to us to decide," Thorkil says, "if we view dandelions as a weed or as a nutritious herb with many values." Software giant SAP just hired sixty people with autism, and Thorkil's ambitious vision is to create 100,000 jobs for people on the spectrum in the next ten years.

Ultimately, Thorkil's aim goes beyond creating jobs: he wants to convince the "neurotypicals" that people are more than their disabilities. "I wish people were more curious rather than keeping their distance. Be curious—find out what their world is like! When you spend time with autistic people, you learn to see the world from a vulnerable perspective. We are all dandelions."

Harnessing the full potential of our cognitive abilities

We don't really need to know exactly how our brain works as long as everything runs smoothly, just as we don't need to know how electricity is generated to plug in our computer. But when we want to harness the full potential of our cognitive ability or learn how to prevent a short circuit, a basic understanding of our cognitive command center becomes vital.

For decades, scientists believed that the development of the brain was completed in adulthood. Now we know that the brain is a dynamic, ever-evolving system that keeps forging new connections. Experts call this "neuroplasticity," and savants have played a crucial role in proving its possibilities.[11]

We have proof that retraining the mind even changes its physicality. For instance, taxi drivers in London have significantly larger hippocampi than those who don't drive taxis (the hippocampus regulates spatial navigation and acts as an "inner GPS").[12] For Gabby Giffords's rehabilitation, too, this plasticity is crucial: the doctors hope that pathways in the left side of her brain (the side injured by the shooting) can regenerate themselves.

Now, we can't know for sure, because fancy MRIs didn't exist when Temple was little, but I bet that her brain grew more in some areas to compensate for deficits in, let's say, her speech department. "That's because there is still some bandwidth there," she says. "My visual tract is four hundred times the size of other people's. That's not neuroplasticity, it's innate. You probably can't achieve my visual skills by training your mind, but we can construct side streets in our brain. I was able to train my social skills and my speech, because half the wiring was still there."

Temple's brain is about 15 percent larger than the average brain, possibly because the neurons grew faster in certain areas to make up for damage in others.[13] Her cortex is significantly thicker than most people's, which explains her outstanding memory. Her brain is actually overconnected, meaning her neurons are firing at a higher rate. The psychiatrist who diagnosed her as brain damaged when she was a toddler could hardly have been more wrong.

Genius against all odds

While Temple was born with savant potential, scientists estimate that there are a few dozen people worldwide who acquired savant faculties through brain trauma. For instance, Derek Amato from Denver, Colorado, suddenly played the piano like a virtuoso after diving headfirst into a shallow swimming pool.[14] Orlando Serrell effortlessly acquired a "calendar brain" after he got struck by a baseball in the left side of his head at ten years of age.[15] Both would not want to undo the trauma if they were offered the choice; Amato calls it his "beautiful disaster."

I spoke with Jason Padgett, who suffered a severe brain trauma after being attacked and kicked hard in the head in front of a bar near Seattle, Washington. Jason broke off all contact with the outside world, quit his job as a salesman, and for almost four years shut himself off in the solitude of his house, tacking blankets over the windows to prevent light from entering, and trying to endure the panic attacks, flashbacks, and phobias common to PTSD. His body's stress response system got stuck on high alert.[16] He went from being an extremely outgoing party animal to a loner who could not tolerate the company of other people. His perception changed fundamentally: the college dropout who never managed math is now obsessively fascinated by the infinite decimal number pi and perceives the world in geometric patterns.

Jason feared he was on the verge of madness and spent long nights researching brain traumas on the Internet. What he found astounded him. "The most helpful thing for me was to read about other people who had been through similar experiences," he told me. Like many trauma survivors, he had assumed he was doomed to live with the flashbacks forever. The brain damage had activated a part of his brain responsible for mathematical and geometrical thinking. Eventually, he was able to diagnose himself as a savant and synesthete,[17] a diagnosis that has since been confirmed by experts. Since the attack, Jason is able to produce highly complex mathematical drawings, and though he paid a price for his talent with stretches of excruciating pain, he would not want to turn the clock back if he could. While he describes his former self as an ego-oriented pleasure seeker, he has become a much more compassionate person and feels a natural empathy toward other people with brain injury or so-called disorders. With the help of pain experts, Jason trained himself in meditation and mindfulness, and he credits this with helping him regain control over his world. Most fascinating, perhaps, is Jason's belief that all of us have the potential his injury accidentally unlocked.

What are we missing?

These stories open up some mighty questions: How can an injury or an oddly shaped frontal lobe so fundamentally change us, our behavior, what we like, and how we perceive the world? Who are we really? Are we at the mercy of our brain cells, or can we steer them in our favor?

Temple loves these types of stories, real-life proof of the power of our minds. Since the advent of modern imaging, her own brain has been scanned multiple times, and she marvels at its odd shape and the explanations it holds for her unusual talents.

She agrees with Jason and many neuroscientists that our brains have prodigious capabilities that we simply don't know how to unlock. One of her favorite examples is the famous "invisible gorilla" video by University of Illinois psychologist Daniel Simons.[18] He asks viewers to watch a video of two teams playing basketball and count the number of times the team in white passes the ball. Half of the viewers whose minds fixate on the players never notice the giant gorilla that walks straight through the playing field!

It makes you wonder about all the things hiding in plain sight we miss! In a way, we only see what we are *expecting* to see. Autistic people and animals pay attention to all kinds of details that escape most of us though our senses are perfectly capable of perceiving them. Temple is convinced that photographic memory or extraordinary recall in autistics and animals are not a matter of different eyes and ears, but primarily of paying attention and that the rest of us, to some extent, can also activate these abilities. The extraordinary talents of some autistics or "accidental savants" might be mere hints at the potential dormant in many of us.

These examples allow us not only to marvel at the infinite possibilities a resilient person can uncover, but also give us a rare insight into the various ways we can relate to pain and fear. Temple has followed neuroscience as closely as she's followed animal sciences, looking for clues to get a better handle on her own brain.

For instance, she has learned to reason herself out of panic attacks. It helps her to know that the cause for her anxiety lies *inside* her brain, not outside (though she readily admits that she is also being helped by anxiety medication). She is not anxiety-free, but anxiety *aware*, and thus more in charge. Similarly, his research on brain trauma helped Jason Padgett understand that his radical shift in perception was not a precursor to madness. In the same way, brain trauma patients are often relieved when they are shown a scan of their brain and can actually *see*, for instance, the lesions in their center for impulse control. It shows them there is no demon inside of them, but rather a broken circuit in the command center that needs extra attention.

Much like Temple Grandin and Jason Padgett retrained their cognitive abilities, we can literally reshape our cognitive setup, strengthen areas of our brain that are useful for sound decision-making, and weaken the pathways that are the turnpikes of fear.

The chemistry of fear and pain

Let's talk about the brain when it encounters fear and pain, because these processes are intimately connected with trauma. When we are in a very stressful situation, our adrenal glands release adrenaline and cortisol. Understanding the chemistry behind our emotions helps us gain insight into what we can do when we become overwhelmed.

With the advent of advanced imaging techniques, researchers have been able to peek into the "black boxes" of trauma survivors and study how extreme stress changes our brains. Two findings stand out: when people with PTSD are reminded of the trauma, the fearmonger amygdala becomes overactive, while areas of the prefrontal cortex that are responsible for decision-making shrink.[19] In other words, fear takes over at times when we don't need it and clouds our rational thinking. After the stress is over, the amygdala might not restore itself back to its normal size.

However, people who have experienced trauma without developing PTSD "show more activity in the prefrontal cortex"[20] and better "communication between the reasoning circuitry in the cortex and the emotional circuitry of the limbic system brain."[21] What does this mean? "It's as if resilient people can have a very healthy response to negative stimuli," says Dennis Charney, a psychiatrist at the Icahn School of Medicine at Mount Sinai in New York who has conducted several brain-imaging studies of rape victims, soldiers, and other trauma survivors."[22] How can we replicate such a healthy response?

Retrain your brain

While Temple and many PTSD patients find that their amygdala, the fear center in their brain, is significantly enlarged, studies have shown that meditation has the opposite effect: it actually shrinks the amygdala.[23] Harvard neurobiologist Sara Lazar and her colleagues recruited people who had never meditated before and guided them through an eight-week stress-reduction program where they meditated for thirty to forty minutes every day. The scientists found that the subjects' hippocampi, important for learning and for emotion control, grew stronger, while their amygdalae shrank. "There was actually a neurobiological reason why they felt less stressed," says Sara Lazar. "Meditation can literally change your brain."[24]

The key is that meditation rewires our brain in exactly the way that galvanizes us for stress and challenging situations.

A few years ago, I participated in a study at UCLA. Eileen Luders, a young German-born professor, slid me into the brain scanner. She was looking for signs that years of meditation had actually physically changed people's brains, and she found evidence: the longer the people she examined had meditated, the thicker their cortex had grown, an indication that the brain can process information more quickly. Her studies also suggest that the connections between brain cells are stronger in meditators.[25]

Why does mindfulness have such a profound effect? Because our brains are trainable. Not unlike puppies, our brains just need consistent attention, focus, and correction when they wander off. We can shape our brains at any stage in our life and literally create new pathways[26] with every thought we think and every emotion we feel.

We've already talked about Fadel Zeidan's studies on how meditation changes our perception of pain. His team showed that meditation works equally well in reducing anxiety,[27] which is crucial for healing posttraumatic stress. After a trauma, the threat might be long gone, but the fear keeps us prisoner. Richard Davidson, the founding chair of the Center for Investigating Healthy Minds at the University of Wisconsin, was able to prove that the brain waves in highly trained meditators are oscillating in such powerful amplitudes that they can ignore pain and replace negative emotions with positive states of joy and happiness.[28] In fact, when Davidson and his colleagues first asked the monks to meditate on loving-kindness and compassion, they initially thought their machines were broken, because the meditators' positive emotions were off the charts. And at least one of them, the Tibetan master Mingyur Rinpoche, was able to meditate himself out of severe panic attacks that had plagued him since he was a child.[29]

Medication versus meditation

I don't want to suggest, though, that trying to muscle or meditate your way out of brain trauma and panic with willpower alone will always work. Mingyur Rinpoche is a virtuoso of meditation; his father was one of the foremost Tibetan meditation masters, and he has easily spent 50,000 hours in his life practicing meditation. I mention him to show the potential of our mental training and what we can achieve with the right effort and the right guidance, not to evoke the expectation that we could expect to sail through a panic attack with a few deep breaths.

With a brain bent on panic, we might need additional help. We have not discussed medication much, because it is such an individual question that can only be reviewed with a qualified doctor. But anxiety medication is one of the most common treatments for PTSD. Some psychologists think that medication inhibits posttraumatic growth, but that's too much of an overgeneralization for me. "Some of my patients can't sleep, can't eat, can't think clearly," says psychotherapist Susan Ollar, who is herself a longtime meditator. "When your mind is so agitated, sitting still would be a very tall order." Medication may help take the edge off anxiety and restore a sane equilibrium, a basis from which we can explore paths such as mindfulness meditation. Temple, for instance, recommends meditation as a way to calm anxiety and aggression in autistic children, but freely admits that she would not be able to function without the help of medication, especially in crowded airports and at busy conferences.

Solace at the stables

But what helped Temple most was her connection with animals. "Animals saved me and kept me going all through my childhood and puberty." She was not born as a natural animal whisperer, but then her mother sent her to a boarding school for gifted yet troubled teenagers. The school offered riding, and though the principal could only afford to purchase abused horses that were easily spooked and dangerous to ride, Temple spent every free minute at the stables. Pairing troubled teenagers with frightened horses sounds like a recipe for disaster, but Temple could relate. In a way, she too was easily spooked and hard to handle. The school finally hit upon a magic wand to keep her focused: if she acted out, she would be barred from the stables. So she learned to cry instead of fight, and this is actually advice she still gives today: "Learn to cry. Let it out. Kids who cry can work on computers; kids who smash the computers can't."

We know too little about how exactly animals actually help us navigate panic attacks and stress, but when the army paired PTSD-afflicted veterans with service dogs, they found that dogs can replace drugs.[30] Trauma therapists have had great success with canine and equine therapy, though thorough studies are still lacking. Does the mere presence of the canine companions bring a feeling of safety? Is it the "trust hormone" oxytocin that calms and opens us? Oxytocin has been called the "hormone of bonding and belonging": it works as a direct antidote to the stress hormone cortisol. Not only do mothers release it when they look at their babies but we also get flushed by it when we look lovingly at our dog. Service dogs can be trained to sense panic attacks and comfort their handlers by licking them when anxiety kicks in. They have greatly helped many autistic children and people suffering from ailments ranging from depression to diabetes. Dogs can sniff out cancer, alert diabetes patients before their blood sugar drops too low, and save lives. Maybe most important, animals don't judge. No matter how eccentric we are, they love us unconditionally.

And often the bond goes both ways: Temple has dedicated her life to alleviating the suffering of animals in slaughterhouses and cattle stations. She played a major role in implementing more humane standards within large fast-food companies such as McDonald's. "We have to treat animals well," she says. "If I showed you the slaughterhouses I constructed, you'd be amazed how humane they are. We all have to die at some point. My cows have the best life, often a better life than a show dog that is left alone all day. Nature is merciless. When a deer gets attacked by a wolf in the woods, it dies a more cruel death than a cow in a facility I designed." But she also admits that when she visits a cruel facility, she breaks into tears as soon as she is out the door. "I don't cry in front of the managers, but sometimes I cry all the way home."

I can relate to Temple's kinship with animals. Animals were my best friends all throughout my childhood. I have learned to train dogs, and my rescue dogs have taught me a great deal about myself, my ability to handle stress, and how to remain calm in challenging situations. Once a grown deer in California got spooked into the ocean and swam in a frenzy until it began to slip underwater. Two neighbors and I paddled out and managed to reach it just in time. Swimming to the shore with that deer was a rare moment of deep connection with a wild animal. It could have killed me with a hoof kick, but instead it stared intently into my eyes and held perfectly still, as I held its belly up with one arm, stroking the water with the other. I'd bet it knew I was trying to save it from drowning.

A trauma therapist for horses

I think of how connected we are to animals one hot, dusty morning in Woodland Hills, California, as I watch horse whisperer Buck Brannaman work a colt. "Don't live in the past!" Buck instructs the owner as he leads the young horse to prance backward and sideward. Buck, six feet five inches of cowboy confidence, makes "breaking" a colt look so easy.

Twenty students are struggling to imitate his sure moves with their own colts in the arena as he thunders, "I don't even wanna hear, 'Oh, Buck, I think he's been abused.' Or, 'Buck, she was born in a rainstorm, that's why she's afraid of water.'" His voice sounds amused, only slightly taking the edge off his sarcasm as he challenges, hollering, "Don't give me *that*! You're *here now*!"

Buck can speak with authority because he is intimately familiar with fear and abuse. He grew up with a violently alcoholic father who mercilessly drilled Buck and his older brother Smokie to be childhood ropers. Things got infinitely bleak when their mother passed away while the boys were little. The cute boys doing elaborate rope tricks were adored as childhood celebrities, and at age seven, Buck became the youngest professional roper ever. But a small misstep in his routine could lead to hours of nightly beatings. Often, in a drunken stupor, Buck's father would unleash his belt for really no reason at all. Buck remembers acutely the nights when he feared for his life, when he thought he would not live to see the sunrise or when he escaped to spend the night outside cuddled with his dog in the doghouse, hoping his father would not find him.

One of his teachers became suspicious when Buck refused to undress at sports class. The deep welts and belt marks he discovered all over the boy's body were so ghastly that there was no time to lose: he found foster parents who took Buck and his brother in that same day.

Buck knows what it is like to fear for one's life, to be terrified, confused, and overwhelmed. Which makes him a superb horseman, because he empathizes with a colt that is too afraid to listen to its owner, and he approaches to take over the reins.

When Buck watches the "traditional" brutal way of breaking in colts with force, he recognizes the damage it does to both horses and humans. Abused horses and abused children are not that different, he reckons: insecure, ready to bolt, always expecting the worst. As a teenager, he did not trust people, but instead spent all day at the stables. Now Buck spearheads a revolution in natural horsemanship, an exercise in mutual trust and partnership.

Buck admits that he "never really got over the hurt" his father caused him, but he decided to learn from the experience and become everything his father was not: a decent human being, an honest husband, a loving father to his three daughters. "I like to live in the moment. You can't live in two places at once," he says in the award-winning documentary about his life. "You never forget, but you don't have to stay in that dark place. It made me who I am."[31] By overcoming the demons of his childhood, he found his calling.

Now Buck does for horses what Richard Tedeschi recommends for traumatized patients: He understands. He's there. He offers safety and a new perspective. He reconditions.

Richard Tedeschi and Lawrence Calhoun saw the similarities when they learned how horse trainer Monty Roberts describes the process of "joining up" with wild and abused horses, which involves a gentle invitation to connect by understanding and responding to the messages in the horses' behavior. "He is essentially an equine trauma therapist who practices the same fundamental principles of relating that we see as necessary in working with human trauma survivors."[32]

Make a four-legged friend

I'm a huge fan of animal therapy. It's not the right path for everyone, but if you feel a kinship with animals and are in a position to care for them (getting a dog is a ten- to fifteen-year commitment!), a trained dog or canine therapy might be a huge help to you. For instance, Gabby Giffords relies on her well-trained Labrador Nelson, and I suggested a service dog for Meggie Zahneis to help her live independently at college. Meggie's parents were skeptical at first, and it took eighteen months for the nonprofit Canine Companions for Independence to find and train a dog for her, but now she and the black Labrador retriever mix, Odette, are inseparable. Odette helps her get around campus, alerts her to dangers when her hearing aids fail, and even facilitates connections with other students, because who doesn't want to ask about that cute puppy?

In Temple's case, not only does she find comfort in the company of animals but she also actually learns *from* them. As a teenager she found an antidote for her anxiety when she observed cattle at her aunt Ann's ranch relax in a squeeze chute—a metal crate where the cattle are held tight for vaccinations. As soon as she saw it, she knew she wanted to build a similar machine for herself. She was craving touch, but like many autistics, she couldn't bear it. Temple created her own "hugging machine" out of primitive plywood that would close in to "hug" her. She calls it her "hugging meditation." The machine allowed her to be in control of the pressure, and to calm herself. Her teachers tried to prevent her from using it, but Temple wouldn't let go of it. She found this was the only remedy that would ease her anxiety. "The machine helped me to relax instantly, and I have become a much more social person because of it."

Now she hardly uses it anymore, but her method has been universally embraced as a calming treatment for autistic children. This was, in fact, the machine she presented to that famous professor at Harvard.

Temple believes that autistic people (and animals) relate to fear and pain differently, but that we all can learn to tolerate it better. She is asking a fascinating question: "How *much* does your pain hurt?"[33]

How the mind controls the pain

Temple became curious about the sensations of pain when she heard repeated accounts from parents of autistic children who reported that their kids acted indifferent to pain and cold. This obviously didn't stem from a physical inability to feel, because the children were overly sensitive to touch and sounds, just like Temple. "There is a lot of evidence that the physical sensations are the same, but they are interpreted by the brain in a different way."

I am bringing this up because when I am in pain, certainly the last thing I think about is that I have a choice how I feel about it. By design, pain grabs our full and immediate attention. But as we have seen in the stories about Rhonda, Meggie, and Alain, how we perceive pain can be influenced by many factors, from our habits and our culture to our genes.

Temple tells me that animals and autistic people have another brain feature in common: their frontal lobes are either less developed or not fully functioning. Some studies suggest that pain is related to prefrontal hyperactivity,[34] and psychiatrists were able to free patients from severe, chronic pain by surgically disconnecting their frontal lobes—a procedure commonly known as a lobotomy. The inventor of this surgery, António Egas Moniz, even won a Nobel Prize for his discovery (probably not one of the Nobel Committee's finest decisions). The results seemed miraculous: Patients who had been crouched in excruciating pain before the surgery were suddenly observed to be relaxed and active afterward. The surgery did not change the pain itself, only "their *feelings* about the pain. They didn't *care* about it anymore," says Temple.[35] The emotional reactions that accompanied the pain were suddenly absent.[36]

Learning from a Labrador

We certainly don't need to undergo a lobotomy to experience a relief. There is pain, a certain amount of inevitable physical pain when, say, a surgeon cuts into our body, or when we stub a toe. And then there is how we *process* the data our nerves are sending us. We can learn to process it differently. We think the pain is in the toe, but it really sits in the brain. This is because several separate systems inform us about our pain: the nervous system tells us about the location and the kind of injury, and a separate emotional system cries, "Ouch! How terrible!"

This is crucial information for anybody interested in dealing with pain. Let me put Temple's question a slightly different way: how much does *your* pain hurt?

Temple recalls a hysterectomy she had to undergo after a cyst had grown to the size of a baseball. "I've had pain that's been really, really terrible," she admits. Temple is convinced that, "on a physical level, the sensory perception is the same. What might be different is how the painful sensation is interpreted in the brain. Some people seem more disabled by pain than others. How people react to it emotionally varies. I wasn't just gonna get all depressed over it."

Again, we are not talking about *suppressing* our feelings, but about methods we can use to rewire our brain: meditation, hypnosis, mental training, psychotherapy, art, exercise, and somatic healing are but a few.

"Exercise, exercise, exercise," is what Temple prescribed herself.

While Temple couldn't pick up her physical exercise program for the eight-week recovery period after surgery, she managed to write four book chapters during her convalescence. "Other people stayed in the clinic for six weeks and got all depressed. I decided I wasn't gonna let that happen," she states matter-of-factly. "I went into the office every day and I got a lot of writing done." She had planned out her research meticulously in advance, put her research material in accessible places ("I couldn't lift up big tomes or reach up to higher cabinets"), and focused on making her deadline.

Temple also needed far less pain medication than most patients. "I just took one prescription painkiller after the surgery, and that was it. I didn't need anymore."[37]

Temple attributes this to her mental attitude. "One of the things that are different for me is: other people get all hung up when a part of their body has to be cut off. I wasn't hung up on that. I said to myself, I'm like a dog that gets over it easily." She half jokingly compares herself to her friend's Labrador, rather than a freshly operated-upon human.[38]

When I ask her if she would take a miracle pill that could cure autism, she shakes her head. "I have other things nobody else has. For instance, I am able to solve problems. Mankind needs people who solve problems. I have found my niche; I wouldn't change it for the world."

9. Breathe

"You don't find wholeness till you're ready to be broken"
Roshi Bernie Glassman, a Jewish-born Zen teacher, furthers healing in places of horror[1]

Ring the bells that still can ring
Forget your perfect offering
There is a crack in everything
That's how the light gets in.
—LEONARD COHEN[2]

One winter day I got stuck with Richard Gere in Kathmandu, Nepal. He was traveling with friends of mine, and a snowstorm grounded their plane to Bhutan. We spent a delightful day in Kathmandu, exploring the local art shops. While he gracefully accepted the wishes of enthusiastic fans to give autographs, he talked about his hope that maybe Bhutan would be the one place on earth where he could travel incognito. Television was still a novelty in the tiny Himalayan kingdom, so he hoped the Bhutanese would not yet know him. When I met him again after the trip, I learned that he had had no such luck: Bhutan had videos, and just about every Bhutanese had seen *Pretty Woman*.

Fifteen years later, though, Richard Gere did indeed stumble upon the secret of how to be invisible, even in the midst of New York. In the film *Time Out of Mind*, he plays an elderly alcoholic who ends up on the streets. Gere wanted to shoot the film documentary-style, and he was worried his A-list status would attract too much attention.

No need to worry. Disappearing in plain sight is easy: instead of crossing the Himalayas, all Gere had to do was not shave for a few days, don a dirty cloak, and ask people for spare change. Nobody recognized him, because nobody looked him in the face. "I could see how quickly we can all descend into territory when we're totally cut loose from all of our connections to people,"[3] Gere, a long-term supporter of the homeless, realized.

Ellen Burstyn made a similar discovery when she lived on the streets of Manhattan. The actress did not do it for a movie role; she attended a street retreat. She slept under a bridge at night, with the autumn cold creeping into her makeshift cardboard bed and rats running a busy shift right above her head. However, the part she found most challenging was begging for subway fare. A couple of wealthy thirtysomethings at an upscale café handed her a dollar bill, but they never looked her in the face. "They gave me what I asked for, but I was disregarded. I wasn't seen," Ellen realized, and vowed to never pass a homeless person ever again without connecting.[4]

Nobody recognized two of the best-known actors of our time, though they did not wear makeup or an elaborate costume. By simply blending in with the homeless, they became instantly invisible. "It wasn't that folks didn't notice me; they could see someone asking for change from two blocks away," says Richard Gere.[5] "It was that they saw the embodiment of failure—and failure is something that people fear will suck them in."

This experience is universal: We prefer to shut out the forlorn and forsaken. We do not want to acknowledge suffering. We don't want to look it in the eye.

This chapter is about what happens when we let suffering in.

Cracking is more important than the mending

The man who organized Ellen Burstyn's street retreat is Roshi Bernie Glassman, the founding teacher of the Zen Peacemaker Order. He is part of this book because he does the opposite of what most of us do: he is not afraid to witness suffering, but goes toward it, accepting it, working toward healing it.

Bernie, seventy-six years old, just returned from Rwanda. He is on his way to Europe for his twentieth visit to Auschwitz. While meditation teachers commonly hold their retreats in beautiful places of nature and solitude, or at least in a quiet room to minimize distractions, Glassman takes his students to focal point of conflicts: Rwanda, Auschwitz, the West Bank, the Bronx.

Bernie softly hums Leonard Cohen's lyrics about the crack that lets in the light. "That pretty much sums it up," he says, "that's what it's all about: taking off the armor, becoming vulnerable." Meditation masters often like to talk about wholeness, but Bernie chooses to emphasize "the cracking experience. A crack is a very powerful experience. Many people remain very hard. They don't crack, or they try not to crack. The cracking is as important, or more important than the mending, because the healing can't start without the cracking."

This is precisely the point why he takes people to the streets: to crack, and to connect. "A lot of people can't *encounter* homeless people. They feel they can't say, 'Hey, hello, how are you? What's going on?' They change to the other side of the street. But when you live on the streets, you're one being, man."

I admire Bernie both for *what* he does and for the *how*. His insights give us crucial hints how to approach the things in life we are afraid of. Though he is a Zen teacher by training, his students include Jews, Christians, Muslims, Sufis, Native

Americans, Hindus, and nonbelievers. He does not call them students, but friends, and the only common denominator among the people who join his Zen Peacemaker Order is their wish to make a difference in the world, whether it is through prison chaplaincy, contemplative care, programs for challenged youths, or some other creative avenue. The international nonprofit now has eighty-three affiliates in twelve countries.

For a mathematician with a PhD, Bernie starts his adventures with an unusual premise:

Dare to not know

Pretty much every expert and teacher I meet is eager to teach what they know. Bernie invites us to start from a place of not knowing. This is a basic principle of Zen Buddhism, and Bernie has made it the bedrock of his entire approach. "Knowing means you're attached to a concept. Let go."

We might think we know what it is like to be homeless, to be ill, to be at war. To be American, to be Jewish, to be Buddhist. Bernie challenges us to start over. "When you haven't seen a person for two minutes," he quips, "don't assume it's the same person. They are different now."

Not knowing is about seeing things, people, and situations for the first time, fresh and open. It is surprisingly challenging to leave our habits at home. Have you tried it?

People who join Bernie for the street retreats leave behind their comfort zone: no credit cards, no comfy sleeping bags—no exceptions. They plunge into the unknown, and let the streets with their unwritten rules become their teacher.

For starters, they have to ask their friends and family for the participation fee (which will be donated to the homeless), and often this act of begging marks the first chink in the armor: most people find it extremely uncomfortable to ask others for money. On Bernie's first street retreat in 1991, twenty people joined him, some of whom had never meditated a day in their life. "I did it because I wanted to connect with the homeless. When you're homeless and begging, people completely ignore you; you simply don't exist," he says. "Once you have been ignored like that, you can no longer do the same to other people; it becomes impossible to look away. The effect of that street retreat was so strong in helping us experience interconnectedness that I made it a permanent part of my life."

The experience is much more intense than people realize. The retreatants sleep under bridges, beg for their food. "I don't know anybody who has done a street retreat who hasn't had profound experiences," Bernie says. Except when they try to skirt the rules and bring their North Face sleeping bag and their Starbucks card. Then they miss out. Because the point is not to shield ourselves, but to become comfortable with being outside our comfort zone. "I have a yardstick for how broad your enlightenment is," Bernie says. "The yardstick is how well you serve others."

Afraid to enter the room

Maybe the insight that healing could arise from bearing witness dawned early in his life. Bernie was born in 1939 in Brooklyn, New York, to Jewish immigrants from Romania and Poland. "I was a change-of-life baby, so my father was much older. I did not have much of a father present." He was mainly raised by his four older sisters, because his mother fell gravely ill when he was eight years old. As his mother lay dying, his father would not go into her room. "He was afraid of death. We know if people sit with a loved one, everything changes.

But he wouldn't confront it." As a little kid, he felt helpless. "I couldn't help him go into the room."

Could it be possible, he has wondered ever since, that the fear of facing suffering can be worse than the actual encounter with suffering itself?

Since then he has not only taken Ellen Burstyn to the rats of Manhattan and Richard Gere to peace talks with Palestinians and Israelis but also has helped thousands of people enter the spaces they fear. "I don't think of fear as being *bad*; it's just another one of the emotions that come up. It mostly has to do with us not bearing witness."

One sunny morning, in the library of the Zen Center of Los Angeles, Bernie explains that the Chinese word for compassion consists of two elements. "One Chinese character stands for compassion in the normal sense and the other for the removal of fear. That's a very important practice. So many people have so many fears when they come to the streets. They are afraid of the homeless, afraid something happens to them, afraid of suffering. The only way I know how to remove their fears is to bring them to the places they are scared of. When they come, it's gone."

Bernie lives by three essential principles that have become the backbone of everything he does and the founding tenets of his Zen Peacemaker Order: not knowing, bearing witness, taking action.

Bear witness

Bernie defines "bearing witness" as "to open to what is. Not to shrink away from any situation that arises. Not to judge. Whatever it is, that's the moment. Just deeply listen to whatever is happening. *Be* what is happening. In that process, healing arises."

This is precisely what many trauma therapists recommend. But it has to be done gently, in the right dose, with loving support.

When we don't like something, we try to avoid it or we check out emotionally. "So when we do a bearing witness retreat, it means not running from it. Instead, we're looking at *that*, looking at running from it, looking at trying to get rid of it."

Bearing witness refers not just to street retreats, or the homeless, but to the fullness of life unfolding inside and outside. Bernie includes meditation in the retreat, because he emphasizes that meditation not only happens on a cushion, in isolation, but also in the midst of life, and that the attitude we bring to meditation extends to everything we encounter: can I be present with what is?

"When we bear witness to the unfolding of our daily lives, not shrinking from any situation that arises, we learn," Bernie says. "And the places of injustice become places of connection and healing."

Launching social reform rather than rockets

Bernie is an unusual meditation master by any standards. He wears a faded Hawaiian shirt and baggy jeans that are held up by suspenders printed with pink cartoon pigs, his thinning gray hair pulled back in a ponytail, and a clown nose in his pocket. Whenever situations get too stuffy and serious, he puts on the clown nose and cracks some jokes. He is a clown with a serious mission.

By trade, Bernie is actually a brilliant aerospace engineer. He has a PhD in applied mathematics from UCLA, and worked for McDonnell Douglas in 1960, serving as a project director for the first manned mission to Mars. But soon his vision centered more on launching an inner revolution than launching rockets into space.

A book on his college reading list, *The Religions of Man*, had one page about Zen Buddhism, and that one page was enough to get Bernie intrigued. He made friends with a young Japanese monk at the Zen Center of Los Angeles, Taizan Maezumi Roshi, who became his main teacher.

Soon he transformed into an increasingly enthusiastic Zen student, more fascinated by the workings of his own mind than the intricacies of mathematics. He built himself a meditation room in his garage, out of earshot of his first wife Helen and his two children, and threw himself into the world of meditation with the zeal of a young novice.

He accomplished the traditional Japanese-style Zen training, meditating for many hours, many days, many months, which turned into years. Eventually he became Maezumi Roshi's successor. "I was very strict back then," he says, wiggling his raised index finger. "If you came to me with emotions, I would have said, 'Stop it! Just sit!'" Now he gives a different answer. "Be with it. Bear witness to whatever arises. If fear arises, bear witness to the fear. If pain arises, bear witness to the pain. *Become* whatever arises."

Recognize the fleeting nature of all thoughts, all things, all emotions

When we experience pain, suffering, depression, or grief, they often seem like monumental blocks of solid rock that have the weight to crush and bury us. But the truth is that they are made up of infinitesimal moments. Our minds are wired to see continuum, sometimes even tricking us into taking completely different faces or shapes to be the same.[6] We string together a steady version of reality much like we let ourselves be captivated by the individual film frames of a thriller.

What meditation and staying present teach us is that feelings and perceptions are not solid, but just visitors passing through; nothing but flickering glimmers.

Even the most intense emotions are just made of exactly that: moment by moment by moment. They are fleeting, volatile, forever changing—pixels projected onto the screens of our mind. We can bear the pain, because it is ephemeral. We can break the chain reaction and press the pause button at any time.

We find gaps, and just like small cracks in a rock widen over time until the rock crumbles, we can use these gaps to chip away at that suffocating monster, a breath at a time.

Bernie says that he must have done "hundreds and hundreds of traditional meditation retreats." He had deep meditational experiences, glimpses of awakening. He experienced the profound insight that we are all connected. Yet this insight came with an unexpected side effect: it led him to ponder how to alleviate the pressing issues all around him. Blissing out on a cushion while people in the same part of town did not have enough to eat seemed fundamentally fraudulent. How could he help the homeless who surrounded him? How could he contribute to peace? How could he heal his own family's wounds and those of his ancestors who had perished in the Holocaust?

Bernie jumps up to demonstrate his understanding of interconnectedness. He raises his left arm. "Let's say my right arm has a gash. Now my left arm does not hesitate, 'Should I help? But I'm late for a meeting. And what about my clothes? Will I get blood on my sleeve if I try to help? What if I get sued?' No, the left arm simply reaches over to stop the bleeding." That's interconnectedness. That's how Bernie attempts to reach out to the homeless and the forlorn: he envisions it as taking care of different parts of one body. So he arrived at the third of his principles: taking action.

"I found that when you bear witness to a larger scene, your experience of connecting is more powerful than when I am just looking at myself." The traditional Zen retreats, he says, "turned out to be pretty much about *me*. Now I am much more concerned about society." Instead of choosing the peacefulness and isolation of a Zen monastery, Bernie chose life. And not just any part of life, but the most challenging: prison wards, skid row, and war zones.

His vision is bigger than just alleviating the homelessness around him: he was looking for an idea to abolish homelessness altogether. For the better part of a year he researched his options, and it became clear to him that starting another soup kitchen or shelter was not the answer.

A sweet recipe for the homeless

You might have tasted Ben & Jerry's Chocolate Fudge Brownie ice cream. But you might not know that buying a pint supports a bakery with a unique hiring policy. The brownies in the ice cream are made at Greyston Bakery in Yonkers, New York—the bakery Bernie founded after deciding that what the homeless needed most were jobs. Greyston hires anybody who walks through the door willing to work. Education? Felonies? Age? Who cares? No resume required. "I don't care about their background. All I care about is, how is your work *now*?" says Bernie. The company motto, written in bright purple letters on the wall, reads, *We don't hire people to bake brownies, we bake brownies to hire people.* Bernie delivers his delicious indulgences—including a cheesecake named the best in New

York—to gourmet restaurants, Whole Foods, and even to the White House, but few people know that the baked goods have been made by people who were homeless or felons. "For me, what was so fantastic is that the best cheesecake in New York, which means the best in the country, was made by people that our country considered garbage—that threw away those people, didn't consider they could do anything. I just love that."

Bernie deliberately chose to locate the bakery in a part of town that was shunned—next to a brothel, on a street littered with crack vials and syringes. He has helped thousands of ex-convicts, single moms, and felons without a high school diploma get back on their feet. "Nobody would give me no job when they saw my rap sheet," says Dion Drew, a convicted drug dealer who was looking to start a new life but could not convince any employer to give him a second chance. Tears start rolling when he speaks about Greyston. "They saved my life. Without them, I would either be dead or in prison right now." He was about to start dealing again when he got the job at Greyston. At first, he worked night shifts packing boxes, slowly making his way up to lead manager. Now he has a wife, a bank account, and a baby girl who wants to become a baker like him. "Greyston has done a complete three-sixty on my life!"[7]

Why does this work? First of all, because the brownies are so delicious that the bakery makes $13 million a year. Second, because the employees work in teams, and the teams are paid according to team performance. If someone does not pull their weight, is late, drugged, or lazy, the team will kick them out. It's a for-profit bakery, not a kindergarten.

But the profit goes to the Greyston Foundation, which supports housing, an AIDS hospice, communal gardens, childcare, and a home for those who are too challenged or mentally ill to hold down a steady job. What began in 1982 in Bernie's kitchen with the first brownie recipe is now a sweet recipe for getting the homeless off the street. When Greyston started, Yonkers had the country's highest per-capita homeless population. According to Bernie, the homeless rate has since been more than halved, while it continues to rise in most other cities.

Bernie still works in the bakery two days a month. "I love working there!" he beams.

His three tenets are written all over the walls, a daily reminder to start each day fresh: not knowing, bearing witness, taking action.

Auschwitz, a place of horror and healing

The three tenets are really put to the test halfway across the globe, in the abandoned barracks of Auschwitz, Poland. Bernie finds the place itself, with its steely skies overlooking miles of barbed wire and crumbling extermination compounds, "so terrifying that no matter how much we prepare for the visit, no matter how much we've read about it or pondered, it overwhelms us." Even if, like Bernie, you've seen the exhibits more than once, there's one thing he can still count on: "Your expectations, your preconceptions, your most basic belief systems concerning love and hate, good and evil, will be annihilated in the face of Auschwitz. In fact, after seeing the countless photographs of dying camp inmates and the high piles of their belongings pillaged by the Nazis, and after visiting Birkenau and viewing the remains of that meticulous technology developed for the purpose of mass extermination and genocide, we stop thinking altogether. As writers and philosophers have already said, there's no language for Auschwitz." Bernie adds, "There are no thoughts, either. We are in a place of unknowing. Much of Zen practice, including many teaching techniques used by Zen masters, is aimed at bringing the Zen practitioner to this same place of unknowing, of letting go of what he or she knows. All we can do is see the endless train tracks on the snow, feel the icy cold of a Polish winter on our bare hands, smell the rotting wood in the few remaining barracks, and listen to the names of the dead."[8]

Most people find it overwhelming to visit Auschwitz once; why does he keep coming back? "I'm still learning," Bernie says. "Every time I go there, my experience deepens." He calls it "plunges, or going to the places where the brain can't fathom what's happening."

Twenty years ago he took his late wife Jishu Holmes to Auschwitz, and she fainted on the first day. Seeing the dilapidated rows of barracks under the hard gray sky, reading the long list of names, some of which sounded familiar, was just too much. "She was overwhelmed with emotion," he remembers.

And yet he speaks of Auschwitz as "a place of horror, but also of healing." How can he possibly call Auschwitz a place of healing?

He wouldn't say in and of itself Auschwitz is doing the healing. "The healing can't happen if you want to stay away from pain and suffering. It probably won't happen if, like most people, you go to Auschwitz, look over the exhibits, and return to the buses for a quick getaway. When you come to Auschwitz, stay a while, and begin to listen to all the voices of that terrible universe—the voices that are none other than you—then something happens."[9]

Every one of his retreats has a theme. "Auschwitz is a place where we deal with how we deal with *others*."

We all have our clubs we belong to, our peers, our nationality, our culture. There are people we don't let into our club—maybe the homeless, or the rich, or the Germans, or the

Muslims. Hitler and the Nazis were determined to stamp out entire cultures that were different. So for Bernie the remedy lies in doing exactly the opposite: bringing people together who could hardly be more different. The people on his retreats are always a diverse bunch: young, old, gay, straight, white, black, veterans, pacifists, Jewish, Muslim, Christian, Buddhist, Sufi, German, Polish, American, French, Israeli, Palestinian.

Spending the week with such a varied group of people can be challenging. "Stuff comes up," says Bernie, "because people have different cultures. Some want to stay quiet, others want to chant and talk. And we deal with what arises. The healing comes out of that. We become more connected with others; our club becomes much bigger."

His whole retreat is set up to help that confrontation. Twenty people on staff support a hundred participants. They change the schedule or offer counseling when things get off track from the three tenets.

Why do people spend their vacation in a monument of human cruelty?

Bernie remembers a Munich woman who came to his Auschwitz retreat a few years ago. On the first day she introduced herself by confessing she'd been thinking of coming for fifteen years, but she had been afraid. "She was afraid she would meet a Jew or a Polish person, because her grandfather had been running a camp." Of course, there were plenty of Jews in Bernie's group, and also a man from Krakow, Poland, who said he'd been thinking of coming to the retreat for ten years but he had been afraid. "He was afraid of meeting a German person." On the fifth day, the Munich woman and the Krakow man were hugging. "So, for more than a decade they carried that fear with them and that's now gone. That's healing arising from coming together."

Bernie and his group spend most of the day sitting at the

railroad tracks where Coco Schumann arrived sixty years ago. They remember those who came by train and never left. It is the selection site where Coco was chosen to survive and his best friend Fricek Weiss selected to die.

A name like our own

Compassion literally means "with suffering." Sometimes the group sits in silence. Often they take turns reciting the names of the people who died here. They light candles and chant the names of the infants and the very old, the names of the gays and the Jews, the gypsies and the political prisoners. Everyone gets his or her turn. "Sometimes one resembles the name of a coworker back home, or of a friend. Sometimes the chanter pauses. She's come across a name that's exactly like her own. For telling names is like telling stories. When we recite the name out loud, dead bones come to life, the bones of men, women, and children from all over Europe. They lived, some grew up, some married, some had children, and all died. Their names become our names, their stories, our stories."[10]

And yet, I say to Bernie, some people's hearts crack and they get destroyed by it, and some people's hearts crack and they open up and a process of healing begins. What makes the difference? How can we help the people who are cracking?

"For me it's the same in both cases: to nurture in the best way I can. In my experience, by bearing witness, things will arise. So I don't have any plan what to do beforehand to make happen what I like to have happen. I don't look at anything as a panacea or the only way of doing things. That's the approach I have taken."

A woman from a small village in Bavaria attended the retreat for several years. The first year, she did not say anything in the counsel groups. The next year she told her story: her grandfather was the mayor of that Bavarian village, and he killed or deported every single Jew who lived there. The third year, she came back to tell she had instated an annual day where the village read the names of the deported; the fourth year, she found out that there was a woman who had escaped. She tracked down the family. The woman was no longer alive, but her family was in Israel. At first the son didn't want to talk to her, but then he did. The encounter changed both lives.

Another participant was raped by her SS grandfather and his Nazi friends. "She lives in California, and she had been in therapy for a long time," relays Bernie. "She decided to come to our retreat; her therapist thought it was a good idea. After she returned, her therapist wrote to us and said she had more healing than in all the years of therapy. And then there are people who leave mad."

Mad?

At one retreat Bernie included an imam he often works with, a tenth-generation Palestinian married to a Jewish woman. Bernie asked the imam to give a talk one evening. "A participant from California got upset. How dare I allow a Palestinian to talk? This was after I had already talked about the theme of the retreat, bringing people together. I listened, and I said, 'Is that so, hmm?' I brought them together, and they spent a lot of time talking. At the end of the retreat, he said, 'It was a very powerful retreat, but still, you have no right to bring a Palestinian here.' Maybe it moved something in him? I don't know. He was still angry."

This is how wars continue—by seeing the past injustice instead of the present opportunity.

The aggressor in us

One year a German meditation instructor came up with the idea to pray for the camp guards, too. Unrest ensued. Half the people threatened to leave. Chanting the names of the dead, fine, but including the perpetrators? No way. "You made a lot of people very upset," one participant yells at Bernie. He nods. "That's the point," he says, "that's exactly the point."

Bernie acknowledges that "the guards have wound up with huge trauma after Auschwitz, too. We don't separate out the bad guys and the good guys." Therefore he includes "a practice of recognizing the aggressor within us."

Ordinarily, our compassion comes with built-in limits, like a limited warranty that expires when we leave our comfort zone. Our ego is savvy about excluding a lot of big players. You have got to read the fine print. It only includes our cliques. Bernie, however, aims for a very vast compassion that includes everyone and everything.

"If you experience the interconnectedness of all life, how can you exclude one part?" Bernie reasons. "If I take my own body, I can say, well, my ass is such a yucky thing. But that's me. If I don't take care, that's gonna cause disease for the rest of it."

To Roshi Bernie, bearing witness means that "we become each and every aspect of that situation. When we bear witness to Auschwitz, at that moment there is no separation between us and the people who died. There is also no separation between us and the people who killed. We ourselves, as individuals, with our identities and ego structure, disappear, and we become the terrified people getting off the trains, the indifferent or brutal guards, the snarling dogs, the doctor who points right or left, the smoke and ash belching from the chimneys.

When we bear witness to Auschwitz, we are nothing but all the elements of Auschwitz. It is an act of letting go. What we let go of is the concept of the person we think we are. It's why we start from unknowing. Only then can we become all the voices of the universe—those that suffer, those that inflict suffering, and those that stand idly by. For we are all these people."[11]

Nobody says this is easy. But it is life-changing.

Practice loving-kindness for others

Whenever I teach loving-kindness meditation, I begin by guiding people to send loving-kindness to themselves. You can send healing to your cancer, love to your illness, peace to your inflamed immune system, worthiness to your self-esteem. Eventually we widen the circle. We include those close to us in our circle of loving-kindness, then people we feel neutral about, and finally maybe even extend to some we find difficult. (Please consult the meditation in the guide in the back of the book for more details.)

The imperative of Jesus, Buddha, and uncountable spiritual teachers to love everyone might seem like an impossibly tall order. But at some point we learned to cut people out, so it must be possible to learn to let them back in.

"No one is born hating another person because of the color of his skin, or his background, or his religion," Mandela famously wrote in *Long Walk to Freedom*. "People must learn to hate, and if they can learn to hate, they can be taught to love, for love comes more naturally to the human heart than its opposite."[12] I think of the invitation he extended to one of his jailers, who had helped imprison him for twenty-seven years, to his inauguration as South Africa's president.

I think of Malala Yousafzai, who said that if she retaliated with violence toward the person who shot her, there would be "no difference" between her and the Taliban. "You must not treat others with cruelty. You must fight others but through peace and through dialogue and through education."[13]

Of Coco Schumann, who chose to take refuge in music rather than in rage.

Of Tulku Pegyal and Garchen Rinpoche, who included their torturers in their prayers.

Of Thich Nhat Hanh, who was expelled from his home country of postwar Vietnam because he refused to take sides.

Of all the many people around the world who choose, daily, to forgive rather than to retaliate.

Beyond their different religions and cultures, they recognize the alchemy of loving-kindness. Occasionally I meet someone who tells me that loving-kindness is a weakness. I think the people in this book prove the opposite. Friendship trumps betrayal, trust triumphs over mistrust, the logic of the heart beats the violence that arises out of hatred. Kindness is a strength and a powerful force for change—maybe the most powerful force for peace there is on the planet.

PART III

MAKING A DIFFERENCE

Helping ourselves and others

Dear Pain,

Ah, there you are! I hadn't expected you back quite so early. Sorry, I've been kinda busy. I am not ready to indulge you today—I've made plans with my tribe. Catch me if you can.

—Occupied

10. Adrenalize

"The magic formula"
Helping others helped rock star Rick Allen get back into his game.[1]

> *How wonderful it is that nobody need wait a single moment before starting to improve the world.*
>
> —ANNE FRANK

When I walk into the Marriott in Woodland Hills, California, I am not quite sure what to expect. I have never participated in a drum circle before, and now I am supposed to drum with one of the best in the world, "Thunder God" Rick Allen? Def Leppard has just finished their summer tour, playing in front of 600,000 fans. They are one of the most popular bands on the planet, with more than 100 million records sold. Their drummer casually strolls into the ballroom, wearing an old pair of jeans and a faded brown T-shirt. I notice a rosary around his neck.

"Just pick a drum!" Rick's wife Lauren Monroe points to an array of strangely shaped goblet drums as the ballroom slowly fills with about a hundred men, women, and children. Most of them simply signed up for the event on Rick's web page like I did.[2] I pick up a hardwood djembe, balance it on my heels, and solicit its first deep beats. "You don't need to hit them so hard," Rick instructs. "The drums are kind of like wineglasses; balance them delicately."

Rick kicks off his shoes. He drums barefoot. Soon we're off with the beat, the drums start talking to each other, and I give my body over to the rhythm.

"Breathe and relax!" Lauren shouts with her nurturing voice over the beat. "The reason why we use the drums is not just because it's fun, it sounds great, it's an uplifting feeling, but also, the drums bring us into the present moment. If you play the drums and find you lose yourself in the moment, that's great. That's the point. We want you to get into the moment, and not be in the past or in the future, just in the moment."

So, why does one of the world's finest drummers drum with novices like me?

"Believe it or not, I'm actually here for myself and for all of you," says Rick during a break. "Being with you here, the combined experience helps me to become healthier and more whole. I can't really do this without you."

Spinning out of control

For a moment his thoughts fly back to the last day of 1984, ten minutes before midnight. The then twenty-one-year-old was racing to a New Year's Eve party at his family home in Sheffield, Great Britain. An Alfa Romeo would not let him pass, and Rick lost his cool. In a risky maneuver, he accelerated his Corvette Stingray to overtake, but spun out of control in a narrow turn and flipped over several times. He was thrown from the car, and his seat belt severed his left arm just below the shoulder.

He says he just wanted to disappear, and he could not imagine ever again showing himself in public. He had not only lost a limb but also the very ability for which he was loved and admired. Or so he assumed. "On the face of it, and I thought so at the time, it was a terrible thing." Rick was certain that his career with Def Leppard was over before it had even fully taken off. But then thousands and thousands of letters poured in from all over the world. Could it be possible his fans still loved him without his ability to drum? Or maybe they truly loved him *and* he could still drum up a storm?

His friends noticed that he was rocking out in his hospital bed, with his feet mimicking the drum kicks. They pulled him out of his depression by encouraging him to try drumming with his right arm and his feet. Rick experimented with electronic drums, and just eight months later he showed off his new skills at the Monsters of Rock festival. A year later he recorded Def Leppard's monumental *Hysteria* album, then *Adrenalize*. "This outpouring of love from the world at large quickly tuned me into the support I was getting from my family and my band. Instead of feeling fearful, I started to move forward, simply because of the support I felt behind me. It was really profound, the shift that occurred."[3]

He looks at the accident now with a vastly different perspective. "My life as it was back then, I felt it was really unsustainable." He had been going too fast, not only literally that evening but also figuratively. "And the experience I went through actually became a huge blessing."

Resilience is a group effort

Have you noticed what all the life stories on these pages have in common?

In a way, the people featured could hardly be more different. They are young and old, outgoing and introverted, world famous and unknown, writers and musicians, soldiers and scientists. But all of them share one crucial factor: They had help. They did not do it alone.

When resilience expert Ann Masten looks back at five decades of research, she notes a glaring truth. "I cannot think of one person who did it by themselves. A lot of what makes the difference for people is the support they are receiving."[4]

Coco Schumann had nothing and no friends when he arrived in Theresienstadt, yet through music and his outgoing nature he made fast friends everywhere he went. In the end, it was his friendships that decided his fate more than once: his friends saved him from starvation by dishing out extra rations of meat and bread, and once they warned him before his entire block was sentenced to death, giving him precious ten minutes to escape and save his life.

Temple Grandin had a mother who believed in her and refused to surrender her child to an institution. Buck Brannaman was saved by observant teachers and compassionate foster parents. Rhonda Cornum gathered strength from her mission with the army. Alain Beauregard credits his survival not only to his doctors but also to his teacher, his friends, and his ex-spouse who took him in when he was too ill to fend for himself. Meggie Zahneis acknowledges she might not be alive today were her parents not so caring and protective.

"If people put you in a crib and ignore you, you never develop the potential," says Ann Masten. "We are so shaped by the interactions we have with the environment, in the form of chemicals, food, relationships, and so forth; I think there are big limits on what is inborn. Throughout life, our close relationships with caregivers, friends, romantic partners, and others build and sustain our resilience."

The process of strengthening our resilience begins in the womb and immediately after birth, through the nourishing presence of our parents and caregivers. Our brains develop at least partly in response to how those around us talk to us, how they touch us, how attentively they encourage us.[5]

Unlike some of her colleagues, Ann Masten does not believe in a "resilience trait." She is convinced that resilience is a team effort. Bouncing forward after a crisis depends not only on our own resources but also at least as much on our connection to the people that surround us and how well we are able to gather support.

Therefore Ann Masten's short list of resilience factors includes some of the individual core skills we already talked about, such as intelligence, problem-solving skills, self-control, self-efficacy, the belief that life has meaning, and the motivation to succeed. But on top of her priorities are factors that lie beyond the individual, such as effective caregiving, capable parenting, other close relationships, close friends, effective schools, and caring communities.

The gift of connecting

When we experience a trauma, we are hardly the only one who suffers. Almost inevitably, trauma corrodes our connection with the world around us, our friends and family. This is especially true when the trauma has been inflicted by others, but it is not necessarily easier when we inflicted it upon ourselves, like Rick Allen, or when forces beyond our power have taken everything away.

"Traumatic events call into question basic human relationships. They breach the attachments of family, friendship, love, and community," says trauma therapist Judith Herman. "Traumatized people feel utterly abandoned, utterly alone, cast out of the human and divine systems of care and protection that sustain life. Thereafter, a sense of alienation, of disconnection, pervades every relationship, from the most intimate familial bonds to the most abstract affiliations of community and religion."[6] Trauma totals our trust.

Our best protector from trauma is also our best ally on our road to recovery: the ability to connect. Rick was lucky that his friends and fans flooded him with affection at a time when he wanted to disappear from the face of the earth, but most of us need to consciously make an effort to reach out. This, then, is the task at hand: to reestablish trust in ourselves, in the workings of the world, in others. One of the best things we can do for ourselves is "hanging out with other healthy brains," as psychotherapist Linda Graham put it. What's important is not the number of friends, but the *quality* of the support. Support can come from friends, family, support groups, our church, or professionals. The best kind of support encourages us to focus on our strength, to take our life into our own hands, and helps to bring out the best in us.

Reach out

We don't need to be Miss Social Butterfly and have a fan club or a busy party life. What matters is simply that we have one or two people in the world we let under our skin—friends we can call at three in the morning and who will drive all the way out to us in the rain.[7] Find these two friends. If you already have them, cherish them. And be one of these friends for someone else.

Rick Allen advises, "Reach out to a friend, or a family member. Anybody that can talk you off the ledge. Because there is hope, and I think the key to that is really being of service. It is helping somebody else who has been through something equally as traumatic."[8]

Rick learned this lesson the hard way after he recovered from the crash. Though he was carried by the love of his fans, he refused to deal with his mental issues. He went on to world fame with his band, busy with tours and travels. He did not speak about the accident, and he did not seek help. He admits, "Plain and simple, I was afraid to talk about what I've been through. I was unable to find the words to describe what I've been through. Let alone I couldn't get my head around that my experience could help someone else."[9]

As psychotherapist Susan Ollar has warned earlier, most everyone who carries a hidden trauma without addressing it will at some point come to a dead end.

Rick's emotions and rage exploded publicly at Los Angeles International Airport in July 1995. According to court documents, he dragged his first wife, Stacy, into an airport restroom after an argument, choked her, and struck her head against a wall.

The torment of rage

Unfortunately, violence is all too frequently part of trauma. We long to connect, but feel misunderstood. We detest violence, but are prone to aggressive outbursts. "Because of the difficulty in modulating intense anger, survivors oscillate between uncontrolled expressions of rage and intolerance to aggression in any form," writes Judith Herman. She describes a veteran who felt very compassionate and protective toward others, but who exploded into anger and irritation toward his family. "His own inconsistency was one of the sources of his torment. . . . Similar regulations occur in the regulation of intimacy. Trauma impels people both to withdraw from close relationships and to seek them desperately. The profound disruption in basic trust, the common feelings of shame, guilt, and inferiority, and the need to avoid reminders of the trauma that might be found in social life, all foster withdrawal from close relationships. But the terror of the traumatic event intensifies the need for protective attachments. The traumatized person therefore frequently alternates between isolation and anxious clinging to others."[10]

That Rick was sentenced to attending AA meetings and seeking counseling after his blowup marked the real beginning of his turnaround: he could no longer avoid dealing with his issues. "I never realized the enormity of the mental challenges I was faced with. I didn't realize there was anything wrong with me," he later told his second wife, Lauren. "Either I was in denial, or I was an asshole before my accident and I was just a bigger asshole afterwards. I started to realize that there were things about me that were different. My reactions to certain situations . . . my fuse was really quite short, and I was just starting to see the issues I hadn't really dealt with."[11]

Rick comes across as down-to-earth, easily accessible, and completely genuine. He humbly calls himself "still a work in progress." He now speaks openly about his vulnerability, and the big change that occurred after he started connecting with other amputees. In hindsight he describes the accident as "a huge blessing. The experience of working through it has made me a better drummer, and a stronger person for that matter."

Courage on the challenging journey

Rick tells me about a trip to Walter Reed hospital in 2006 that changed his life. Meeting fellow amputees, he realized how much he had in common with them: the posttraumatic symptoms, anxiety attacks, the inability to tolerate loud noises (yes, despite being in a rock band). He detailed his experience in an interview with ABC: "I was moved by their courage, their suffering, and by the very challenging journey many of them had ahead. I spent time talking to as many warriors as I could—listening, learning, and sharing my own experience of losing my arm and having to rebuild my life."[12]

And he found his life's purpose.

"Back then it was just about playing drums, and now it's bigger than that. It's about how I can share my experience, connect with other people, inspire other people. If I can remember that life purpose every day, it makes life much easier for me. It's a choice. I can choose to isolate or I can choose to use my life experience to inspire others."[13]

Shifting the focus away from us

"The best way to find yourself is to lose yourself in the service of others," said Mahatma Gandhi. We not only benefit from being helped, we also benefit from helping. It's a two-way street.

Temple Grandin now helps millions of animals and autistic kids. Buck Brannaman saves horses. Rhonda Cornum not only gathered strength from her mission with the army but also works actively toward strengthening the army. Alain Beauregard holds workshops to help others through the experience of severe illness. Meggie Zahneis has vowed to be an advocate for other children.

"Psychotherapists frequently find that their main task is to help patients shift their focus away from themselves," writes psychologist Julius Segal. Segal quotes Viktor Frankl's specific technique—he calls it "dereflection"—"to divert patients from spending precious time endlessly searching for the neurotic sources of their anxiety and depression. Instead, he directs their attention to the healthier parts of their personalities and encourages them to dwell on the meaningful things they can do and the contributions they can make. [Retired Stanford psychiatrist] Irvin Yalom agrees that it can be vitally important to get stress-ridden individuals to stop thinking about themselves and to start thinking of others."[14]

Part III of this book is about making a difference. "If you got any kind of blues, I feel for ya," Bob Dylan said.[15] "I know life is hard but you don't need anyone to tell you how to feel better. I'm gonna tell you the magic formula: Whatcha got to do is go out and help someone more unfortunate than you. Go to an orphanage, play football with the kids, go to retirement homes, go to soup kitchens, go into prisons, go see some people, there's people everywhere who aren't as well off as you. No matter how bad you have it somebody got it worse. Instead of adding to the sadness in the world, why not lend a hand, help somebody out? And not just on Christmas, why don't you give it a try year-round?"

All the protagonists you'll meet in the final stretch of this book found their turning point when they decided to ask for help and eventually reached out to help others.

Since his first visit to Walter Reed, Rick has reached out to teenage cancer patients, children with special needs, at-risk youth in crisis, families of domestic violence, and veterans who have served in Vietnam, Iraq, and Afghanistan.[16]

Rick now regularly invites participants from the Wounded Warrior Project to Def Leppard concerts. He and Lauren founded the Raven Drum Foundation and the Resiliency Project to build a community for survivors to connect. They see the drum circles as an important step in the healing process, and they use their Resiliency Radio to share their own struggles and encourage others to share theirs.

"One of the main issues is that the warriors won't ask for help. And we are really here to highlight the fact that you're not a coward if you ask for help."[17] He adds, "My desire is to encourage a support system for warriors, destigmatize PTSD, share their stories and offer alternative ways to pave the road to resiliency and health. PTSD does not control us; we have the power to control it."[18]

The power of the circle

To make a difference, Rick Allen uses what he loves most—drumming. "Playing drums in a group is a very ancient form. When we play, we find a dominant rhythm, and that dominant rhythm carries everyone. Nobody can say, 'I don't have rhythm.' Everybody has rhythm."[19] Even his five-year-old daughter Josie, nestled between him and Lauren, keeps time.

Drums have been used for thousands of years in healing ceremonies and sacred rituals, for communication and connection. "Just the physical aspect of drumming starts to anchor us, the thoughts we have, we spend so much time thinking about the future and worrying about the past . . ." says Lauren at the gathering in Woodland Hills. "Set the intention to support one another. There is not anyone in this room who has not experienced sorrow and pain; we are all alike in that regard."

There could be no image more potent for the third part of this book than the circle. We are connected. Even when we feel disconnected, we actually are still part of the wider circle. "It's impossible to feel lonely in a drum circle," says Lauren. "The impact of what we do is actually creating a new paradigm of healing. We don't look at the symptom, but at the whole person, and how we can elevate the spirit and the physicality and the emotional aspects of someone to health. It`s like when we're sick, instead of looking at what part of us is sick, we look at what is well, and we move from there."

We have spent a lot of time in this book talking about

the mental and emotional challenges, but the body plays an equally crucial part in healing. The body is our life's recording device—it stores every memory, emotion, and trauma.

When I attended a workshop with therapist Linda Graham, she reminded me that, "We need to rewire the *entire* network: thoughts, emotions, body. Rewiring goes all the way down to the bodily sensations." Trauma experts such as Peter Levine believe that we need to learn to access and relax the places in us where we hold the physical memory of the trauma.

Especially when a trauma has been physical, coming back into the body can be scary, but truly healing.

Reconnect with your body

"As many of us know when it comes to trauma, that connection between mind and body is lost sometimes, because it is too painful to be in your body," Lauren acknowledges. "Slowly we can retrain our mind and our nervous system to be more present. Drumming is a great way to do that. We find that using breathing and drumming together to teach people how to be more present in their healing journey really has a profound effect." Lauren is a musician, but also a healer who studied ancient healing techniques with shamans and tribal healers in Brazil, Mexico, North America, and New Zealand. "Mindfulness practice is one of the keys we offer, learning how to bridge the doorway between mind and body. We're offering things up, and releasing them."

Whether it is through drumming or somatic healing, yoga or hiking, the body holds a key to healing. This is done most safely with the help of an experienced therapist. A friend of mine who suffered through a sexually abusive relationship and a severe eating disorder reconnected with her

body through yoga and mindfulness. For you, it could
be dancing, hiking, or exploring nature: whatever speaks
to you and your senses.

And then we're off again. The beat accelerates in the drum circle, and for a few precious minutes Rick Allen shows off his rock star skills. Next to him is a drummer in a wheelchair who uses his arms instead of his legs.

I forget that I am here to write a book. My hands shimmy by themselves, tap the djembe, and we all bop in one concentrated dance of beats. At times Lauren guides us in brief visualizations, reminding us to keep ourselves grounded in our breathing.

The rhythm mounts to an earsplitting crescendo and then, with a bang, silence.

Total. Silence.

We take our hands off our drums, sit back, and listen to the stillness. The people in the ballroom who did not know each other an hour ago now feel connected in one powerful circle of healing.

"Just breathe. Listen and observe. It's not with the drums, it's between the beats. That's where the healing happens," says Lauren. "The power lies in the transitions. We learn to go from the noise and the rhythm to the silence."

Silence has never felt more powerful. Stillness never sounded louder. We take a deep collective breath and release it with an outbreath.

And the weight of the past drops off our shoulders, if only for the length of an exhale.

11. Shine

"One of the bravest cats I know"
How top surfer Jesse Billauer returned to
the US Open after he was paralyzed by a
wave[1]

The only true disability is a crushed spirit.
—AIMEE MULLINS[2]

J esse Billauer is a Pisces, and the ocean his natural habitat.
We *have* to meet on the beach in Southern California. He
grew up here, belongs here, on the shore under the picture-
perfect California sky. "The ocean is my home," he says with
a broad grin. "I feel more comfortable in the water than I do
on land." His eyes' sparkle matches the ocean. He habitually
scans the horizon for decent waves. Surfing, to him, represents "freedom, independence, endless possibilities."

Growing up in Pacific Palisades and Malibu, Jesse used to
rise with the sun to catch as many waves as he could before
school. His brown curls bleached by the constant exposure
to sun and sea, this quintessential California beach kid spent
every free minute either in the water, on the soccer field, or
playing basketball. Because of his fearless grace on the board,
the phenomenal athlete caught the eye of sponsors when he

was barely twelve years old. By age seventeen, he already had more trophies than he could fit on his shelf. His friends compared him to his idol, pro surfer Shane Dorian.

The perfect wave

Jesse preferred surfing solo, but on March 25, 1996, the surf forecast was too exciting not to share the stoke. The seventeen-year-old called all his friends to Zuma Beach at sunrise. Come on out! It's gonna be epic!

He remembers the wave because it was so flawless. The swell, eight feet tall, rolled toward him and he was perfectly positioned to catch it. He swooshed through the barrel like the pro he was about to become. But he stayed on the wave just a tad too long. The crest hit him in the back and smashed him headfirst into a shallow sandbar. He did not even have time to soften the blow with his hands.

Jesse's body started shaking, then tingling, then went numb. He was floating facedown. Luckily, the next wave tipped him over. "HELP!" he managed to scream, before he got tossed again. "It was the weirdest feeling, like a giant was pulling my arms behind me with great force."

His friends thought he was joking until they didn't see him surface. "You have to hold my head over water," Jesse cried when they reached him. "I can't move."

Friends pulled him to the beach and called 911. A lifeguard cut open Jesse's wetsuit, only to find Jesse reprimanding him. "What are you doing, man?! I need this wetsuit tomorrow!" The lifeguard shook his head. "Bro, I don't think you do."

The next thing Jesse recalls is waking up in the hospital, tubes emerging from his throat and nose, his mother Cecile and his father George anxiously waiting at his bedside.

Never. Ever. Again.

Never. The word "never" entered his life, with the weight of a doctor's voice. "You will probably never walk again."

Jesse Billauer had just been nominated as one of the world's top one hundred surfers by *Surfer* magazine. He was about to go pro the next month. He heard the word "never" and did not hear it. "Impossible" was not part of his lexicon.

He refused to grasp the gravitas of the doctor's diagnosis: C6 spinal cord injury, paralyzed from the midchest down. "I didn't know anybody who was paralyzed. I didn't even know what paralyzed meant." His sponsor brought five brand-new custom surfboards into the hospital, and Jesse pictured himself taking them for a spin. "I was like, this is gonna take a couple of months and I'll be back on the board."

Jesse, now thirty-six years old, smiles when he thinks back to that seventeen-year-old in a hospital bed. "All I could think about was that I urgently needed my friends to get my truck at Zuma so that my parents wouldn't find the pile of condoms in the middle console."

His father's worries were of a different order. "For a day, just for one day, I thought it might be better if he hadn't survived." George takes a deep breath.

"He's proven me wrong every single day."[3]

Superman's greatest achievement

"The biggest problem when people first get injured is that they think their life is over," actor Christopher Reeve told Jesse when they met in 2002. "They can't imagine building a new life. And then you show up and tell them how they can push their limits."[4]

Just like Rick and Jesse, Christopher Reeve lost what he was famous for: his physical prowess. After all, he embodied Superman. Reeve spoke with brutal honesty about the days after his 1995 riding accident when the truth sank in: he would not be able to move his body again. The first lucid words he mouthed to his wife from the hospital bed were,[5] "Maybe we should let me go." His wife Dana began to cry, and responded, "I am only going to say this once: I will support whatever you want to do, because this is your life, and your decision. But I want you to know that I'll be with you for the long haul, no matter what." Then she added the words that he credits with saving his life: "You're still you. And I love you."

Reeve said he never again considered suicide. He pushed himself to learn to breathe on his own, became the spokesperson for spinal cord injury, and singlehandedly multiplied public support for research.

Just six months before his surf accident, Jesse had been struck by a car so forcefully that his own car spun around several times and flipped over, and he was ejected onto the Pacific Coast Highway. "I was lucky I wasn't run over right there," Jesse remembers. Back then, at the hospital, he said, "If I can't walk or surf, I don't want to live." But despite the dramatic accident, he recovered quickly from the whiplash and the bruises. Later, when not walking became a reality, his perspective shifted. Jesse was fortunate, like Christopher Reeve and Rick Allen, to have supportive family and friends who rekindled his hope. The nurses joked that there was no space in the waiting room for anyone else while Jesse was in the hospital, because the room was always filled with his buddies. His life as he knew it was over, but "it was my friends who came and supported me and brought my spirits up. They helped me realize I am still the same person."[6]

Start over

Jesse had to "start life all over again. Like a little kid, I couldn't even brush my teeth, or my hair." He hated not being able to feel his body, to spend most of his time in bed, to have to ask for help, to depend on others 24/7. "I couldn't even go to the bathroom by myself; all these private moments were gone." But he focused on the task in front of him: rehabilitating his body, regaining his strength. "I knew I was on a new journey, a new path, a new life."[7]

A bold move to reach for the stars

Any athlete who wants to compete at the highest level needs not only physical strength but also a specific mental tool kit that distinguishes dabblers from the champions. Nothing could have prepared Jesse for losing control over his body, but in many ways the rigorous discipline of a future pro athlete did actually train him in the skills that mattered most after the accident: discipline, determination, patience, tolerance for frustration, and the boldness to reach for the stars. The same qualities that made him stand out on the surfboard now helped him navigate the tides of pain and fear.

As a teenager, Jesse had spelled out with a preternatural clarity what he wanted in life: to become a pro surfer, own a house with an ocean view, marry, have children, enjoy life. He wasn't going to let breaking his neck get in the way.

George Billauer was impressed with how well his son handled the brutal injury. "When the doctor told him he would be paralyzed, Cecile and I broke into tears. Jesse said, 'You're more paralyzed than I am. You breaking down doesn't help me right now. If you want to cry, please leave the room.'"

George, a chiropractor, reduced his work to half time in

order to take care of his injured son. Few people realize how complicated life as a quadriplegic is: eating, drinking, bowel movements—every daily necessity requires help. Privacy goes out the window.

Jesse focused on possibilities. Life kept beckoning. Soon after the accident, he was impatient to leave the rehab clinic. "I was like, 'Dude, I gotta get out of here! I'm missing out on everything!'"

He did not lose any time. With the help of a tutor, he made up for the missed lectures at high school and graduated with his class. His classmates elected him homecoming king, and Jesse playfully threw his graduation cap in the air from his wheelchair. Six months after the accident, he moved into his own apartment with a caregiver, then to San Diego for college.

Find your passion

Jesse thinks he did so well because he already knew what his passion in life was. For Coco, it is music; for Rick, drumming; for Meggie, writing; for Temple, helping animals. Instead of letting adversity define them, their passion defines them, and the drive to excel at what they do gives them the courage and determination to push through obstacles.

When Jesse is invited to speak in schools, he often guides his listeners in a short visualization. "Close your eyes," Jesse instructs. "Visualize your dream. Find your passion. You never know what's gonna happen. So you really gotta enjoy the moment, follow your heart. Follow your own dreams, not your friends' dreams or your parents' dreams. Don't listen to what others want you to do; follow what *you* want to do. Once you know what you love, life will be more beautiful. Appreciate life. Never give up. Try everything."

Soon after the accident, all Jesse could think about was getting back into the water—his element, his life source. "If I can go surfing lying down, who cares about standing up?" Jesse convinced his pro surfer friends, Rob Machado and Kelly Slater, to help him. They worried about his safety. What if he fell into the water? He'd be drifting like a piece of wood! But Jesse kept urging until they finally relented and drove him to the beach. At first, he failed miserably. He had no strength, kept rolling off the board; he could barely lift his head. "The waves are rolling in on us, and he's just laughing the whole time. Just his whole attitude, like, cool, no worries. Got under water, got rolled around, big smiles!" remembers Rob Machado.[8] "He has total trust in me. That's pretty radical. For me, that was so intense."

Then a perfect peeler rolled in. Jesse's buddies floated behind him, holding the board. As the wave moved in, they pushed Jesse's board expertly into its crest. Catching the wave flushed Jesse with bliss beyond belief. "These are top athletes, dude," Jesse raves, shaking his head in disbelief. "Any surfer would be thrilled to go out surfing with them. And here they are, taking time out of their surfing time, to take *me* out!"

Jesse can breathe on his own and move his arms a little. He still has not gained enough strength to cut a steak, but he has trained his upper arms—his "guns," as he proudly calls them—so that he can balance on the board. Constant advances in new technology help, too. WaveJet built him a motorized surfboard. With the push of a button, the engine propels him into the surf.

What does it mean to be back in the ocean?

"Freedom, independence, getting away from it all. I feel a lot of burning sensation in my body, but when I'm in the water, it's gone. I feel buoyant, light."

Sometimes Jesse ponders, "How unlucky am I to be part

of that very small percentage of people who get hurt?" That number, though, is actually not that small. According to the Christopher & Dana Reeve Foundation, one in fifty Americans, or 5.6 million people, live with some form of paralysis in the United States.

Then Jesse catches himself and asks, "How lucky am I? I gotta make the best of it. I just gotta roll, have fun. I love surfing, watching the waves, looking at beautiful women. I am living for the now. My body is what it is, but I'm still enjoying my life. I can't do a hundred percent of the things I want to do, but I'm really not worried right now."[9]

He believes that we are all "only temporarily able-bodied." Sooner or later an illness or old age will catch up with us, so why not enjoy the moment and be as kind as we can?

"Never met a bigger athlete spirit"

"I have been fortunate to hang out with many of the great athletes of several generations, from Muhammad Ali to Martina Navratilova," says long-distance swimmer Diana Nyad. "I'm not sure I've ever met a bigger athlete spirit than Jesse Billauer. To spend time in Jesse's presence is to experience the intoxicating charisma he radiates. Here's an individual who has found the profound courage to beam a sincere smile, to find reasons to live a grateful life, and to refuse to waste the life . . . albeit radically different than the life of his dreams . . . he has been forced to live." Diana Nyad became the first person to swim from Cuba to Florida without a shark cage—at age sixty-four. She is an inspiration to many athletes, yet she feels inspired by Jesse. "You cannot read about Jesse Billauer, nor read his direct words, nor go to hear him speak, nor play a round of poker with him, nor watch him still surf with the help of friends who push him down the waves, and not wish that you could only feel half his positive passion for your own life."[10]

Walking or not

For a few years Jesse explored the possibility of walking again. He joined an innovative program at UCLA, until the initiative was transferred to Kentucky. Strapped into a full-body harness, he trained his muscles to take steps again. At one point he even experimented with a drug that was only available in Mexico, but it did nothing for him. "He left most of the research to me," George says, "but eventually he did not want to be the guinea pig. A lot of people in his condition are trying very risky methods that are unproven. Jesse decided he was too busy living his life."

This is not a story about a miraculous recovery. Rather, this is about a meeting with a man who has done an amazing job at playing the cards life dealt him. This avid poker player is *all in*.

Accept what is

"It is what it is," Jesse says matter-of-factly. "I am not walking. Oh, well. If I walk, I walk. If I don't, I don't." Jesse shrugs his shoulders. "I focus on the quality of life more than I focus on a cure. I want to live my life now and do the things that I love."

As Richard Tedeschi and other posttraumatic growth researchers have found, the ability to accept situations that cannot be changed is crucial for adapting to traumatic life events. They call it "acceptance coping," and have determined that coming to terms with reality is a significant predictor of posttraumatic growth.[11]

Jesse and his grandmother Engelina spent long hours talking about what is important in life and how to not give up. She knew from personal experience. Engelina's parents were deaf and mute. During the Holocaust, Engelina lost all her family but one sibling. She survived five different concentration camps before the British army freed her from Bergen-Belsen. "You have to look forward, not look back," Engelina told Jesse.

In 2005, Engelina took her sons and grandchildren to visit Bergen-Belsen and other concentration camps. The experience contributed to Jesse's resolve. "If my grandmother could survive the Holocaust, I can survive this."

Determined to rise above

Jesse keeps himself too busy to "sit around and feel sorry for myself," but when he has time to ponder, he writes poetry.

> *I am determined, determined to rise above challenges.*
> *I am strong, strong enough to face my weaknesses.*
> *I am wise, wise to decide right from wrong.*
> *I am I, through my own eyes.*
> *I am brave, brave as my grandmother in the Holocaust.*
> *I am love, love that has been given to me throughout life.*
> *I am rolling on, as a story not yet finished.*

Go volunteer for someone else

When people ask Jesse how he keeps his spirit positive, his advice is clear-cut: "The best thing is: go volunteer for some people who are less fortunate than you are. There is always someone less fortunate. There is always someone who has something worse than you."

Life rolls on

Jesse is now doing what Rob Machado and Kelly Slater did for him: giving other challenged athletes the courage and opportunity to surf. Life Rolls On, the charity he founded in 1999, has become his motto, his message, his survival plan. It began as a fund-raiser to cover the enormous costs of his rehabilitation, but the first events were such a success that his brother and father soon suggested expanding the scope. Of all dates, they organized their very first big surf event on the morning of September 11, 2001. Laird Hamilton and his wife Gabby Reece, Kelly Slater, Rob Machado, Tim Curran, Dan Malloy, Ross Williams, and other surf stars showed up. "The Twin Towers were burning, and they still came," says Jesse. "The support was overwhelming. That shows you the strength of these events and the community, how tight we are."

Today, thousands participate. Organizing his annual surf event in Santa Monica, California, Jesse excitedly wheels between the microphone tent, the sponsor stands, and the volunteer groups on the sand. This is a surf event like no other: more than a hundred surfers line up in their wheelchairs. Anxious moms hover over their four- and six-year-olds. No one is too young, too old, or too handicapped to participate. Kelly, a blond six-year-old, catches my attention as she quivers with excitement and fear. Most of the surfers can't swim or even move their limbs. Volunteers help squeeze their limp bodies into wetsuits and then they're off: the able-bodied surfers form a line into the ocean. One by one, surfers hoist the paralyzed people onto surfboards, then push and pull them out into the open sea. At least six or seven experienced surfers mind each handicapped newbie. They steer the boards from behind and if necessary, hold the bodies in place. The reward is the return journey. When their minders catch the wave, they gather speed, and the newly minted surfers shoot back to the beach, their eyes wide with the thrill. "It's like a roller-coaster ride, just way more fun," squeaks Kelly after her first ride. "Can I go again?"

One family comes every year. The father used to surf with his daughter. After a stroke, he thought the fun days in the water were over. Now the Life Rolls On event is the highlight of his year.

Jesse Billauer jokes he has invented a new sport and play-fully dubs himself "the Laird Hamilton of quadriplegic surf-ing."

So much more than just catching a wave

Life Rolls On has become the go-to organization for adaptive surfers. Jesse hosts more than a dozen events each year on both coasts, and he personally oversees every single event, all of which are free for participants. Each event costs about $15,000, but Jesse insists on financing them with sponsorship money.

"I get to feel that freedom, that joy of being in the ocean. When people come to us, they get to know that it's an option for them, too," says Jesse. His payback is when he sees "the kids in their chairs go back to school and they are the stars. They show videos of themselves skateboarding in the wheel-chair or surfing. Now they're looked at as the cool kid. They thought of themselves as the outcast before; now they're at the top of the food chain."

It is about so much more than just catching a wave. "Surf-ing is just the catalyst for them, it's about boosting their con-fidence. So it's more about building a community, building relationships, and letting them know there is a lot more out in the world they might not have known about. For instance, some people in a wheelchair don't think they can ever get married or have a girlfriend; they see me and my wife and they have hope they can find someone, too. Surfing is just the medium that can bring us together."

There are many organizations that help challenged athletes get back into their game, and they do amazing work: Disabled Sports USA, the Challenged Athletes Foundation, Make A Hero, Achilles International, to name a few. The Paralympics are a celebration of human endurance; blind mountain climbers scale Mount Everest; double-amputees ski black runs; paralyzed skateboard artists demonstrate stunts. My favorite athletes include Arizona psychologist Jessica Cox, who was born without arms and has become the first pilot to fly a plane with her feet; and Minda Dentler, the first woman ever to finish the Ironman World Championship in Kona in a hand bike. Like my grandfather, Minda was paralyzed by polio as an infant, and she failed at her first Ironman attempt but kept training and finally succeeded in 2013.

As Mexican painter Frida Kahlo said as she struggled to regain her ability to walk after a bus accident, "Feet, what do I need you for when I have wings to fly?"

Bad things happen to good people

Jesse regularly gives speeches at schools and events, usually to 99 percent able-bodied people, mostly teenagers who are of the age Jesse was when his accident happened. Oftentimes a gasp ripples through the audience when Jesse describes how his head hit the sandbank. The realization surges through the crowd that they, too, are anything but invincible.

"I always thought bad things only happen to bad people," Jesse says, "but bad things happen to good people."

Once a teenager came up to Jesse after his talk at a school.

The teenager confessed he was struggling with suicidal thoughts and had planned to kill himself, but Jesse's optimism had cast a light on the possibilities he was throwing away. "I will never think of killing myself again," Jesse remembers the boy saying. "If you can just change *one* life like that . . ." Jesse says proudly, "that's why I do this."

Forgive yourself

Jesse finds it easier to accept his fate because he caused it. "I was lazy. This injury happened because I did not pay attention. If someone else had caused the accident, I might be more angry." He does not waste time reproaching himself. "Once in a while I'll be super bummed out. Damn, why did this happen to me?! But, there is never any doubt in my mind that I'm not gonna give up."

Jesse accepts responsibility for making a mistake, but notice how he does not beat up on himself.

"Resilient individuals tend to view mistakes as experiences for learning and growth," psychologists Robert Brooks and Sam Goldstein note.[12] Accepting responsibility is a crucial step in the recovery, but blaming ourselves again and again is not.

Forgive yourself, and move on.

Jesse brims with life. Soon after he figured out how to balance on the surfboard with his elbows, he wanted to take the challenge up a notch. He begged his friends to take him to Fiji to surf ten-foot breaks. "What could go wrong?" his father quipped before they headed out.[13] Jesse convinced his surfer friends to tow him with their Jet Skis into one of the world's most dangerous surf breaks. They hesitantly gave in after much arguing, blown away by Jesse's determination.

The giant waves Jesse negotiates are dramatic, but Jesse's grin is as monumental as the waves. His friend, Grammy-decorated singer-songwriter Jason Mraz, calls him "the most incredible surfer." Soon after his Fiji adventure, Jesse went diving with fifteen-foot sharks in Mexico, then skydiving. Never showing an iota of fear, he bursts with joy at every milestone.

"Jesse has more energy and drive to do things than anyone I know," Jesse's friend Brett Sanson says admiringly. "He gets up at five to go fishing, then surfing, later in the evening to a concert. He does not want to miss a thing. A lot of people say, 'Oh, I'll do that later.' With Jesse it's always, 'I'll do that *now*!' "

Things *can* go wrong. Jesse fractured his femur surfing in Hawaii. He got a hairline fracture in his tibia while surfing in Nicaragua.

"He has destroyed the word 'excuse,' " his friend Ben Harper throws in proudly. "He is one of the bravest cats I know, and every time you know someone this brave, it enriches your soul, it enriches your life."[14]

Take risks

Taking meaningful, calculated risks is a sign of resilience. This might seem counterintuitive, because taking a risk is what got Jesse into trouble in the first place. If he had never wanted to go near the ocean again, nobody would have blamed him.

Yet throughout this book you encounter people who are willing to risk failure again after they have been dramatically injured. That Rhonda was willing to deploy again, that Bethany Hamilton returned to surfing after the shark bite, that Rick continued drumming with one arm, and that Jesse insists on surfing some of the trickiest waves on the planet, might seem like sheer madness, but by exposing themselves, they empower themselves.

"A resilient individual is one who is willing to take calculated, necessary risks and to capitalize on opportunity," resilience expert Karen Reivich explained at the army boot camp in Philadelphia. Taking risks is a side effect of the self-mastery we spoke about earlier: resilient people believe that they can handle the fallout, knowing full well how hard this can be.

Nothing can sway him

It is Jesse's zest for life that attracted Samanta "Sam" Pearson to him. When he first spotted the gorgeous stockbroker in his apartment elevator three years ago, he wasted no time: he told her she was beautiful and asked for her number. She instantly noticed his striking eyes, but most of all his confidence. At the time Sam did not know anybody in a wheelchair, and she hesitated, but was also intrigued. "I wanted to know his story." On their first date he took her surfing, and Sam, thirty-four, fell in love with his fiery spirit.

"He's a very, very passionate person. Nothing can sway him. He knows what he wants and he goes after it. He doesn't take no for an answer. If he can't do it, he'll figure out another way to fulfill what he's trying to fulfill. Nothing is too big a task for him."

Sam now joins him in running Life Rolls On, enthused by the close-knit community. She calls the events "life-changing, and not just for the participants, but for everybody who helps."

Some of her friends told her point-blank that she was crazy to date someone in a wheelchair, but Sam speaks honestly about the challenges. "We had to figure out how to be intimate. Being intimate is an emotional, mental, and physical connection. Am I going to miss that real raw physical connection I could have with someone who is not paralyzed? I had to think about these things; what am I giving up and what am I getting in return? To me, the emotional is much more important. Sometimes I hit a roadblock, realizing I am gonna miss certain things. But what do I want the most? He really respects me, understands me, and cares about me. I think the injury made him value life more. It's so attractive to know somebody like that."

Sam is a very physical person. She loves to run, hike, and work out in the gym. When he realized how much hiking meant to her, he crowdsourced a $16,000 all-terrain wheelchair and surprised her by showing up for a hike. While Jesse can't run with her, he will drive her to a race, cheer her on from the sidelines, and then wait for her at the finish line. "None of my previous boyfriends have done that—*none*!" Sam raves.

Their biggest adventure yet

On his wish list for life, Jesse has ticked off all the items that were on top: he has been surfing at every US Open for the last ten years, and when he hits the waves, the crowd goes wild. He owns a house close to the ocean, he just married Sam, and together they prepare for their biggest adventure yet: their first baby.

Even if fathering the baby involved a plane ride to Miami to a fertility clinic that specializes in spinal cord injuries, who cares? Sam had to realize that Jesse had this baby planned, too. He wants a boy and has picked out the name years in advance: Dorian Blue Billauer. Dorian, because surfer Shane Dorian is his idol. Blue, because it's the color of the ocean, which represents freedom. "Soon I'll have my own little helper who can push me in the waves," he beams.

He surely accomplishes the last and arguably the most important point on his list: he enjoys life, to the fullest. He has always been an overachiever.

12. Forgive

"I will be joyful, dammit!"
Why Cindi Lamb isn't MADD anymore[1]

> *Find a place inside where there's joy,*
> *and the joy will burn out the pain.*
>
> —JOSEPH CAMPBELL

Early Saturday morning before breakfast, in a barn in rural Cecil County, Maryland, a strong soprano is already belting out the happy tune Judy Garland made famous:

> *Forget your troubles, come on get happy*
> *You better chase all your cares away*

Cindi Lamb is rocking into her weekend, her whole body vibrating with the rhythm.

The fact that Cindi wakes up and feels like singing first thing in the morning is an accomplishment; that she can dance at all is a miracle. "They told me I would always walk with a limp," she says. "But if you tell me there is something I cannot do, my reaction is, 'Really? *Watch this!*'"

The world's youngest quadriplegic

Many Americans know the first part of Cindi Lamb's story: On the morning of November 10, 1979, Cindi strapped her five-month-old daughter Laura into the car seat to fetch groceries at a store in Frederick, Maryland. She was driving the speed limit, fifty miles per hour. Though it was only eleven a.m., thirty-seven-year-old Russell Willows had already downed a few beers and two pints of Canadian Mist whisky before making his way home in the uninsured Charger he had borrowed from his girlfriend without her permission. On the narrow country lane, Willows swerved across the centerline at seventy miles per hour and struck Cindi's new pickup truck head-on. The impact of the crash propelled Cindi through the windshield and broke the straps of Laura's baby seat, hurling the baby against the dashboard and crushing three vertebrae in her neck.

Miraculously, all three survived. Willows was the least injured, Cindi had fourteen broken bones, and Laura was paralyzed from the shoulders down. She became the world's youngest quadriplegic, defying the doctors' prediction that no infant so young could survive such catastrophic injuries.[2]

Soon, details emerged of a fiasco utterly predictable and preventable. Willows was on probation for armed robbery and had more than thirty traffic violations on his record, including three prior arrests for drunk driving. He had no insurance and no license, but that didn't keep him from getting behind the wheel.[3]

As soon as her broken legs had healed enough to leave the hospital, and while taking care of her injured daughter, Cindi spearheaded a campaign against drunk driving, initially called the Laura Lamb Crusade. An interpreter for the deaf and a Tupperware manager, Cindi had no experience as an activist, but she figured, "One day Laura is going to ask me, 'What did you do about it?' At least I wanted to be able to give her a good answer."

Cindi banded together with Candy Lightner, who had lost her teenage daughter in a drunk driving crash. They launched Mothers Against Drunk Drivers (MADD).[4] Laura was a captivating, charming girl who had inherited Cindi's big blue eyes and infectious smile. Together the trio changed the world.

In the 1980s, drunk driving was the leading cause of death for people under thirty-four, killing a victim every twenty-three minutes,[5] but nobody had successfully funneled the families' outrage into meaningful political action on a national level. The beverage industry touted the mantra that drunk driving was a matter of personal freedom. Laura Lamb was a game changer. When Cindi wheeled cherubic Laura into the public eye, the toddler's limp body rendered that personal freedom argument instantly obscene.

Fighting the odds

Cindi had every excuse not to launch an emotional political campaign. She drove over an hour each day to Johns Hopkins Pediatric Intensive Care Unit to be with Laura, despite overwhelming pain from her own injuries. "I had such a difficult time trying to care for my son in all of this," Cindi recalls. Alan Junior was just ten months older than Laura. Cindi's marriage to her husband, Alan Lamb, imploded six months after the crash. He moved out, taking little Alan with him, a decision Cindi "regrets to this day."

Suddenly she was a single mom, torn between caring for her injured child and the necessity of earning a living. She never took a cent of child support from Laura's father, nor did she claim a welfare check. "My dad always said, 'You pull yourself up by your bootstraps,'" she states matter-of-factly. "You take care of yourself."

Cindi transformed herself into a formidable activist, appearing on *60 Minutes, 20/20, The Phil Donahue Show, Good Morning America,* and at countless rallies. With Laura next to her during a press conference about lowering the legal blood alcohol content for drivers, Cindi recited a moving poem she had written as a plea to prevent further crashes:

> *I have a different Laura now; she's stronger than a tree.*
> *She cannot move her body, but she can move you and me.*
> *I shed my tears in bed at night, but I don't cry alone.*
> *There are thousands of parents whose kids will never come home.*
> *Please remember Laura Lamb, she fought the odds and won.*
> *She's taught us how to fight the odds so that all kids can walk and run.*

Within five years, MADD grew to 600,000 volunteers; by the 1990s, MADD was America's favorite charity.[6]

MADD's activists were instrumental in lowering the legal blood alcohol content to 0.08 (it was 0.15 in Maryland at the time), raising the legal age for drinking alcohol from eighteen to twenty-one, convicting more drunk drivers, and changing the cultural paradigm. Cindi estimates that the changes initiated by MADD have saved 250,000 to 300,000 lives since MADD's inception in 1980.[7]

Sometimes, when Cindi talks about MADD, she challenges people to consider, "Who are these 300,000 people that are now walking the face of the earth that otherwise would have been killed by a drunk driver if it weren't for thousands of MADD volunteers? Is it your mom? Your brother? Is it you?"

Cindi couldn't save her daughter, but she helped to save thousands of others.

Active engagement as a lifeline

While not every parent is ready to take on the world and willing to speak about their tragedy in public, for some, active engagement becomes a lifeline. Candy Lightner, Cindi's MADD partner in the early years, says that one of the reasons she so immersed herself in the cause was "to avoid the painful grieving over her daughter's death."[8]

I have spoken with many parents who channeled the unbearable grief of losing a child into activism. Some claim transforming their sorrow into a lightning rod for change saved their own lives, when the purpose and maybe also the busyness of taking up a cause served as an antidote to the utter despair. Ultimately, though, they still had to work through their grief, buoyed by the newfound alliances with other survivors. Psychologists have observed significantly less depression among parents who reinvested their energy into helping others.[9] This was the only way they could find any meaning in a meaningless tragedy: as a call to advocate for change.

Commit random acts of kindness

"People often ask me what they should do when they are distraught," says Cindi. Her answer is exactly the same as Rick Allen's, Jesse Billauer's, and Meggie Zahneis's: "Help someone else who is worse off than you are. It always works."

It does not have to involve full-time activism. My sister-in-law Tami and her husband Brett have declared the anniversary of their daughter's passing a "Random Acts of

Kindness Day." On the saddest day of their year, they call for kind gestures to strangers and friends, anything from helping an elderly person shop for groceries to distributing warm clothes to the homeless. This way, they cultivate positive moments while remembering their daughter. They are watering flowers in the desert.

You are not alone

It is crucial to recognize that one is hardly alone. This was, in fact, the teaching the historical Buddha Shakyamuni gave to an inconsolable mother who came to him with the corpse of her son, wailing and threatening to throw herself off a cliff. She begged him to revive her son. He told her to go from house to house and to collect a mustard seed from every family where nobody has died. She went from door to door, and everywhere she heard variations of the same tune. "We just lost our brother," or "No, not here, we lost a family member not long ago." Eventually, she understood—she was not the only one.

When my sister-in-law Tami lost her child, her despair was so all encompassing that her family worried greatly she would choose to join her daughter "on the other side." Tami and her husband Brett have always been compassionate people. Rather than becoming absorbed in the overwhelming pain of their loss, for them the loss brought to the forefront the suffering we all have in common. When such a tragedy strikes, it is easy to become isolated in a cocoon of despair. Almost everybody who suffers greatly feels they are alone in the world and that nobody else can understand the depth of their despondency. From the moment their daughter fell ill, Tami and Brett made a point of visiting the bedsides of other toddlers in the hospital who never received visitors. Living through the stress of seeing their daughter through six heart surgeries made it all the more important to them to support others in distress.

Eventually Tami found a purpose in volunteering for Compassionate Friends, the self-help group for bereaved parents. For Tami, it was a safe place to cry and vent. This might be too much to bear for some: Brett found it hard to continuously overhear the phone calls of other bereaved parents—it was like death arriving at their house several times a week all over again.

There is no right way to grieve, no judgment in each path chosen. Each one of us needs to find our own way into healing after loss.

"This is how you get unstuck, Stuck," writes Cheryl Strayed to a grieving mother. "You reach. Not so you can walk away from the daughter you loved, but so you can live the life that is yours—the one that includes the sad loss of your daughter, but is not arrested by it. The one that eventually leads you to a place in which you not only grieve her, but also feel lucky to have had the privilege of loving her."[10]

Focus on what you have in common

Focus on what you have in common with others. Join a group, any group, where people will listen and try to understand you. Many find a support group that focuses on their specific trauma the most helpful. For others, it's a church or a nonprofit they want to support. Finding the right group might take time. What sets Cindi apart is that she did not stop after visiting five churches, or ten. Even after one church gave her a cruel welcome, she did not give up on finding a community that was right for her. Please don't give up looking; your group is out there. And it can save your life.

Cindi lives in the countryside now, surrounded by rolling hills, in an idyllic oversized barn with a firehouse-red roof. The sign next to her desk reads, *Well-behaved women rarely make history.* Two Nigerian dwarf goats, two stray cats, two Jack Russell terriers, and ten chickens compete for her attention and affection, along with her husband, Gordon Wiley, and her mom, Millee Bush, an exuberant, quick-witted eighty-five-year-old in neon green sneakers. "My mom has been my best friend since I was a little girl. She is *always* on my side."

Gordon stokes a fire outside to relax on Friday night, while Cindi looks back at sixty years that have included more tragedies than most people have seen on TV.

The success with MADD is not why I include her in the book. I include her because of how she eventually came to meet the drunk driver whose actions mangled and finally killed Laura.

Promise to kill

After the accident, Cindi was seething with anger. Though both her legs were still in casts and she was pushed into the courtroom in a wheelchair, she managed to lunge at Willows, and the court police had to yank her off him. She hated him with all her might, and he returned the sentiment by threatening to silence her for good once he got out of prison. "I hated you every time you came on TV, and you would say my name over and over again," Cindi remembers him saying later.

The two simmered in their separate lockdowns of hate. Willows did five years behind bars: two for the accident, and three more for violating his probation. (Later, even he admitted that he deserved a harsher sentence.) After he was released, he was busted for driving drunk once again, for which he was locked up for three more years in 1987.[11]

Cindi refueled her hate for him with every helicopter ride to the hospital when Laura stopped breathing, with every seizure that necessitated another emergency intervention, and during the countless nights when she woke up multiple times to turn Laura's flaccid body from one side to the other. Did he have any idea what it was like to care for a paralyzed toddler? Did he ever contemplate that this exuberant girl would never feel a hug, play patty-cake, or ride a bike? Could he empathize with the lack of sleep a single mother feels when she has to get up at all hours during the night? Laura could not regulate her temperature; she had to be kept warm in winter or cooled in summer. "For several years I was crazy from the lack of sleep," Cindi remembers.

In the meantime, she got on with her life, worked as an advertising manager for a radio station, and married a handsome transmission builder who fell head over heels for the perky blonde and her adorable daughter. "Ray never saw the wheelchair and the respirator," Cindi recounts proudly. "All he saw was Laura and me."

By the time Laura was three, she could hardly breathe by herself anymore and needed the help of the respirator almost constantly. Only then did the Lambs qualify for in-house medical help. Twenty nurses began to rotate daily through their six-hundred-square-foot home on the Chesapeake Bay, changing diapers, suctioning Laura every twenty to thirty minutes, providing chest physiotherapy, girding her with full-body braces, dashing to the hospital when Laura was shaken by seizures and wracked with broken bones due to atrophy and osteoporosis. "But through it all, Laura never once complained. Not a word," Cindi remembers. "Fact is, Laura was known for her light—her joy and love. She always wanted to be around people. But most of all, she loved to dance. I would hold her and we would dance around and around and around while she giggled with squeals of delight. She was just a bucket of joy."

The nurses afforded Cindi the space to invite some cheer back into her own life, and she instinctively knew that this was crucial for her own survival. She began performing in dinner theater, singing and dancing in temporary reprieves from the intensive care unit her house had become.

Recharge your batteries

I include this example deliberately, as you might wonder how Cindi could sing and dance when her child was suffering. Anyone who cares for a severely ill person knows that it is vital for caregivers to recharge their own batteries. If they run out of energy, everyone suffers. Don't ever tell a caregiver not to look after themselves or not to invite joy in their lives.

The birthday shock

On February 12, 1986, which happened to be Cindi's birthday, a man and a woman from the health insurance company showed up at her house. Instead of a birthday gift, they delivered bad news. "We can't cover Laura anymore." The insurance limit—$3.2 million—had been used up. The home care—twenty nurses rotating to monitor, ventilate, and protect Laura around the clock—cost $40,000 a month, and had become too expensive. Laura was to be placed in an institution. Cindi protested with all her might, "No way! I won't let my child be taken to an institution."

Together with her brother Steve, she hatched a plan to write a duplicitous bestseller that would earn enough royalties to pay the nurses: *The Glove Box Guide to Drinking and Driving*, to be placed in every car. It didn't come to that.

On the evening of March 9, Cindi was performing with her theater group when she received an urgent call from the nurse. Laura had a seizure. During seizures, the brain does not receive enough oxygen. Laura's seizures usually lasted a minute or so; this one lasted over an hour. Cindi "knew right away what this meant." She rushed to the Johns Hopkins Hospital, as she had done a zillion times before.

Three days later, on March 12—the day she was to be transferred to the institution—Laura passed away.

"I don't think that's a coincidence," says Cindi. "I don't believe *anything* is a coincidence. God has a plan."

Sex, drugs, and alcohol

Laura's death propelled Cindi into a depression so severe she contemplated putting a gun to her head. The tiny house turned into a huge, empty gap. No more nurses, feeding tubes, or diaper changes. No more Laura.

On a hot Sunday afternoon a few months after Laura's death, Cindi was quenching her sorrow with beer and TV. Rodney Dangerfield's comedy *Back to School* came on, and Cindi had her aha moment: she would go back to college to complete her bachelor's degree in health science education. She followed through on this plan, and since 1991, has been teaching students in two local community colleges about sexuality, sports, health, and nutrition.

"I teach sex, drugs, and alcohol," she jokes, "things I know about!"

An eye for an eye

All these years, she had been playing out a recurring fantasy in her mind: With the help of friends, she would ambush Russell

Willows in a parking lot when he staggered out of his favorite bar. Killing him meant letting him off too easy. She would have her friends pin him to the ground, facedown in the dirt, and she would break his neck with a crowbar.

Did he have any idea what it was like not to be able to eat, breathe, or move on his own?

An eye for an eye, a broken neck for a broken neck, right?

After twenty-three years of fantasizing about smashing his bones, she called information and got his number. She was not exactly sure why, but she had begun to write a book about her life. To complete the memoir, she needed to interview the man who caused this tragedy. He still lived in Frederick and was hesitant to meet, but Cindi kept calling. Eventually he agreed to a breakfast at Denny's, along with their spouses, and Cindi finally got to ask him the question that had weighed on her mind all this time. "Why did you do this to my daughter? Why?"[12]

She started sobbing while he sat silent. Cindi tried hard to control her emotions, but the outrage spilled out of her.

"How many midnight ambulance trips and helicopter air-lifts do you think Laura and I went through? And collapsed lungs, pneumonia, tube feedings, cyanosis, suctioning every twenty minutes, broken legs and arms from a tiny atrophied body, heart failure, seizures, green and yellow mucus, infections, and fevers, and on and on and on." She tried to calm down, leaned across the table, and whispered, "And then, to top it all off, after playing tug-of-war with God for six long years, Laura dies!"

Cindi came unglued. She continued to pummel him with the gory accounts of a physically wrecked, limp little girl. "Over twenty years of pure hatred and loathing poured out of me like molten iron. I just couldn't stop." Until her husband Ray grabbed her arm and shouted, "That's enough!"

Could you forgive?

Then it was Russell's turn to speak. The son of alcoholics, he had started to drink at a young age, battling his own demons. He had joined the military at eighteen, was dishonorably discharged for fighting, and spent the next decade in and out of jobs, getting into trouble, trying in vain to keep in check the vast amount of anger that lingered in him. If the police had done their job, he admitted, he would have been locked up in jail long before the car crash. Behind bars, with a murderer in the cell to his left and a manslaughterer in the cell to his right, he had plenty of time to contemplate.

After a bad stretch during which he lost everything dear to him—his wife, contact with his son, and his home—he quit drinking, and was now ten years sober. "So I've had ten coherent years to think about you and your daughter," Cindi remembers him saying. "I think about it every day and every night. I feel bad always. You don't know how many times I wished and prayed that it had happened to me instead of your little girl. I wished I could bring her back. And I have been praying that someday we could meet, because I've wanted to tell you how sorry I am. It probably sounds stupid to you now, but I am sorry. I know this is crazy to ask, but do you think you could forgive me? Ever?"

Cindi could see his sorrow and feel his sincerity. "Yet with each tinge of pity I might have felt for him, the snapshots of a suffering Laura, a broken family, and the remains of my tattered heart pulsed through my body." Forgiving him seemed equivalent to spitting in her daughter's face. Looking at him, she saw wretched snapshots of Laura's suffering imprinted on his features, and she said, "No, I won't forgive you. Not now, and I doubt I ever will." But she understood that he, too, lived in hell every day.

Ray drove Cindi home. Once again, Cindi self-medicated, submerging the emotions with a six-pack of Miller Light followed by a couple of shots of Absolut vodka. The same beverages that caused her such unending grief had also been numbing the constant ache inside her. And this is so common: when facing a challenge, the first reaction of 75 percent of men and 30 percent of women is to reach for a pint of high-proof.

Does it help? No.[13]

Do many of us do it anyway? You bet.

"I began to recognize that I was trying to stop the pain and find solace in a beer can, in a shot glass. I knew I was heading for danger." Cindi knew all the warning signs of alcohol dependence by heart; she had taught this information to her college students for over twenty years. "My hatred was eating me alive. I couldn't stand it anymore. I felt like I was being flushed down a toilet, swirling and spiraling downward, getting really close to being sucked down the hole for good. Something had to change."

Cindi felt a spiritual need was not being met in her life, and she began church shopping. For a year, she visited over a dozen churches. "So many churches seemed so dry, so lifeless, so pointless. The pastor at one church told me that because I did not baptize Laura before she died, she was not in heaven. I wanted to just give up."

Uncompromising compassion

This is rural Maryland, where the Amish rise and retreat with the sun, walking barefoot, working their meadows with their traditional horse carts, refusing electricity, central heating, and cars. Cindi takes me to a vegetable stand by the roadside, where a kind-faced Amish woman sells us juicy peaches and tomatoes. Gordon and Cindi remember well how, in 2006, an armed milkman shot ten schoolgirls in the nearby West Nickel Mines School, a one-room Amish schoolhouse—killing five of them before turning the gun on himself. The Amish forgave the shooter the same day, instantly understanding that the killer and his family, too, had suffered great loss and pain. They comforted the shooter's family and invited his widow to one of the funerals. Their forgiveness and mercy was so uncompromising and absolute that it shocked the world in international headlines. "That's *compassion*!" Cindi's husband Gordon exclaims, his voice ringing with incredulous admiration. "It's mind-boggling and admirable that they could do this."

Both Cindi and Gordon admit their inability to muster such instant generosity. "I know it says to forgive in the Bible," Cindi seconds. "I always knew I should do it, but when you suffer such a great loss it is really, really hard. I could not do it."

The visitor

Cindi had been brought up Christian, but her faith faded and as a teenager she decided the Bible was "just made-up stories."

However, when Cindi lost consciousness after the car crash, she felt "hands under my thighs and torso lifting me up. I was like, wait a minute, this is not the ambulance guy." She felt she was in "a different warp, not on earth anymore." Much like physician Rhonda Cornum, Cindi's rational, scientific mind had always thought out-of-body stories were subjective experiences due to adrenaline and endorphins. Experiencing a near-death experience herself, however, she could no longer doubt it was real. "I was going up and I could feel everything dropping off me—my bills, my painful marriage, all my physical burdens—until I turned into a sphere. All of a sudden I started feeling love, or rather, I *became* love, the kind of ultimate mother-love, how you always wanted to be loved. I transformed into a sphere of light and energy."

She hoped she could just keep going and leave her worldly troubles behind, but then "all of a sudden something stopped me, I felt like a hand pressing my head down. I couldn't keep going. When I came to, I was back in the crash. Laura was on the floor in her puffy yellow snowsuit, gasping for air and crying. Laura! I needed to be there for Laura."

Since then, she has come to accept the presence of something greater than herself. "It's not a case of me *believing* in Jesus Christ, *believing* in an afterlife. I *know* Jesus was here. I *know* there is more!"

Still, she could find no church large enough to hold her sorrow.

A year after the meeting with Russell Willows, while sitting in her office, out of nowhere "the visitor" came. She remembers the exact moment: August 26, 2001, at nine thirty in the morning. She was overcome by a feeling of love and unity. "God snatched me up," is the only way she can describe the moment, "power-washing" her with a divine presence, or "a spiritual orgasm, to put it in worldly terms."

After the "God-snatching," everything shifted. "I changed from the inside out." She raced to a nearby church, the Edgemere Church of God, to share her experience. People were just forming a praying circle, and welcomed her; she joined and stayed. She has been singing and praying with them ever since.

Another six months later, while driving to college, she was listening to a Christian broadcast about forgiveness. She wishes she had jotted down the words, for she cannot remember them now, but the idea of forgiveness suddenly penetrated her heart and touched her core. "I sat in the parking garage at Towson University and I forgave. I meant it. It was over."

She describes the experience as "tons and tons of lard falling off my shoulders. I was just *so relieved*!"

The common denominator: pain

Cindi called Russell Willows to set up another meeting, but didn't tell him why. She scheduled it for the day she was going to be baptized, drove to Denny's, and without much ado, told him, "I forgive you with all my heart."

This is how Cindi remembers the meeting: "Russell finally looked me in the eye, and then down at the floor. He took in a deep, long breath, held it, and when he let it out, that breath hit the floor like a building. It was audible. His shoulders slumped forward, like it was the very last breath he had to give. I will never forget the sound of that one breath leaving his body, that massive thud." He looked at her and said, "You'll never know what you have done for me."[14]

She squeezed his hand. "We have something in common. Pain. We both have had immense pain in our lives. I think it's time we dumped it. I'm dumping my pain right here and now, at the counter of Denny's in Frederick. And I want you to do the same." He nodded.

Russell confessed that he, too, had found God, though maybe not in a formal way, and that he had been praying for Cindi's forgiveness every single day of his ten sober years.

Cindi was blown away. "Whew! I was shocked to realize I had just been answering *his* prayers. I still get chills just thinking about when he told me that."

They hugged, she drove to church to get baptized, and then she threw herself a baptismal party that evening to celebrate with a hundred friends.

Forgive

"Forgiving him was like getting out of prison," says Cindi. "I shouldn't have been in prison to begin with. Everything changed that day. Everything changed that day that God snatched me up, and everything changed the day I forgave him. That change continues to this day!"

Just like resilience, forgiveness isn't something that we either have or don't have. It's a skill we practice. We might think forgiveness is all about the other person, but it actually benefits us the most. For instance, when researchers interviewed 10,000 Americans, they found that those who described themselves as "holding grudges for years" were also suffering disproportionately from heart attacks, high blood pressure, stomach ulcers, back pain, and headaches.[15] There is a clear link between forgiveness and better health, fewer medical symptoms, and better sleep.[16]

But forgiveness cannot be forced. Cindi had *wanted* to forgive for many years. Her forgiveness seems to have come about suddenly and miraculously, but if you read closely, you notice that it was a long process of nurturing her heart to become big enough to include the man who killed her daughter. The British Forgiveness Project[17] offers a wealth of inspiring stories of people who arrived at forgiving their perpetrators, and a "Forgiveness Toolbox" with many of the elements Cindi used: broadening our understanding to include others' perspectives; building bridges by relating to another person's pain; empathy, curiosity and courage; accepting responsibility; letting go of anger and bitterness; and finding our own path, regardless of what other people expect of us.

"Forgiveness is not an occasional act, it is a constant attitude," said Martin Luther King Jr.

I wish this could be the whole of Cindi's story, with a happy closure and an uplifting morale of forgiveness. But she's gone through much more.

A decade after the first car crash, Cindi's car was run over and flattened by a truck while she was stopped at a stop sign. This time, the driver was smoking a joint at the wheel. "At six thirty in the morning!" Cindi emphasizes. "First I get hit by a drunk driver, then by a pothead!" She was trapped in the wreckage for three and a half hours, screaming for Laura in brutal flashbacks until she realized she was alone this time.

Panic attacks haunted her after the second crash. She had always assumed panic attacks only befell wimps, but no, this was real. A therapist helped her get back behind the wheel.

Both crashes have left lasting physical effects: jumbled discs, severe arthritis, and "bulgy-eye pain" so paralyzing that on bad days she is unable to walk at all. On some days she questions her will to live. She just had back surgery to repair major nerve damage, but she will always have to deal with relentless pain in her lower back, hips, and knees. When her daily pain medication wears off in the afternoon, she struggles to keep her cheerful composure. "Am I still forgiving him now, when every corpuscle in me writhes with unconscionable pain?" she asks. "Yes, of course, I do. It's done. But it's a struggle."

She kept in touch with Russell Willows for some years, but then she heard that he fell off the wagon. In 2007 he lost his son Gary to liver cirrhosis and started drinking again.

Fighting fire with fire.

Life hasn't treated Cindi kindly either. First she lost her father to prostate cancer in 1996; then her brother Steve, at fifty-seven, succumbed to a sudden heart attack while lounging in his easy chair. A year later, on a camping trip celebrating their twenty-eighth anniversary, Cindi's husband Ray suddenly grabbed his chest and died ten minutes later in front of her. "I could *not believe* this was happening to me *again*! What kind of God would take your child, take your dad, take your brother, and now take your husband, too? I was so outraged with God! Your plan, God? *Really?* What the hell kind of plan is this?"

Refuse to be a victim

Cindi quotes Nietzsche's famous adage, "What doesn't kill us makes us stronger." While each death was devastating, nothing was as devastating as losing Laura. "So I say to myself, well, I was able to deal with *that*, so I should be able to make it through *this*."

This is what posttraumatic growth means to Cindi, "You get stronger from it and more determined." The more people told her to put Laura in an institution, or that she would always walk with a limp because she broke so many bones, or that her face would droop because of nerve damage, "The more I became rebellious. My rebelliousness saved me. I am just not going to succumb. I refuse to be a victim."

Knowing a gift when you get one

Cindi attributes her resilience to her parents and the loving home atmosphere they created. "I was raised wonderfully," she says. "My parents had a tremendous romance for forty-five years, I grew up in an environment where my parents were always hugging and kissing. Looking at life optimistically, because your parents are optimistic, that's a good basis in life." Her mother is an adorable and chipper presence in the house.

After her husband's death Cindi became close with her husband's best friend, Gordon. They fell deeply in love. Within two weeks Gordon asked for her hand, and they married six months after Ray died. The neighbors still gossip, but Cindi is unfazed. "I have never been happier. Gordon is a gift. I know what gifts are and I recognize when I get them. Today is a gift!"

Laugh for any reason

More than anyone else I've ever met, Cindi, her mom, and Gordon constantly count their blessings, all the time. They remind each other of the little things they appreciate in life, point at the yellow gardenias flowering lushly, and marvel at everyday wonders that most people take for granted—a good cup of coffee in the morning, the sun, the sky, and each other. "The biggest component in our relationship is laughter," Cindi says before breaking into a heartfelt, full-belly laugh. For no reason. Other than that having laughter in your life is a good reason in itself.[18]

The idea that laughter is medicine has now been confirmed by studies that show how laughter triggers the release of happiness hormones and brain waves similar to the epiphany experienced in a meditative state.[19]

Viktor Frankl called humor "another of the soul's weapons in the fight for self-preservation" and "a trick learned while mastering the art of living."[20]

Cindi has started a side business as an entertainer. She sings at events and birthdays, and often at fund-raisers for charities. She constantly looks to help others in need. "I have had so much crap in my life, there must be at least ten people running around with no crap in their life," exclaims Cindi. "I figure it must be an easy road from now on!"

I am startled to learn that she especially likes to sing at funerals. "Because I've been to so many funerals, I've been in their shoes and I understand their needs."

Friends have asked her many times: "How can you still sing? Why are you still happy?" To which Cindi answers, "God, sex, and beer!" She laughs, but then turns serious. "It's God, my mom, and Gordon that saved me."

A church party like no other

One Sunday, Cindi invites me to her church. Driving through the countryside with her is a study in joyfulness. "Look at that!" the bubbly blonde exclaims every few minutes, pointing at a whimsical farm, a bald eagle circling above us, or the soft swells of the meadows she must have passed millions of time. "Isn't this *awesome*? Love it, love it, *love* it!!!"

Even when we hit a cloud of freshly dispensed manure, she shouts, "Smells *lovely*!" I am pretty sure she revels in delight all the same when no one is with her.

Edgemere Church of God is a redbrick church in a blue-collar neighborhood. In her beautiful, deep, pitch-perfect voice, Cindi belts out "Get Happy," the same song she practiced early that morning in her barn. A hundred churchgoers rise from their benches, clapping and cheering; one woman dances through the aisles waving colorful flags. I have never seen a church party like this. "We sing praises to God like he's standing right next to us, like it's midnight on New Year's Eve in Times Square," Cindi quips about the buoyant crowd. "When I walk in here, I feel like I'm being hugged from my hair roots to my pinky toes. How can you not jump up and down with joy when we're celebrating God?"

Forget your troubles, come on get happy
You better chase all your cares away

It could be the theme song of her life.

"When I sing, I'm no longer Cindi, I do forget all my troubles. I'm consumed by the Holy Spirit. If I can just bring some joy to someone else!"

She does not sing *despite* her hardships, but because.

A cathartic passage into the past

After church, we drive back to the Chesapeake Bay and turn down a quiet side street, pulling up to the quaint beach hut where Cindi took care of Laura in the last years of her life. When Cindi first picked me up from the airport, she broke down crying, confessing how afraid she was of revisiting painful passages from her past, but now she is eager to return. It was her idea, a very emotional homecoming that she simultaneously anticipates and dreads.

Luckily, the new owner is a charming fisherman who is delighted to show us around his picture-perfect beach pad. Cindi is thrilled to discover he kept the bathroom tiles her brother Steve had laid. That the house is still standing proudly is a testimony to resilience in itself after Hurricane Sandy washed away a good chunk of the shoreline. "This is a cathartic visit," she exclaims, oscillating between tears and smiles.

"You just can't crumble," Cindi says. "The word that appears the most often in the Bible is not God, not love, not ethics, it's joy. JOY!"

After a few days with her I realize that Cindi's joyfulness is not just her nature, but a deliberate effort to keep her soul afloat, and not to drown in the ocean of misery that has risen to flood her life. "I am responsible for my thoughts, and I work hard to keep them upbeat," she says. "I will be joyful, dammit!"

Pastor Suzi Nowak introduced Cindi in church as "the most cheerful person you'll ever meet."

13. Love

"Nobody can do it alone"
America's civil rights icon Maya Angelou
turned clouds into rainbows[1]

> *I have decided to stick with love.*
> *Hate is too great a burden to bear.*
> —MARTIN LUTHER KING JR.[2]

How can this end well? A girl, three years old, is sent across the American plains like a postcard. Responsible parents don't even let their kids walk to kindergarten alone, but night-club singer Vivian Baxter is getting a divorce, and her brats are now a burden. So Maya and her brother, four, find themselves in a train car all by themselves. The journey takes days. Fellow travelers feed them potato salad, and conductors help them switch trains. Name tags on their wrists prevent them from getting lost: "Marguerite and Bailey Johnson Jr., from Long Beach, California, en route to Stamps, Arkansas"[3]—a dusty, cotton-picker dump, where racial segregation is so ubiquitous that Marguerite—Maya Angelou—later joked that blacks were not even allowed to eat vanilla ice cream, only chocolate.

Thus begins Maya Angelou's biography, and this ominous start is only the beginning to a life that will come to know many more incredible episodes, as well as epic battles to erase "the ugly graffiti on the walls of her psyche," as Bill Moyers once said about her.[4]

Nightclub dancer, singer, prostitute, pimp, journalist, actress, director, Martin Luther King Jr.'s right-hand woman, America's national conscience: Maya Angelou's life has woven the strongest fabric for her thirty books—thirty mirrors she held up to America. She was a pioneer in many disciplines: the first black streetcar conductor in San Francisco; Hollywood's first black director; the first black poet to read at a presidential inauguration; the first black woman to describe her life in such captivating, drastic terms that her book made the bestseller list for two years in a row. Barack Obama revealed that his mother, a huge fan of the poet, named his sister Maya after her.

Posttraumatic growth is something Maya Angelou knew all about. Despite the many episodes of violence and loss in her life, she learned never to give up. "When it looks like the sun wasn't gonna shine anymore, God put a rainbow in the clouds. Imagine!"[5] She hummed the lyrics from an old African American folk song. "I've had a lot of clouds, but I have had so many rainbows."[6]

She even had the ceiling in her Harlem town house painted with clouds in a light blue sky. When we talked in the autumn of 2013, Maya Angelou spoke deliberately, every sentence piercing the air as sharp as a pencil. It was one of the last interviews she would give before we lost her bright light just seven months later on May 28, 2014.

During our talk, she sometimes gasped for air because of a collapsed lung, but her passion and candid humor blazed. She confronted her age and arthritis with the same kind of gung ho spirit she brought to life. "When I wake up with pain, I just tell the pain, 'Get out! I did not invite you into my body!'

I actually say that out loud," Dr. Angelou rasped in her deep voice, as she looked back on her life with wisdom and verve.

A hurricane and some fierce storms

As abruptly as Vivian Baxter had deported three-year-old Maya and her brother, she ripped them out of Stamps four years later and transplanted them to Saint Louis. The kids rejoiced briefly in the reunion with the bubbly nightclub singer. Maya Angelou described her mother as "a hurricane in its perfect power."[7]

Baxter's boyfriend, Mr. Freeman, took advantage of the mother's night shifts and preyed on young Maya, raping her before she turned eight. He ordered her to keep silent, threatening to kill both her and her brother. But when her mother discovered the bloodstained underwear, Maya revealed the name of the rapist. Mr. Freeman was sentenced to a year in prison—and, unbelievably, released the next day.

A few days later the police found his body behind the slaughterhouse, beaten to death. "I thought my voice had killed him," said Dr. Angelou. "That was my seven-year-old logic, so I stopped talking. My mother's family and my mother tried their best to woo me away from my mutism, but they didn't know what I knew: My voice could kill."[8]

Spanking didn't get Maya to talk either, so Vivian Baxter shoved the sullen, taciturn girl off to her grandmother in Stamps again. This, said Dr. Angelou, "was the best thing that could happen to me!" For five years after the rape, she did not speak. Instead she withdrew into the universe of books, reading every tome on the shelves in the minuscule Stamps library. Perhaps in these speechless years she uncovered the force of language that she later unleashed on artists, civil rights leaders, and presidents. She learned by heart the wise lines of Edgar Allan Poe and Shakespeare's sonnets, convinced that Shakespeare must have been a black, barefooted chit like her—how else could he have known about abuse and calamity so intimately?

A course book in mastering posttraumatic growth

Maya Angelou is in this book for many reasons. I admire her for her vigorous, emphatic art of writing, for her unabashed self-confidence, her untiring work for women and blacks. A rare and rich treasure of wisdom, she is one of the greatest icons of the civil rights movement and one of the most distinguished African American authors. Her life's achievements were acknowledged with three Grammys, the National Medal of Arts, and the Presidential Medal of Freedom. But I think she also deserved a Nobel Prize for posttraumatic growth. Her life was her greatest piece of art.

Her biography reads like a course book in mastering the vicissitudes of existence. She gave this book its title because when asked how she rose above hardship, she defined her emergence as "bouncing *forward*, going beyond what the naysayers said."[9] Speaking about the "blessed components of resilience," she said, "A person who resists being tied down and bound and made less than herself is able, by resisting, not only to be better than the naysayer would believe, but she's also able to lift up the naysayer."[10]

Taking up the battle

Innumerable studies tell us that children like Maya Angelou, who were sexually abused or raised in a climate of poverty and violence, are more prone to posttraumatic stress, depression, addiction, and other severe emotional and physical issues. They are less likely to succeed in society, find and hold well-paying jobs, and develop healthy long-term relationships. Their disadvantage is compounded by the kind of unstable parenting and racial violence that Maya Angelou grew up with. Scientists show that neglect in early childhood leads to lasting changes in people's brain functions, making them less stress-resistant and more fearful as adults.[11] For decades, researchers believed that abused children were doomed to fail.

More than a million children are abused every year in the United States alone,[12] so we better figure out fast how to protect and promote them. "As the world gets concerned, how do you shift the goal from surviving to thriving?" asks child psychologist Ann Masten.

Maya Angelou had an answer.

"Take up the battle. Take it up!" she rallied. "This is your life, this is yours! You make your own choices. You can decide life isn't worth living. That is the worst thing you can do. How would you know? Pick up the battle and make it a better world. It can be better, and it must be better, but it is up to us."[13]

Stretch, stretch, stretch yourself

Before you interject the obvious—that we ordinary mortals cannot hold a candle to Maya Angelou's fiery grace—let me tell you that she wouldn't have accepted such an excuse. "If a human being dares to be King, or Gandhi, Mother Theresa, or Malcolm X, if a human being dares to be bigger than the condition into which she or he was born, it means so can *you*. You can try to stretch, stretch, stretch yourself."[14]

Not only did Maya Angelou prove her own words, but the country's foremost child resilience expert, Ann Masten, too, vetoes the notion that resilience is rare and reserved for exceptional children with extraordinary talents such as Maya Angelou. "Resilience is common and grounded in ordinary relationships and resources" is the uplifting upshot of Masten's decades of research.[15] That's why she calls our innate capacity to bounce forward "ordinary magic."

The first psychologist to discover that a surprising number of at-risk children do well was Norman Garmezy, often lovingly dubbed "the grandfather of resilience theory."[16] In the 1960s he observed that many children of schizophrenics had grown into successful, happy adults, and he wondered what made the difference for them.[17]Ann Masten collaborated closely with Garmezy at the University of Minnesota. "We focused on the gloomy for such a long time. It really bothers me that when people hear about the evidence on trauma, child abuse, and in utero exposure to alcohol, they *assume*, 'Oh, I must be totally damaged.' People pick up this idea, but there are many opportunities for reprogramming in the course of life. Resilience does not mean you don't have any scars, but I am continuously amazed by the human ability to reinvent ourselves."

Reboot your life

"As human beings, we're reprogrammable to a degree the pioneers of resilience couldn't even have imagined. We are dynamic systems; we can change," asserts Ann Masten. She likens the process to a computer restart. "Sometimes when things are all tangled up, you reboot it, you start over, and things straighten themselves out."

You are not a statistic. Don't let anybody tell you that your past defines who you can grow to be.

So, how do we hack into the programming code of this resilience reboot?

Masten and Garmezy spent decades looking at the factors that set resilient children apart, such as intelligence,[18] personality, and self-mastery. But as we discussed in chapter 2, one factor stands out above all: the support of a loving adult.

Of all the "many, many resilient people" Ann Masten has met over the course of four decades, she's noticed they unfailingly have had one thing in common. "You just don't see examples of people who made it on their own." When parents and teachers fail a child, in the end it does not matter so much who steps up, but that *someone* steps up and encourages the child to believe in herself, whether it is siblings, neighbors, or friends. "One woman's unexpected helpers were homeless women," Ann Masten recounts. "Though they were not doing that well themselves, they intervened in that girl's life. They told her, 'You can be somebody,' and they went and got help. They played an important role. I think this is a very hopeful notion."

Find your mentor

In *Raising Resilient Children*, Robert Brooks and Sam Goldstein describe "a basic ingredient in nurturing hope and resilience in our children as the presence of at least one adult who communicates to a child, through words and actions, 'I believe in you and I will stand by you.' "[19] The late Dr. Julius Segal called such a supportive person a "charismatic adult." As we discussed earlier, just one supportive adult could outbalance risky genetic factors in maltreated children. "The power of one adult to change the life of a child," Brooks and Goldstein urge, "must never be underestimated."[20]

What we mustn't forget is that these supportive adults often didn't appear in a child's life by luck or magic. Resilient children are especially good at forging connections, at reaching out, at recognizing trustworthy people and asking them for help.

Childhood is a time when we are most vulnerable and in need of support; but at any stage of life we still need people who value us, act as confidants, and stand by us no matter what.

Liberation through love

Maya Angelou came to exactly the same conclusion: "Nobody ever does it alone. Experience allows us to learn from example. But if we have someone who loves us—I don't mean who indulges us, but who loves us enough to be on our side—then it's easier to grow resilience, to grow belief in self, to grow self-esteem. And it's self-esteem that allows a person to stand up."[21]

Young Maya clearly suffered from the knowledge of having been rejected by her birth parents. The thought that her mother "would laugh and eat oranges in the sunshine without her children"[22] was too much to bear. She and her brother pretended their mother had died.

What life had in the cards for her didn't look promising. But there was one crucial difference: "My grandmother! She was the greatest person I ever met. I thought she was probably God! She loved me unconditionally." Maya is convinced that these injections of self-confidence made all the difference. Her brother Bailey, too, was a loyal companion to whom she could entrust her deepest secrets. "I am grateful to have been loved and to be able to love," she said. "Love liberates."[23]

"Sista, you gonna teach!"

Maya Angelou called her grandmother "Momma." When Maya refused to speak, Momma didn't chastise her, but simply handed her a small notebook with a pencil attached so that Maya could communicate with notes. "My grandmother said to me, 'Sista, these people making fun of you and calling you dummy—Momma don't care. You gonna be a teacher. You gonna teach all over the world!'" Maya Angelou remembers. "Amazing! I used to sit there and think, 'This poor ignorant woman! I'll never speak!' Of course, now I have dozens of doctorates and teach all over the world. It's a blessing."

Maya's mother had been unable to understand the depth of her daughter's trauma, and could provide no comfort. But Maya's grandmother, her brother, and neighbors in the tight-knit, poverty-stricken community of Stamps, accepted her for who she was, mute and all. "They really believed in me, and that made all the difference," Maya Angelou told me.

A well-educated neighbor, "the aristocrat of Black Stamps,"[24] Bertha Flowers, finally impressed upon Maya that she could not possibly love poetry if she did not read it aloud. Hiding behind the chicken coop, Maya tried to read a few lines in secret. "She gave me back my voice."

And so Maya learned, "Anything that works against you can also work for you once you understand the Principle of Reverse."[25]

"You can do it!"

A supremely intelligent and intuitive child, Maya was adept at finding help and resources, proud of her special skills, increasingly sure of her self-worth and intelligence. While her town was threatened daily by racial violence, Maya Angelou attracted the attention and support of elders in the community who took her under their wing, gently challenging and nurturing her, and expanding her horizon by introducing her to the books that became her lifeline.

Her grandmother and the community taught her crucial lessons. "They taught me to stand up for myself, to be my own best friend, to protect myself. They encouraged me to encourage myself." The difference this loving support made was integral to Maya Angelou's understanding of her self-worth.

Her family didn't do the work *for* her, but they nudged her enough so she could muster the courage to stand up for herself. "And I not only have the right to stand up for myself, but I have the responsibility. I can't ask somebody else to stand up for me if I won't stand up for myself. And once you stand up for yourself, you'd be surprised that people say, 'Can I be of help?'"

This is exactly what charismatic adults do. "That's one of the roles of these adults, to say, 'You can do it, let's try it, let's go step-by-step!' Ann Masten says, animatedly. "The mentors, the positive supporters in kids' lives, they energize our motivation."

Be a rainbow in someone else's cloud

Supporting resilience in others is the supreme way to nurture resilience in ourselves. "What are the components of resilience?" I asked Maya Angelou. She responded without hesitation, "A desire to make change. A desire to make change in your own life and in the lives of the people around you—to better, improve the life."

At the beginning of Part II we discussed how 40 percent of Americans feel as though they have no purpose in life. Here is a purpose: help others. "It is a no-fail, incontrovertible reality: If you get, give. If you learn, teach."[26]

What if you feel you have nothing to give? "We all have more to give than we give," said Maya Angelou. "At the very least you can always give good thoughts."

With this motto, she managed to not only turn her clouds into rainbows. "The thing to do, it seems to me, is to prepare yourself so that you can be a rainbow in someone else's cloud. Somebody who may not look like you, may not call God the same name you do, may not dance your dances, but be a blessing to somebody."[27]

The decision to "no longer stand by"

Whenever she received an award, Maya Angelou thanked everybody who had helped her—God, teachers, rabbis, priests—but especially her late grandmother, Annie Henderson. Maya Angelou's eyes welled up when she thought of this indomitable woman who instilled in her a strong sense of self-worth. Her grandmother, the only black woman to run her own store in Stamps, was a God-fearing, robust, dignified force unto herself. While she did not cuddle Maya and was prone to punish misdeeds with severe beatings, she impressed upon her granddaughter a strong sense of right and wrong, the trust that God would protect her, and the wisdom of tolerance. And yet, Maya had to watch helplessly when this woman, her protector, could not protect herself from the humiliation and racial slurs of white children who would storm her grocery store. Maya responded by throwing rocks at them, but eventually she understood that the rocks only hardened, rather than extinguished, her rage.

Through these experiences, Maya transformed from a quiet, submissive victim to a more outspoken, tenacious activist. At age seventeen, when she was told that the streetcar operators of San Francisco didn't accept blacks, she sat in their reception area every day for three weeks, ignoring nasty racial slurs, until she was given an application. Eventually, she made her decision to no longer stand by "with no chance of defense," but to take up her weapon of wisdom: a pen.

In her famous autobiography, *I Know Why the Caged Bird Sings,* she gave an account of her rape. She hoped that it would help other survivors of violence. "You can survive rape. You never forget it—don't even think that. But you can survive it and go on."[28]

Dr. Angelou called rape "a dire kind of evil, because rape on the body of a young person more often than not introduces cynicism, and there is nothing quite so tragic as a young cynic, because it means the person has gone from knowing nothing to believing nothing. In my case I was saved in that muteness . . . And I was able to draw from human thought, human disappointments and triumphs, enough to triumph myself."[29]

Dr. Angelou has become a "modern-day Shakespeare" for millions, her books a trusted source of wisdom through which those who suffer find kinship.

Trying to make a better world

Carrying this message of triumph into the world was exactly why Dr. Angelou kept writing, speaking, and giving. Up to the last months of her life, she filled her schedule with teaching, empowering women, and receiving awards. "I'm a teacher who writes, not a writer who teaches," she defined herself. For more than three decades, this woman who never attended college taught American studies at Wake Forest University in Winston-Salem, North Carolina. Thirty universities from all over the planet awarded her honorary titles, and she celebrated the status by asking even close friends to address her as Dr. Angelou. "I have created myself," she said proudly. The experience of the crucial difference supportive adults made in Maya's life when she was a withdrawn child impressed on her the lifelong commitment to act as a charismatic adult for others. "I would like to be of use. Anyone who can't be of use is useless. I'm not here for no reason. I am here for a purpose. So, I am a member of different organizations, trying to make a better world. I am of use, yes, people can count on me. I will do the best I can."

I asked her the question that guided me throughout my research. "Why do some people come out of traumatic experiences such as loss and abuse broken and defeated, while others soar and emerge wiser and more compassionate?" I was taken aback by the answer, expecting, I guess, a "softer" response. "We overrate what the world owes us. We really think that people owe us, that we are entitled to raises and kind treatment and even success. Well, the truth is, I don't know that we're entitled to anything. I just know that when someone is kind and generous to me, I'm very grateful. Nobody owes me anything. So when I get something, I am very pleased and I try to give it away as soon as possible. I try to add to it and give it away to someone else who needs it."

Develop an attitude of gratitude

Dr. Angelou called this "an attitude of gratitude. I think we have to be grateful. Grateful that we have *a way* to develop it. You could have died last night, you know. Be grateful. And show us the good face. Stand on the good foot. People like you better. You're more welcome. And you like yourself better." She laughed. Rather than reveling in the injustice and brutality that stamped her life, she chose to focus on the achievements. "If I live my life with self-confidence and kindness and don't get anything back from that, I'm not overcome. I have so much. I can't believe how blessed I am."

Maya Angelou learned early on from her grandmother: "Whining is unbecoming. It's just ugly. It also lets a brute know that a victim is in the neighborhood. The brute who was gonna mind his own business or victimize someone else says, he says, 'Oh, here's a victim!' And you get hurt. So it's dangerous." Just like Coco Schumann and many others in this book, she had to learn to stay strong and bite her tongue when survival in a hostile environment became her first priority.

The advice she received from her mother was to counter-balance the bleak with the blessings: "Laugh as much as possible. Laugh as much as you cry."[30]

Not invincible, but strong

Developmental psychologist Emmy Werner found "protective factors" for the children who did well, mainly in three areas: in the child, in the family, and in the community.[31] Maya Angelou had all three, just as Werner describes.

From the 1950s to the 1990s Werner followed 698 children in Kauai, Hawaii, from birth to midlife, conducting a landmark longitudinal study that examined the impact of biological and psychosocial risk factors. She discovered that one in three children were vulnerable, yet "even among children exposed to multiple stressors, only a minority develops serious emotional disturbances or persistent behavior problems."[32] Of the children living in troubled families, two-thirds "who had experienced four or more risk factors by age two developed learning or behavior problems by age ten or had delinquency records and/or mental health problems by age eighteen. However, one out of three of these children grew into competent, confident and caring adults."[33] These latter children were A students in school, developed friendships, and by the time they reached age forty, every single one of them had a job, a steady income, and zero trouble with the law. "Their very existence challenges the myth that a child who is a member of a so-called 'high-risk' group is fated to become one of life's losers."[34]

Emily Bazelon cautioned in the *New York Times*, "When it comes to abuse victims, though, this finding is rarely trumpeted, for fear that saying abuse isn't always inevitably harmful is tantamount to saying it's not always bad."[35]

No child is invincible, but we need to change the ways we think about abused and neglected children. They are stronger than we think. They need love, not prejudice. "Some of these kids come out of it, saying 'I've seen the worst there is, nothing is gonna throw me after that,'" says Ann Masten. Can we see them as survivors instead of victims? This does not mean that they did not *suffer*, or were not hurt. Tedeschi's fitting description of posttraumatic growth comes to mind: more vulnerable, yet stronger. But focusing on their strengths, rather than their humiliation, helps them reinvent themselves.

When Werner followed up with the Kauai kids in adulthood, she noticed a common thread: "the *opening of opportunities* in the third and fourth decade of life led to enduring positive changes among the majority of teenage mothers, the delinquent boys, and the individuals who had struggled with mental health problems in their teens." Among the most potent forces for positive change for these youth in adulthood were "continuing education at community colleges and adult high schools, educational and vocational skills acquired during service in the armed forces, marriage to a stable partner, conversion to a religion that demanded active participation in a 'community of faith,' recovery from a life-threatening illness or accident, and, to a much lesser extent, psychotherapy."[36] Most of the people who managed to turn their life around in later years were women.[37]

Masten calls them the "late bloomers," and Maya Angelou was one of them. Dr. Angelou recalled how, when seventeen years old and pregnant, she stood in front of the building in San Francisco that housed the beginning of the United Nations, staring enviously at the important politicians and translators who flooded in and out of the building, and dreaming herself into a bigger perspective. "I knew I had a penchant for language," she said. "If I wasn't six foot tall, black, unmarried, and uneducated, I knew I could go in."[38]

For a few dark years Maya did drift into poverty and crime, working as a prostitute and a pimp. Her dream was to become a dancer, but she wrecked her knees. She chose instead to sing (though it wasn't her passion) and quickly garnered an enthusiastic following. In Hollywood she worked with icons such as Billie Holiday, Harry Belafonte, Roberta Flack, and Sidney Poitier, sang in the chorus of *Porgy and Bess*, and became "Miss Calypso."[39]

Forgiveness as the greatest gift

Maya Angelou's greatness began to shine through when she was given a stage on which to sparkle, and even her mother came around to see her daughter blossom: "When I was twenty-two, my mother told me, 'I think you're the greatest woman I ever met. You're very kind, and you're very smart.'" Maya was startled at first, but then wondered, "'Suppose she's right? Suppose I'm gonna be somebody?' I had those loves."

Her relationship with her mother is also a testimony to the force of forgiveness. Despite the early abandonment, Maya forgave Vivian Baxter her many obvious shortcomings. At the age of fourteen she came to live with her and they slowly developed a bond. "I think we all suffer," Maya Angelou told me. "Some people seem to fall in love with the suffering and cling to it. Then it's very hard to get any work done, very hard to survive like that. You have to be honest with yourself: That action hurt me. That was unkind. And then go on about your business. But at least admit it. Dust yourself off and get on with your way. Forgiveness is the greatest gift you can give yourself."

Baxter, who had been a "piss-poor mother" of the young child by Angelou's standards, later forged a new relationship with her daughter. She even delivered the baby—Maya Angelou's only child, Guy Johnson.

Abused children can become loving parents

Ann Masten rejects the popular notion that abused children are likely to become abusers. In her home state of Minnesota, NFL running back Adrian Peterson has been accused of severely beating his four-year-old son. "People are saying, well, he is just doing what his parents did to him." Ann Masten has heard this many times. But just like Maya Angelou and Buck Brannaman, the great majority of survivors have resolved to treat their children with the love and care they wished they could have had growing up.[40] "It's generally accepted that if you're in the pattern of being abused by one or both parents, that's what you're going to do when you grow up," Buck says. "I don't agree. I believe the deciding factor all boils down to free will. People have the choice. Self-discipline prevents that streak from coming out. You need to be vigilant to guard against a slow growth in the wrong direction. You need to be cognizant of how you behave toward your wife and children. Not a day goes by when you don't think about how you want to be and how you don't want to be. It's always in the back of your mind, a burden that you carry."[41]

Ann Masten believes that, "Most people who experience

this do a much better job as parents or become particularly good parents."

However, she notes, "We are overwhelmed with children who don't have that kind of supportive adult." She recently returned from India and found it devastating "how many children there are who don't have anybody. The parents are overwhelmed with getting food and shelter." She reminds us that we must not forget the communal support we often take for granted: a bus to get to school (not to mention schools to attend), libraries to borrow books from, and so on. "If there is no school and no library, no matter how intelligent a child is, it is much harder for her to develop her potential."

Indeed, where would Maya Angelou be without that library in Stamps?

"The glorious task of reclaiming the soul"

In the fifties, another mentor entered Maya Angelou's life: Martin Luther King Jr. "He was the best we had, the brightest and most beautiful,"[42] she said after her first encounter with him. From him she learned: "We, the black people, the most displaced, the poorest, the most maligned and scourged, we had the glorious task of reclaiming the soul and saving the honor of the country. We, the most hated, must take hate into our hands and by the miracle of love, turn loathing into love. We, the most feared and apprehensive, must take fear and by love, change it into hope. We, who die daily in large and small ways, must take the demon death and turn it into Life."[43]

Maya Angelou matured into a strong-willed civil rights hero. She recounted with deep satisfaction that her life catapulted her to the hot spots of black history—Ghana, South Africa, Harlem, marches in Washington, and into the midst of the 1965 riots in the Watts neighborhood of Los Angeles.

In the summer of 1959 she organized the legendary Cabaret for Freedom, a fund-raiser for Martin Luther King Jr., and became the coordinator of his organization, the Southern Christian Leadership Conference (SCLC). After a short stint as a journalist in Egypt, she made friends with Malcolm X in Ghana. She agreed to help him build his Organization of Afro-American Unity, but Malcolm X's assassination in 1965 put an end to her involvement. The demon death became a steady shadow, with forty-nine deaths in Watts alone. Martin Luther King Jr. enlisted her to organize a march in Washington for him. She agreed, but postponed her departure until the day after her fortieth birthday. On the evening of her birthday, April 4, 1968, King was shot to death in Memphis. His murder catapulted Maya Angelou into a ruthless depression.

For many, many years she wouldn't celebrate her own birthday, but instead spent the day commemorating King with his widow Coretta Scott King, praying "for this country."

Blacks during these decades of segregation, abuse, and violence had a choice, just like any oppressed group has—they could choose submission or resistance, silence or violence, or shades in between. Maya Angelou veered among all these options at one time or another, but in the end she chose love. It seems a superhuman effort that all these decades of violence didn't turn her bitter and hateful. She felt that turning cynical meant handing a victory to the aggressors. "All my work, my life, everything I do is about survival, not just bare, awful, plodding survival, but survival with grace and faith. While one may encounter many defeats, one must not be defeated."[44]

Overcoming the fear of death

Fear, though, was her constant shadow. With the death of her beloved grandmother "Momma" in 1953, Maya lost her bedrock. Grief flipped into fear. She recounts anxiously check-ing on her son Guy, then double-checking all the locks in her house and shifting chairs under door handles. "I didn't realize that I was trying to keep death out," she told Oprah Winfrey of this period. "Then I began having trouble breathing. Fi-nally, I had to come to grips with what was the matter with me. I looked at my life and thought, 'I'm afraid to die.' And I concluded that whether I was afraid or not, I would die. It was one of the most important crossroads in my life, because once I realized that no matter what, I would do this thing, the next step was to think, 'If I am going to do the most difficult and frightening thing—dying—is it possible that I could do some difficult and maybe seemingly impossible things that are good?' You'd be surprised what coming to grips with the fact that you will die does for you."[45]

How *does* one come to grips with a big question like this? "First, tell the truth. Tell the truth to yourself first," she said from her home in Winston-Salem. "Admit that you're lonely and you do get afraid sometimes. Admit that you do overcome and that you like yourself better when you're laughing."

After King's death it took her several years to dig herself out of the dark cave of hopelessness and throw herself into fresh projects with renewed fervor. Instead of focusing on the violence and the death toll, she decided to shine a light on the accomplishments of her people. She invented the Black History Month special *Telling Our Stories* to feature black role models such as Kofi Annan, Alicia Keys, and Jennifer Hudson. "We're more alike than we are unalike. When you know that, then you can make a relationship that helps us all to be kinder, truer to each other, more courteous."

Maya Angelou was one of the rare voices of harmony in a divided America, a "global renaissance woman" whose voice did not fall on deaf ears. After she wrote and recited a poem for President Bill Clinton's 1993 inauguration, her books' circulation exploded. When President Barack Obama awarded her the National Medal of Freedom, he recited part of the inauguration poem she had written for Bill Clinton: "History, despite its wrenching pain, cannot be unlived, but if faced with courage, need not be lived again."[46]

Joy! Joy! Joy!

Dr. Angelou celebrated her many achievements "with a happy spirit, joyful that I didn't die last night. I've conducted the Boston Pops! I've danced at La Scala! I spoke at the United Nations!" One of her favorite words was "joy!"—a word she added to her signature when signing her books, with an exclamation mark!

Just like when I traveled with Cindi Lamb, in speaking with Dr. Angelou I heard joy! Joy! Joy!

Almost fifty years after she had admired the United Nations in San Francisco as a young, pregnant, uneducated girl, she did indeed get to go inside and speak in front of the heads of state. For the occasion, she composed *A Brave and Startling Truth*, a poem about rising above and beyond, and we need to hear its soaring message of hope and peace. Its final verse reads:

> *When we come to it*
> *We must confess that we are the possible*
> *We are the miraculous, the true wonders of this world*
> *That is when, and only when,*
> *We come to it.*[47]

Epilogue

You are the sky. Everything
else—it's just the weather.

—PEMA CHÖDRÖN

I love flying, especially the moment when the plane finally breaks through to a clear blue sky after taking off and ascending through a thick layer of clouds. The moment when I become part of the big sky, the endless horizon.

At times when I am grounded on earth and see nothing but clouds, I try to remember: the sun is still there, always. I can't see it this very instant, but it doesn't stop shining, just because little me is on a part of earth that is shielded right now.

This is the traditional image used in Buddhism to explain the truth beyond what we can see: the vast sky that does not become smaller just because our perspective is narrow.

There is a place beyond suffering. Not somewhere out there, but *within* us. We can connect with an awareness beyond pain and fear.

"Have you ever noticed that your awareness of pain is not in pain even when you are?" meditation teacher Jon Kabat-Zinn asks. "Have you ever noticed that your fear is not afraid even when you are terrified? Or that your awareness of depression is not depressed; that your awareness of your bad habits is not a slave to those habits; or perhaps even that your awareness of who you are is not who you think you are?"[1]

There is a wise soul in all of us, even if it's temporarily hidden amid layers of fear and grief and insecurity and anger and hurt. Sometimes the wise soul speaks up spontaneously, breaking through like the plane through the clouds, yet most of the time it needs nurturing and acknowledging.

A Christian might call it *soul*, a Buddhist *Buddha nature*, a Native elder *the spirit*. It doesn't matter what we call it; what matters is that we honor it. Connecting with this core is part of our life purpose, and a sure way to posttraumatic growth.

No one can break you. Regardless of how we have been hurt and wounded and assaulted, our core remains untouched, can never be spoiled or tainted.

Like the life force of the phoenix.

Poet May Sarton wrote:

> *It struggles now alone*
> *Against death and self-doubt,*
> *But underneath the bone*
> *The wings are pushing out.*

> *And one cold starry night*
> *Whatever your belief*
> *The phoenix will take flight*
> *Over the seas of grief.*[2]

Guide

Five effective exercises for cultivating
courage in the face of adversity

Throughout the book, survivors and experts have high-
lighted helpful strategies to deal with difficulties. In this
section, I especially recommend five simple exercises that
have been scientifically proven to fortify us for challenges,
help us through hardship, and support our recovery. I also go
into detail about these exercises because it is best to actually
sit down and practice them in formal sessions before putting
them to the test in "real" life.

I wonder if these exercises sound so simple that you might
dismiss them as too easy. For this reason, I have added some scientific evidence to further convince you to give it a try. I promise you'll be surprised how effective they are once you explore
them for yourself. Don't take my word for it, try them out!

1. MEDITATE

Take twelve minutes every morning and every evening. Why
twelve? Because a study with marines showed that the cognitive benefits of meditation decreased if they practiced less
than twelve minutes daily.[1] If you are too busy to find twelve,

take twenty. You're breathing anyway, so what do you have to lose?

Find a place that inspires calmness where nobody will disturb you; turn off your phone. If you can't find a quiet place for yourself, you can even sit in your (parked) car or at the kitchen table. Set a timer so that you are not distracted by watching the clock. Becoming aware of the most fundamental thing that keeps us alive, our breath, has profound repercussions for our health, our state of mind, our calmness, and our ability to navigate stress.

Many people think that meditation means to suppress thoughts and emotions, or not to think at all—which is impossible. The mind thinks and knows and churns. The Tibetan word for meditation, *gom*, simply means "to become familiar with," and this is what we do when we meditate: we become intimately familiar with our mind, and we learn to harness its potential. The "mind," in meditation, does not equal "brain." Many Asian traditions understand that mind and heart are intimately connected. If you ask a Tibetan to point to his mind, he will point to his heart. "Mind-heart" might be a better translation, and meditation serves to make both our minds and hearts bigger so that we can hold anything we meet with awareness and love.

Meditation in its most essential form is simply: to be present. To watch what arises, like an old man watching children play. We don't have to get involved; we just watch what unfolds, and remain aware of our breath.

When we initially start sitting quietly, the first thing we might become aware of is how loud and busy our minds are. This is called "the waterfall stage," where thoughts and ideas and fleeting memories pelt us with their pitter-patter.

But eventually, the waterfall turns into a lake. Our mind becomes a clear and deep mirror in which we see more clearly.

Whatever your faith or beliefs, being mindful and present will serve you well in all aspects of your life, especially when it comes to trauma and hardships.

What to do

Sit with your spine straight, but comfortable. You could sit in a relaxed cross-legged position on a cushion on the floor, or on a chair with the soles of both feet firmly planted on the ground. Close your eyes if this helps you focus; otherwise you may leave the eyes slightly open, gazing down softly along your nose. (In the Buddhist tradition in which I have trained, we don't close our eyes completely; we just lower the gaze. If it helps you concentrate, you may close your eyes, but generally we don't attempt to shut off our senses. We just don't follow the impulse to latch onto the sensory input.)

Your shoulders and arms should be relaxed, with your palms resting loosely on your thighs. Keep your mouth slightly open, as if to say "ah." Keep your eyes, ears, and generally all your senses open and alert, yet relaxed. These two words, in fact, encompass the most profound meditation instruction: alert, alert, relaxed, relaxed.

Now turn your attention to your breath. Breathe naturally, but fully. Feel the inbreath entering your nostrils. Follow the breath enter your body, your lungs, and deep down into your belly. Taste it there for a moment. Then feel the breath ascend again. Keep your attention on your outbreath ever so slightly. Let it go. Start over.

Breathe in, letting your awareness follow your breath. Breathe out. Let go. Breathing in, breathing out. Pay close attention.

When we get distracted by fleeting thoughts, sounds, sights, and sensations, we simply return our awareness to the breath. We don't get up to take the call, we don't make a shopping list. There is no need to keep a running commentary; we simply follow the sensations of the breath. Follow it closely, yet spaciously. The breath anchors us, and eventually spaciousness will expand within us.

All we do is to stay present. Not to alter or judge or cure or manipulate, just to observe. Bear witness to whatever arises.

At the end of your meditation, dedicate your session by bowing to yourself and the universe.

If sitting feels claustrophobic, try walking meditation. Focus on the breath and the slow movement of one foot lifting off the ground, then the other. You can also try a restorative version of yoga, which is basically meditation in movement.

Why it works

Meditation trains us in the very skills we need in order to confront adversity and recover from it. Through deep breathing, we learn to regulate stress and calm fear.[2]

Possible side effects of meditation include lower blood pressure, a better-functioning immune system,[3] and a significantly enhanced ability to tolerate pain. Meditation reduces inflammation[4] and even changes gene expression.[5] It can assuage depression more effectively than antidepressants.[6] Meditation has a proven effect on insomnia, anxiety, empathy, and concentration. It improves many of the traits we have identified as core skills of resilience: optimism, self-mastery, control, flexible thinking, and the ability to cope with stress.

Most important, meditators often report an increased sense of purpose and happiness. Richard Davidson at the University of Wisconsin suggests, "It's best to think of happiness as a skill. The current research leads us to the view that if we practice we can get better at being happy."[7]

And what else could be better than galvanizing us for life's trials?

Take it further

Meditation works its magic when we practice regularly. Just like brushing our teeth, practicing every morning and evening is more beneficial than a two-hour marathon on the weekend. It is crucial to develop a regular habit of connecting with our breath, our body, and the present moment. In addition, we can do this exercise whenever we notice we're distracted, whenever we get stressed, whenever we pass the spot where the accident happened, or before we leave the car to enter our office building. Meditation is like a pause button for our overactive minds. I always do it to anchor myself before speaking engagements and important conversations.

For a more in-depth introduction to meditation, I recommend Jon Kabat-Zinn's book *Full Catastrophe Living* and his Mindfulness-Based Stress Reduction courses (MBSR).[8]

Eventually you might want to find a meditation teacher or meditation group to support you. Meditation can be challenging, as it nudges us to be present with whatever comes up, including painful sensations and trauma flashbacks. The support of experienced meditators is crucial to help us navigate through these challenges.

2. APPRECIATE

One of the single most effective practices for our well-being is gratitude. It is easy to feel grateful when life treats us well. But when the pudding hits the fan, appreciation becomes invaluable. We can either dwell on everything that went wrong, rehashing events over and over in our mind, or we can focus on the positive. Many of this book's subjects chose the latter: Meggie Zahneis focuses on "the things I *can* do," Maya Angelou called for an "attitude of gratitude," Rick Allen chose "Life is Great!!" (with two exclamation marks) as his slogan.

And yet, when the going gets rough, it is easy to get down-trodden. To uplift our spirit, we consciously cultivate gratitude.

What to do

Every day, write down three things you are grateful for.

It could be small things—a ray of sun breaking through the clouds, your neighbor bringing you a cup of tea—or big things—a good test result, a little more movement in the legs, a baby's first steps.

Jot down the first three things that come to your mind, and then take a minute to reflect on them. What made these moments great? What does this mean to you? Is there something you can do to contribute to this good thing?

Whether you tell your diary or your computer, getting down a tangible reminder of gratitude is important.

"When this becomes a habit, you've developed the attitude of gratitude," says Karen Reivich.

Why it works

Professor Robert A. Emmons, at the University of California, Davis, calls himself "the world's leading scientific expert on gratitude." To scientifically examine the impact of gratitude, he arbitrarily divided students into three groups. For ten weeks, they were to keep a journal and record their emotional well-being, health, and behavior, anything from going for a walk, to drinking alcohol, to fighting a headache with an aspirin. He arbitrarily asked a third of the students to simply record anything that seemed important (the "neutral" group), another third to especially note down stressful moments (the "stressed" group), and the last third to list five things they were grateful for (the "grateful" group). Surprise: The "grateful" not only reported that they were more satisfied, optimistic, and content with their life, but they also had fewer medical symptoms and invested significantly more time into their fitness.[9] Follow-up studies showed that grateful people get better grades, have more energy, and they even sleep better.[10] In addition, cultivating gratitude improves our mood, and makes us more social and willing to help others.[11]

A feeling of gratitude might not come easily when the world looks bleak. That's why writing the journal is essential in redirecting our outlook. Here, "gratitude" refers not primarily to the immediate gratitude we feel after someone has helped us, but more to a general outlook on life that acknowledges the many things to be grateful for. The gratitude journal gives us a chance to pause to notice the beauty in small moments, acknowledge it, and savor it.

Take it further

Many psychologists offer variations of this exercise. Martin Seligman calls it the "What-Went-Well Exercise"[12]; the army, "Hunting the Good Stuff"; Benedictine monk Brother David Steindl-Rast, "The Good Day."[13] You could start a "gratitude challenge" on social media and share what you're grateful for with others.

Or you could take it another step further and actually express your gratitude. Think of a person you are deeply grateful to whom you have never properly thanked. Write a heartfelt, thoughtful letter in which you describe what you are grateful for and how he or she changed your life. Then read the letter to that person, either over the phone or, even better, in person.[14] People who expressed their gratitude in person showed the largest happiness boost, and it lasted for several weeks.[15]

You're welcome.

what they want in life, and one of the most urgent answers... love. The world's best-kept secret is that while everyone seems to be searching for it, love is always available. I believe that more essential than finding someone who loves us is connecting with our own capacity to love. Without loving ourselves, we cannot find love, at least not the true kind of love where we don't just use others to fulfill our needs. We cannot truly be there for others if we don't take care of ourselves, yet very often we neglect the person we rely on the most: ourselves. By loving ourselves, I don't mean cherishing I, me, and mine. I am talking about making friends with ourselves—a true, honest, warm friendship. Loving ourselves begins with taking care of ourselves: Getting sleep, physical exercise, and eating healthily are basic steps toward sanity. As obvious as this may sound, I have plenty of stressed clients who don't take care of the basics. Often they're too stressed, but even more often, there is a reason they don't prioritize themselves: underneath, they don't feel worthy or deserving. Maybe they made a fatal mistake, or they think they're "just not good enough."

In our modern culture, we hype the ego, yet we hate ourselves. We place enormous emphasis on our means, and less on our life's meaning. What we look like is considered more important than what we *are* like. Self-respect and self-infatuation are two very different traits. They are, in fact, opposites. Accepting ourselves does not mean denying negative feelings or habits we need to work on; but only by not judging ourselves can we work to change them.

What to do

Like in the meditation exercise, sit in a comfortable posture, relaxed and upright. Take a few minutes to settle by paying attention to your breath and the present moment. Then focus on your heart region and think about a person for whom you have very warm, positive feelings. It could be someone you are very grateful to, someone who got you out of a jam. It is best to begin with someone who is alive and with whom you have an uncomplicated, easy relationship, perhaps a child. Allow the warm feeling of gratitude and love to flush over you.

Then replace the focus on the breath with these thoughts:

> *May you enjoy happiness and the causes of happiness.*
> *May you be free from suffering and the causes of suffering.*

You can place the thought on the inbreath and outbreath.

Breathing in, *May you enjoy happiness and the causes of happiness.*

Breathing out, *May you be free from suffering and the causes of suffering.*

Keep repeating the wish for happiness, sending this person warm feelings, maybe in the form of light or love. What does this person look like when she or he is happy?

Next, extend this warm feeling to yourself.

> *May I enjoy happiness and the causes of happiness.*
> *May I be free from suffering and the causes of suffering.*

Spend several minutes sending yourself feelings of happiness and kindness, healing and love, whatever you need. Picture yourself happy. Don't overthink things. You can put your palm on your heart region to help you connect with your innate goodness. Stay with the feeling of warmth and kindness. If your thoughts ramble, simply redirect your attention to the breath and the wish to be happy.

Why it works

University of Texas psychologist Dr. Kristin Neff recognizes three components of self-compassion: kindness, a sense of common humanity, and mindfulness. "An ever-increasing body of research suggests that self-compassion enables people to suffer less while also helping them to thrive," she says. "One of the most consistent findings in the research literature is that greater self-compassion is linked to less anxiety and depression."[16] While harsh self-criticism elevates our stress hormone levels, a brief exercise in loving-kindness for ourselves can lower them. Neff has studied self-compassion for more than a decade and has found studies that show it not only helps trauma survivors to deal better with upsetting events but it also generally enables us to face others' suffering without becoming overwhelmed, and makes it easier for us to forgive.[17]

By practicing loving-kindness for ourselves, we enhance our ability to generate positive emotions, even when we face a distressing situation.

Take it further

One of the things I enjoy most about this practice is that we can do it in formal meditation first, but then we can carry it into daily life. When self-destructive thoughts arise, remember to return to your breath and send loving-kindness to yourself. When you routinely slip into berating yourself for a mistake, put your palm on your heart region and send yourself some kindness.

Sharon Salzberg's classic *Lovingkindness* is an immensely helpful guide for developing loving-kindness meditation.

4. LOVE OTHERS

The first step in loving others is to recognize that we are fundamentally all the same. We all want happiness, and we all want to avoid suffering. Sometimes others try to achieve their version of happiness in ways I disagree with, but when I think it through, I can still send them loving-kindness.

In the words of Buddhist teacher Sharon Salzberg, from whom I first learned the practice of loving-kindness twenty years ago, "The command to love everyone, including those that harm you—as put forth by many great spiritual teachers, such as Buddha and Jesus—has often been viewed as undesirable or even impossible. However, it is worth considering that it is in fact eminently possible and practical to wish true happiness for your enemy, for this is the only way to be free of the torment brought on by them. The benefit of this love is twofold. If it brings happiness to an enemy, this enemy is much less likely to cause harm or frustration to those around him. However, if this viewpoint of love has no immediate effect on your enemy, the mere act of loving brings with it an inner peace."[18]

What to do

Widen the circle. After practicing loving-kindness for yourself for a week or two, begin to extend loving-kindness to others. Start as in the previous exercise, paying attention to the breath, opening up to a loved one, then to yourself. From that place of warmth, extend loving-kindness to family, friends, and neutral people.

May I and all sentient beings enjoy happiness and the causes of happiness.

May we be free from suffering and the causes of suffering.

For "neutral" people, think of people in your life you usually overlook, such as a bus driver, a waitress, or all the people you pass on the street today.

Again, when your loving-kindness meditation gets hi-

jacked by discursive thoughts, don't dwell on them—just return to the breath and the thought,

May we all enjoy happiness and the causes of happiness.

Breathing out, *May we be free from suffering and the causes of
suffering.*

Why it works

Loving-kindness (called *metta* in the ancient language of Pali)
has been practiced for thousands of years, and the phrases I am
suggesting are taken from some of the oldest Asian scriptures.
They have a two-thousand-year-old proven track record, and
I find it assuring that modern science has evidenced the benefits of the practice. In a landmark study, Barbara Fredrickson
and her colleagues showed that "practicing seven weeks of
loving-kindness meditation increased love, joy, contentment,
gratitude, pride, hope, interest, amusement, and awe."[19] The
daily experience of these positive emotions helped increase life
satisfaction and lowered depressive symptoms.[20]

David Kearney at the Seattle Institute for Biomedical and
Clinical Research launched a twelve-week loving-kindness
meditation course for veterans who suffered from PTSD. A
clinical loving-kindness intervention for veterans was a first,
but the results were reassuring: loving-kindness meditation
did indeed decrease the vets' PTSD symptoms and depression.[21]

Loving-kindness meditation shows many of the same benefits in rewiring our brain as mindfulness meditation, yet in
addition it increases our empathy and our ability to be there
for others. A multinational team of researchers concluded
that "training compassion may reflect a new coping strategy
to overcome empathic distress and strengthen resilience."[22]
Loving-kindness decreases our bias toward others,[23] increases
our social connectedness,[24] and is effective long term.[25]

When longtime meditators were exposed to disturbing sounds such as a woman screaming or a baby crying, the scientists found that instead of distress and negative emotions the sounds immediately triggered love, empathy, and compassion.[26] I have met several of the accomplished meditators who participated in these studies, such as the Tibetan master Mingyur Rinpoche and the French scientist-turned-monk Matthieu Ricard, and can personally attest that they are among the kindest, most compassionate and joyful people one could ever meet.

Take it further

Eventually, after several weeks of daily practice, you could widen the circle to include "difficult" people in your life. Don't start with your biggest enemy—just begin to include people you have some difficulties with. Don't expect or force yourself to feel a certain way. It's called "practice," not "perfect." This is not the time to rehash conversations from the past or replay scenes in your mind. Stay with sending them warmth and loving-kindness. Keep it simple. Meditation is our opportunity to stay present and focus on loving-kindness.

Eventually, this practice can become a great exercise in real-life situations. When you want to support someone, but maybe don't know what to say, send them loving-kindness. When a situation tenses up, send loving-kindness. When a conflict arises, breathe loving-kindness. We are not trying to change the outside world, we are just working with our own heart—but in effect, our world might change with us as well.

I don't recommend attempting to send loving-kindness to the people who have hurt you most without guidance and having done the practice for a very long time. But eventually, as Buddha said in the *Dhammapada*, "Hate is never conquered by hate. Hate is conquered by love. This is an eternal law."

5. CONNECT

Often illness, trauma, or loss prompts us to withdraw. We need time alone, and that can be healthy. Yet to connect with others is also an integral part of the healing process. Ideally, we connect with people with whom we can establish mutual trust and understanding. As we have seen in several of the stories, it can be necessary to distance ourselves from people who are depleting our energy or who burden us with unhelpful advice. Yet it is essential that we find at least one or two people with whom we can truly connect. People who have proven to be extremely resilient also happen to be unusually creative in connecting with others.

What to do
Ask yourself:[27]

- Who are the people in my life I feel truly connected to?
- Who are the people who would refer to me as someone they feel truly connected to?
- How would I describe the quality of the connection I have with others?
- Can the quality of the connection be improved, and if yes, how?
- If no one or only one person comes to mind that I feel truly connected to, can I think of ways to connect with others in a meaningful way?

The exercise here is to reach out and connect. Even when reaching out is the last thing you feel like doing, even if you are bedridden or too sick to venture out, you can still connect, be it via phone or the Internet; you can join a nonprofit or a volunteer organization.

Sometimes we are surrounded by people and still feel disconnected. Then just listen. Listen fully, with your ears as well as your heart. Every single person on this planet wants to be heard and acknowledged.

Pick up the phone and make a call to a person or a group you would like to connect with. Follow up, and repeat as needed.

Why it works

Social support is one of the greatest buffers before, during, and after a crisis.[28] Even just holding the hand of a beloved partner lessens anxiety and pain.[29] People with social support live significantly longer, feel less pain, and are more likely to experience posttraumatic growth.[30] It literally hurts to be left out.[31] Lack of social connection is a "greater detriment to health than obesity, smoking and high blood pressure,"[32] and social isolation "is now considered a major health risk."[33]

When Harvard psychiatrist George E. Vaillant examined the lives of 236 successful Harvard sophomores in the famous Grant Study that followed them for seventy-five years, he came to a striking conclusion of what made for a fulfilled and happy life: It wasn't their IQ or family's socioeconomic status, nor the sociability and extraversion that was so highly valued in the initial process of selecting them for the study; even alcoholism and depression "proved irrelevant" for their later flourishing. What made all the difference for both their economic success and their mental and physical health was their empathic capacity and "success in relationships": their ability to love, forgive, and be grateful. "In short, it was a history of warm, intimate relationships—and the ability to foster them in maturity—that predicted flourishing in all aspects of these men's lives."[34] Vaillant summed up the recipe this way: "Don't try to think less of yourself, but try to think of yourself less."[35]

Take it further

I recommend Brooks and Goldstein's *The Power of Resilience* as a guide to strengthening our relationship with others. They encourage us to consider:[36]

- How would you like friends, relatives, and colleagues to describe you?
- Are you interacting with them in ways that would lead them to describe you this way?
- If not, what must change?

This might challenge us to make changes in the way we communicate with others.

A wise friend once told me, "If you feel lonely and cannot find anybody who takes care of you, think of someone who needs care." If you need help, think of someone who needs help more and reach out to them. If you long for someone in your life to support you and can't find this support, try a different approach: support others.

Compassion for others has been universally found to be healing, empowering, and nurturing. People who regularly volunteer for a good cause are healthier and live significantly longer, but only if they do so for truly altruistic reasons, not if they are motivated selfishly.[37] Instead of buying happiness in shops, we are actually happier when we spend money on others.[38] Even toddlers find greater happiness in *giving* treats than receiving treats.[39] So, take up a good cause!

Martin Seligman sums up the vast body of research that evidences the positive power of kindness. "We scientists have found that doing a kindness produces the single most reliable momentary increase in well-being of any exercise we have tested."[40]

Or in the words of the Dalai Lama, "Be kind whenever possible. It is always possible."

Acknowledgments

Through this book, I have made soul friends and heart connections. Whenever people asked me what I was writing about and I mentioned posttraumatic growth, it was like opening a gate to their souls. People started pouring out their hearts, relieved they could talk about a topic they are rarely encouraged to share. I listened to many moving stories about courageous grandparents who had survived the Holocaust, doctors who treated sick children, torture survivors who found new hope, and uncountable personal tales of loss, survival, and strength. When I first started out, I thought these stories of posttraumatic growth were rare. Now I know that they are everywhere.

Only a few of these people are mentioned in the book. Some are referred to in passing, maybe without a name to protect privacy. Thank you all for sharing your secrets with me; I vow to keep them safe.

I thank all the people who opened their hearts and homes to me, and everybody who generously volunteered their time to share their insights:

Dr. Maya Angelou and Tulku Pegyal, whom I wish were still with us; my teachers Roshi Bernie Glassman and Garchen Rinpoche; my heroes Coco Schumann, Dr. Temple Grandin, Alain Beauregard, Meggie, Cindy, Bob, and Nick Zahneis,

Daniel Gray Bear, Brigadier Colonel Dr. Rhonda Cornum, Cindi Lamb, Jesse and Samanta Billauer, Rick Allen, Lauren Monroe, Jason Padgett, and Tara Blocker.

For their help in contributing to my research, I am especially indebted to Colonel Ken Riddle; Lieutenant Colonel Sharon McBride; Lieutenant Stefanie Pidgeon; Major Dale W. Russell; Staff Sergeant Michael Bourgeois; Staff Sergeant Christian Condo-Carpio; Sergeant First Class Justin Rocha Daniels; Tony Gantt; Alice A. Booher; Nadia Capolla; Gordon Wiley; Millee Bush; Pastor Suzi Nowak; Engelina, Richard, and George Billauer; Matt Diamond; Brett Sanson; Jim Banks; Sarah Bloomfield; and Roshi Wendy Egyoku Nakao of the Zen Center LA.

My gratitude goes to all the psychologists and scientists who so kindly shared their extensive knowledge from decades of research with me, most of all Dr. Richard Tedeschi, Dr. Lawrence Calhoun and their research team, Dr. Ann Masten, Dr. Crystal Green, Dr. Susan Ollar, Dr. Karen Reivich, Dr. Roland Staud, Dr. Mitchell Levy, Dr. Felicia Axelrod, Dr. Simon Tanguay, and Dr. Linda Graham, with whom I attended an insightful workshop at Insight LA.

My love Gayle Landes and my dear friend Matteo Pistono read countless revisions; Tami Carter, Carol Moss, and editing magician Deb Norton provided critical feedback. Writers Cheryl Strayed and Samantha Dunn gave profound advice and encouragement that changed the course of the book.

Peter Cunningham, Steven Lippman, and Catherine Gregory are awesome photographers who generously donated pictures to this project to support people and organizations they care about.

Even how this book came into your hands is a result of posttraumatic growth: My wonderful agent Stephanie Tade immediately connected with the topic (thank you, Bob Miller, for introducing us!), and she found the perfect publisher, Zhena Muzyka, who came to know posttraumatic growth all too well when she found herself as a single mother with a critically ill son and six dollars to her name. After pulling herself out of the dale by starting a successful fair trade tea business to afford her son's surgeries, she now heads up this imprint, Enliven, which is dedicated to publishing life-changing books like this one. I could not be prouder to be on their team.

Last but not least, I owe deep gratitude to all the people who caused me suffering. You know who you are. In Buddhism we call you "precious jewels," because you challenge us to grow stronger than we think we are.

Notes

INTRODUCTION

1. I was first alerted to the Estée Lauder and Hanes products by Emily Bazelon, "A Question of Resilience," *New York Times Magazine*, April 30, 2006. www.nytimes.com/2006/04/30/magazine/30abuse.html.
2. "Resilience." Merriam-Webster.com. *Merriam-Webster*, n.d. Web, accessed May 21, 2015, http://www.merriam-webster.com/dictionary/resilience.
3. Amy M. Azzam, "Handle with Care: A Conversation with Maya Angelou," *Educational Leadership* 71 (2013): 10–13.
4. "What Is Resilient?" http://www.army.mil/readyandresilient (emphasis mine).
5. Stephen Joseph, *What Doesn't Kill Us: The New Psychology of Posttraumatic Growth* (New York: Basic Books, 2011), 73, Kindle edition.
6. bell hooks, "Cultivating Openness When Things Fall Apart," *Shambhala Sun*, March 1997.
7. In a letter to wife Winnie Mandela, written from Robben Island, February 1, 1975.
8. Kurt Miller, "Bethany Hamilton, Story of a Hero—'The Current' Film," from the Make A Hero documentary, posted January 24, 2013.
9. Aimee Mullins, "The Opportunity of Adversity." Recorded October 2009. TED video, 21:58, published February 19, 2010, http://www.youtube.com/watch?v=dTwXeZ4GkzI.
10. *The Seven Storey Mountain* (San Diego, CA: Harcourt Brace, 1999), 91.

1. SURVIVE

1. The primary source for this chapter is my visit with Rhonda Cornum on her farm in Kentucky. Her autobiography, now out of print, was an invaluable additional source to fill in some of the details of her capture. See Rhonda Cornum and Peter Copeland, *She Went to War* (Novato: Presidio, 1992).

2. *War*, 11.

3. For a detailed account, see *War*, 163.

4. Ibid.

5. According to the Nebraska Department of Veterans' Affairs, "An estimated 7.8 percent of Americans will experience PTSD at some point in their lives, with women (10.4%) twice as likely as men (5%) to develop PTSD. About 3.6 percent of U.S. adults aged 18 to 54 (5.2 million people) have PTSD during the course of a given year. This represents a small portion of those who have experienced at least one traumatic event. The traumatic events most often associated with PTSD for men are rape, combat exposure, childhood neglect, and childhood physical abuse. The most traumatic events for women are rape, sexual molestation, physical attack, being threatened with a weapon, and childhood physical abuse." "What is PTSD?" Post Traumatic Stress Disorder, by the Nebraska Department of Veterans' Affairs, http://www.ptsd.ne.gov/what-is-ptsd.html.

6. The percentage varies depending on the circumstances of the war, and the disposition of the individual, but also on factors that lie within the control of the army; for instance, the length of the deployment. Some researchers estimate the incidence of PTSD after a traumatic event at around 8 to 12 percent and even after the most traumatic events at rarely exceeding 30 percent. *What Doesn't Kill Us*, 64; George A. Bonanno, Chris R. Brewin, Krzysztof Kaniasty, and Annette M. La Greca, "Weighing the Costs of Disaster: Consequences, Risks, and Resilience in Individuals, Families, and Communities." *Psychological Science in the Public Interest* 11 (2010): 1–49.

   Let me add a few words of caution about the great variability of PTSD rates: I believe it is important to give a general range to get an idea of the prevalence of PTSD, therefore I mention the numbers given by the VA and various researchers. But the rates vary greatly not only depending on the severity and duration of the traumatic event but also on how PTSD is defined and assessed.

7. The American Psychiatric Association (APA) defines the trigger to PTSD as exposure to actual or threatened death, serious injury, or sexual violation. It describes the behavioral symptoms that accompany PTSD as re-experiencing, avoidance, negative cognitions and mood, and arousal. American Psychiatric Association, *Diagnostic and Statistical Manual of Mental Disorders*, Fifth Edition (Arlington, VA: American Psychiatric Association, 2013), doi:10.1176/appi.books.9780890425596.991543.

8. For instance, the prominent trauma specialist and psychiatrist in the US Department of Veterans Affairs, Jonathan Shay, speaks of "moral injury," which he defines as a "betrayal of 'what's right' in a high-stakes situation by someone who holds power." See also Peter A. Levine, *In an Unspoken Voice* (Berkeley, CA: North Atlantic Books, 2010), chapter 3.

9. Viktor E. Frankl, *Man's Search for Meaning* (Boston: Beacon Press, 1959), 20.

10. "Around a fifth of all people are likely to experience a potentially traumatic event within a given year." *What Doesn't Kill Us*, 21.

11. "Cognitive behavioral therapy" is a general name for a multitude of methods employed in psychotherapy, but generally speaking it is based on the belief that we can change maladaptive thoughts to affect and improve our emotions and behavior.

12. Rhonda spoke of the "gate control" theory. In order to explain how thoughts and emotions affect the perception of pain, in the sixties Patrick Wall and Ronald Melzack developed the theory that the dorsal horn of the spinal cord, where the thinner and thicker nerve fibers meet, functions as a "neurological gate," which can either transmit pain signals to the brain or block them. Negative emotions such as fear or anger open the gate wider, whereas positive emotions can close the gate and reduce pain perception. Though the gate control theory was a milestone in acknowledging the influence of mental and emotional factors on pain, the early model is considered outdated.

Nowadays pain is understood as a multidimensional process with a biopsychosocial component that is unique for each individual. See also Sytze van der Zee, *Schmerz: Eine Biografie* (Random House, German edition, 2013), Kindle locations 731–38 and 908–13.

13. *War*, 13.

14. *Trauma and Recovery* (New York: Basic Books, 1997), 159.

15. *War*, 18.

16. Ibid., 14.

17. See also *Flourish* (New York: Atria, 2013), 169.

18. The influential Canadian American psychologist Albert Bandura first discovered the concept of self-efficacy as an essential tool in overcoming trauma. "Among the mechanisms of human agency, none is more central or pervasive than people's beliefs in their efficacy to manage their own functioning and to exercise control over events that affect their lives. . . . Self-efficacy beliefs . . . affect whether individuals think in self-enhancing or self-debilitating ways; how well they motivate themselves and persevere in the face of difficulties; the quality of their emotional life and vulnerability to stress and depression; resiliency to adversity; and the choices they make at important decisional points which set life courses." Charles C. Benight and Albert Bandura, "Social Cognitive Theory of Posttraumatic Recovery: The Role of Perceived Self-efficacy," *Behaviour Research and Therapy* 42 (2004): 1129–48.

19. Martin E. P. Seligman, Steven F. Maier, and James H. Geer, "Alleviation of Learned Helplessness in the Dog," *Journal of Abnormal Psychology* 73 (1968): 256–62.

20. See also *Flourish*, 188–89.

21. "Optimistic persons might be more inclined than pessimists to derive a sense of benefit from adversity. Second, optimism is related to flexible use of adaptive coping strategies. Third, optimism is considered a predictor of perceived capability to manage the demands of a potentially traumatic event." Gabriele Prati and Luca Pietrantoni, "Optimism, Social Support, and Coping Strategies As Factors Contributing to Posttraumatic Growth: A Meta-Analysis," *Journal of Loss and Trauma: International Perspectives on Stress & Coping* 14 (2009): 364–88.

But according to psychologist Gabriele Oettingen and others, positive thinking alone can actually have negative effects if it is not contrasted with realism, because it tricks us into becoming lazy. For a warning manifesto against the impact of reckless overconfidence, see the downfall of Lehman Brothers, and the section about "Overconfidence" in Daniel Kahneman, *Thinking, Fast and Slow* (New York: Farrar, Straus and Giroux, 2013), 199–267.

22. "People who cope well usually have a number of positive factors going for them. For example, they tend to have better financial resources, better education, and fewer ongoing life stressors to worry about; they are also likely to be in better physical health and to have a broader network of friends and relatives on whom they can rely, both for emotional support and for helping with the details and demands of daily life." George A. Bonanno, *The Other Side of Sadness* (New York: Basic Books, 2009), 75.

2. GROW

1. The main source for this chapter is an extensive interview I conducted with Richard Tedeschi in Charlotte on February 28, 2014. I also attended a research session with Tedeschi, his colleague Lawrence Calhoun, and their graduate students. Additional information comes from their many publications and studies, especially *Posttraumatic Growth in Clinical Practice* (New York: Routledge, 2013).

2. Slow Food began as a countermovement to fast food and fast living, focusing instead on sustainable local farming and food production. See www.slowfood.com.

3. Tedeschi and Calhoun developed an inventory to measure posttraumatic growth. The inventory asks for ratings on statements such as, "I changed my priorities about what is important in life," or "I have more compassion for others." Richard G. Tedeschi and Lawrence G. Calhoun, "The Posttraumatic Growth Inventory: Measuring the Positive Legacy of Trauma," *Journal of Traumatic Stress* 9 (1996): 455–71.

4. Joseph notes, "Only a minority of people develop PTSD; of

those, only a minority develop persistent PTSD; and only half of those whose problems are persistent do not benefit from treatment." *What Doesn't Kill Us*, 64.

However, in our attempt to shed light on the resilient folks, we must not overlook that there is a small group of "chronic PTSD sufferers," who do not seem to respond to treatment easily. The landmark National Vietnam Veterans' Readjustment Study found that between 4.5 to 11 percent of veterans suffered from persistent PTSD decades after the war. This group included a high number of minorities, soldiers who committed or witnessed excessive brutality, and soldiers who enrolled before completing high school. The findings sparked a fierce debate about the effectiveness of PTSD treatments and require further research.

Based on various studies, psychologist George A. Bonanno estimates the rate of chronic PTSD for survivors of personal injury, riots, war, and car accidents between 6 and 18 percent. He writes, "Because there is greater variability in the types and levels of exposure to stressor events, there also tends to be greater variability in PTSD rates over time. . . . Although chronic PTSD certainly warrants great concern, the fact that the vast majority of individuals exposed to violent or life-threatening events do not go on to develop the disorder has not received adequate attention." George A. Bonanno, "Loss, Trauma, and Human Resilience: Have We Underestimated the Human Capacity to Thrive after Extremely Aversive Events?" *American Psychologist* 59 (2004): 20–28, doi:10.1037/0003-066X.59.1.20.

5. See *Posttraumatic Growth in Clinical Practice*, Kindle locations 917–19.

6. Gabby Giffords and Mark Kelly, "Be Passionate. Be Courageous. Be Your Best." TED video, 18:48, published April 11, 2014, https://www.youtube.com/watch?v=M6TMSQWI9m4.

7. Quoted after *Posttraumatic Growth in Clinical Practice*, Kindle locations 498–500.

8. W. Keith Campbell, Amy B. Brunell, and Joshua D. Foster, "Sitting Here in Limbo: Ego Shock and Posttraumatic Growth," *Psychological Inquiry* 15 (2004): 22–26.

9. Gabrielle Giffords and Mark Kelly, *A Story of Courage and Hope* (New York: Scribner, 2011), Kindle location 2508.

10. "How people cope with their experiences is important. Some behaviors can help people feel better in the short term but lead to greater difficulties in the longer term. For example, our survey revealed that many of the survivors were using drink and drugs to help them cope—73 percent said that they were drinking more; 44 percent, that they were smoking more; 40 percent, that they were taking sleeping pills; 28 percent, that they were taking antidepressants; and 21 percent, that they were taking tranquilizers. In addition, we determined that those on either prescribed or non-prescribed medications were in poorer psychological health than those on no meds at all." *What Doesn't Kill Us*, 5.

11. Several researchers have drawn an inverted-U relationship between the severity of trauma and the perception of post-traumatic growth, with medium stress producing the highest growth. Steve Powell et al., "Posttraumatic Growth after War: A Study with Former Refugees and Displaced People in Sarajevo," *Journal of Clinical Psychology* 59 (2003): 71,àí83, doi:10.1002/jclp.10117. See Tanja Zöllner and Andreas Maercker, "Post-traumatic Growth in Clinical Psychology: A Critical Review and Introduction of a Two Component Model," *Clinical Psychology Review* 26 (2006): 638, doi:10.1016/j.cpr.2006.01.008.

12. See chapter 4 about Coco Schumann.

13. "In just one example, 61.1 percent of imprisoned airmen tortured for years by the North Vietnamese said that they had benefited psychologically from their ordeal. What's more, the more severe the treatment, the greater the posttraumatic growth." *Flourish*, 161.

14. Interviewing 2,752 New Yorkers during six months following the September 11 terrorist attack, Bonanno et al. concluded that "only a very small percentage of Manhattan residents had trauma reactions that were severe enough to meet the definition of posttraumatic stress disorder. Even more surprising, however, was how quickly that level of trauma declined. Four months after the attack, the prevalence of PTSD in the

New York area had dropped to just a few percentage points, and by six months it was almost nonexistent." *Other Side of Sadness*, 61. See also George A. Bonanno et al., "Psychological Resilience after Disaster: New York City in the Aftermath of the September 11th Terrorist Attack," *Psychological Science* 17 (2006): 181–86. George A. Bonanno et al., "What Predicts Resilience after Disaster? The Role of Demographics, Resources, and Life Stress," *Journal of Consulting and Clinical Psychology* 75 (2007): 671–82.

15. *Flourish*, 159–60.

16. Studies have found sociocultural differences in dealing with trauma, for instance in expressing emotions or admitting the need to seek help, but posttraumatic growth has been observed in a wide variety of contexts and cultures. See Tzipi Weiss and Roni Berger, *Posttraumatic Growth and Culturally Competent Practice: Lessons Learned from Around the Globe* (Hoboken, New Jersey: John Wiley & Sons, 2010).

17. Peter A. Levine mentions a study showing 52 percent of PTSD occurrence following common orthopedic surgery. *Unspoken Voice*, 9.

18. *What Doesn't Kill Us*, 76–77.

19. The issue is particularly sensitive when viewed against the backdrop of the abusive strategies in the past, especially after World War I, when doctors, psychiatrists and sergeants shamed traumatized soldiers and tortured them with electric shocks before sending them back to the front. Milena Fee Hassenkamp, "Psychische Leiden im ersten Weltkrieg," *Süddeutsche Zeitung*, March 19, 2014, http://www.sueddeutsche.de/gesundheit /psychische-leiden-im-ersten-weltkrieg-vom-schlachtfeld-in -die-hoelle-der-nervenaerzte-1.1871045-2. The British psychiatrist Lewis Yealland outlines strategies such as shaming and electric shocks in his treatise *Hysterical Disorders of Warfare* from 1918. See also *Trauma and Recovery*, 21.

20. Referring to his study of survivors after a ship capsizing, Stephen Joseph finds, "It turned out that those who were most distressed were the ones who reported feeling helpless during the accident, who prepared themselves for the worst, who thought they were going to die, and who felt paralyzed with

fear. We also asked the survivors how they coped in the aftermath. Those who were most distressed were the ones who were least emotionally expressive, who lacked social support, and who had experienced other life-events in those preceding three years, such as serious illness, family bereavement, or loss of employment. In the time since we conducted this survey, many other studies have reported similar results. It is now commonly accepted that two major roadblocks to recovery are a lack of social support and a preponderance of other life-events to contend with in the aftermath of trauma." *What Doesn't Kill Us*, 5.

21. *Posttraumatic Growth in Clinical Practice*, Kindle locations 691–93.
22. Maren Westphal and George A. Bonanno, "Posttraumatic Growth and Resilience to Trauma: Different Sides of the Same Coin or Different Coins?" *Applied Psychology* 56 (2007): 417–27, doi:10.1111/j.1464-0597.2007.00298.x.
23. *War*, 91.
24. Joan Kaufman et al., "Social Supports and Serotonin Transporter Gene Moderate Depression in Maltreated Children," *Proceedings of the National Academy of Sciences* 101 (2004): 17316–21, doi:10.1073/pnas.0404376101. Generally, African Americans are more likely to have two long versions (technically called "alleles"); Asians are more likely to have short versions.
25. The researchers of the Grady Trauma Project, which examines at-risk population in Atlanta, assert, "It is now commonly accepted that PTSD results from an interaction of predisposing genetic and environmental risks that enhance the likelihood of a pathological stress response and fear memory following severe trauma. However, almost nothing is known of the nature of the genetic contribution(s) and how they interact with other risk factors." Alex Rothbaum, "Grady Trauma Project," November 13, 2013, http://gradytraumaproject.com/grady-trauma-project. See also Bazelon, "A Question of Resilience."
26. Avshalom Caspi et al., "Genetic Sensitivity to the Environment: The Case of the Serotonin Transporter Gene and Its Implications for Studying Complex Diseases and Traits," *American Journal of Psychiatry* 167 (2010): 509–27, doi:10.1176/appi.ajp.2010.09101452.

27. Kaufman et al., "Social Supports and Serotonin Transporter Gene Moderate Depression in Maltreated Children."

28. Jay Belsky, "The Downside of Resilience," *New York Times*, November 30, 2014. He refers to several not-yet-published studies, including one by Stacy S. Drury of Tulane University, who found that children with two short alleles of the 5-HTT gene did worse in orphanages, but benefited more from high-quality foster care than children without the genetic variation.

29. *Unspoken Voice*, 13–14.

30. Ibid., 14.

31. When Peter Levine speaks about "shaking it off," he does not use the term as a figure of speech, he means it literally: physically releasing the tension by allowing us to shake and quiver, something many trauma patients naturally do, but emergency doctors who are not trained in trauma response often try to prevent that natural response by fixating the patient.

32. *Unspoken Voice*, 15.

33. Ibid., 38.

34. *Trauma and Recovery*, 155.

35. George A. Bonanno seconds, "Resilient people are actually less likely than others to use avoidance and distraction as coping strategies. They are less inclined to evade thinking about the loss, or to deliberately occupy their minds to avoid confronting the pain." *Other Side of Sadness*, 74.

36. *Stitches* (New York: Riverhead Books, 2013), 10.

37. Romans 5:3–4. Tedeschi readily points out his many predecessors in history. This and some of the following quotes are cited after *Posttraumatic Growth in Clinical Practice*, Kindle locations 205–13.

38. Bill Moyers, *Joseph Campbell and the Power of Myth*, PBS, June 21, 1988.

39. *Gabby*, Kindle location 1964.

40. Bethany Hamilton, "I Am Second," YouTube video, 3:17, uploaded March 21, 2011, https://www.youtube.com/watch?v=37l1WfdFNQE.

41. For instance, nearly half the 111 women who participated in a study in Israel felt their religious beliefs had significantly weakened in the wake of sexual trauma, while 8 percent said their

faith had strengthened. Menachem Ben-Ezra et al., "Losing My Religion: A Preliminary Study of Changes in Belief Pattern after Sexual Assault," *Traumatology* 16 (2010): 7–13.

42. See Part II for deeper insights into the Buddhist science of mind for trauma recovery.

43. "Indeed, individuals who had experienced domestic violence or cancer, and who reported knowing a person with similar problems who had changed in positive ways, tended to report higher levels of growth than those who did not know such a person. Thus, the availability of role models in one's own social groups may be as influential, and perhaps more influential, than the distal broad societal themes." Lawrence G. Calhoun, Arnie Cann, and Richard G. Tedeschi, "The Posttraumatic Growth Model: Sociocultural Considerations," in *Posttraumatic Growth and Culturally Competent Practice*, Kindle locations 439–41.

44. A version of this saying is sometimes attributed to Reverend John Watson. Quote Investigator, June 29, 2010, http://quote investigator.com/2010/06/29/be-kind.

3. DIG DEEP

1. According to the US Department of Veterans Affairs, suicides among young veterans have climbed sharply. Janet Kemp and Robert Bossarte, "Suicide Data Report, 2012," Department of Veterans Affairs, http://www.va.gov/opa/docs/Suicide-Data -Report-2012-final.pdf.

 "The number of suicides among 18- to 29-year-old men increased from 88 in 2009 to 152 in 2011. That translates into a 44 percent rise in the suicide rate, which jumped to 57.9 suicides per 100,000 veterans." Alan Zarembo, "More Young Male Vets Are Committing Suicide," *Los Angeles Times,* January 11, 2014.

2. "Specifically, soldiers are taught that resilience is the ability to grow and thrive in the face of challenges and to bounce back from adversity. Fostering mental toughness, optimal performance, strong leadership and goal achievement does this. One important message is that resilience is something that can be obtained by all." Paul B. Lester et al., "The Comprehensive

Soldier Fitness Program Evaluation Report #3: Longitudinal Analysis of the Impact of Master Resilience Training on Self-Reported Resilience and Psychological Health Data," December 2011, http://csf2.army.mil/supportdocs/TR3.pdf.

3. See *Flourish*, 82–83 and 128.
4. Ibid., 127–28.
5. Ibid., 135.
6. The Comprehensive Soldier Fitness program includes several levels of engagement: the online questionnaire *every* soldier takes, online video modules such as the one Tedeschi designed to train soldiers in areas where the questionnaire identified weaknesses, the intensive ten-day resilience boot camp for selected leading soldiers I attended in Philadelphia, and less intensive offshoots of the boot camp training in individual army centers led by soldiers who have completed boot camp.
7. See Prati and Pietrantoni, "Optimism, Social Support, and Coping Strategies."
8. *Flourish*, 158.
9. Reivich and Shatté, *The Resilience Factor* (New York: Broadway Books, 2002), Kindle locations 290–302.
10. *War*, 203.
11. Ibid., 203.
12. *Man's Search for Meaning*, 66.
13. From the opening verses of the *Dhammapada*, loosely following the translation of Thomas Byrom.
14. Albert Ellis first formulated the ABC theory in 1962, and Seligman expanded it in 1990 into the ABCDE theory, adding D for disputation, i.e., providing a rational context for the event, and E for energization.
15. Rhonda explains, "There are four ways: active/passive, constructive/destructive. Active constructive communication builds trust, loyalty, and positive emotions, and the other three communication styles do not. For example, imagine you are the commander and your driver comes in and says, 'Guess what, my husband just got a new job.' When the commander practices active constructive responding, he pays attention and shows genuine interest, so he'll say something like, 'Oh great, when is he starting? And what does that allow you to do?'

With the active destructive style, the commander says, 'Oh no, does that mean you're not going to be able to work weekends?' That makes the person feel undermined and doubting." For a more detailed explanation, see *Flourish*, 48–51.

16. See *Flourish*, 146–47. See also Elaine Hatfield, John T. Cacioppo, and Richard L. Rapson, "Emotional Contagion," *Current Directions in Psychological Sciences* 2 (1993): 96–99; Robert R. Provine, "Laughter," *American Scientist* 84 (1996): 38–47.

17. There is plenty of evidence of the link between genuine smiles and positive outcomes of negotiations, etc. For instance, women who were showing a genuine smile in their college yearbooks had better relationships, more satisfying marriages, and generally more success over the next decades. Consider also the fascinating experiment by George A. Bonanno and Anthony Papa, who measured the smiles of college students after showing one group a comedy and another group an extremely sad film. "It turned out that whether the students smiled or not after the comedy didn't matter much; the link between smiling and long-term health was evident only after the sad film. In other words, being able to smile at something funny is well and good, but it doesn't tell us much about how healthy a person is. What really matters, in terms of our long-term health, is the ability to crack a grin when the chips are down." *Other Side of Sadness*, 38.

18. The so-called Losada ratio was first discovered by the Brazilian psychologist Marcel Losada. Barbara Fredrickson, *Positivity: Top-Notch Research Reveals the 3-to-1 Ratio That Will Change Your Life* (New York: Harmony, 2009).

19. "Youth spend an average of >7 hours/day using media, and the vast majority of them have access to a bedroom television, computer, the Internet, a video-game console, and a cell phone." Victor C. Strasburger, Amy B. Jordan, and Ed Donnerstein, "Health Effects of Media on Children and Adolescents," *Pediatrics* 125 (2010): 756–67, doi:10.1542/peds.2009-2563.

20. Ibid.

21. "For example, among survivors of a disaster at sea, the men who had managed to escape by cooperating with others showed relatively little evidence of post-traumatic stress

disorder afterward. By contrast, those who had 'frozen' and dissociated tended to become more symptomatic later. Highly symptomatic as well were the 'Rambos,' men who had plunged into impulsive, isolated action and had not affiliated with others." *Trauma and Recovery*, 59.

22. The army is promoting meditation on its own websites. e.g.: "'Mindfulness is a simple but ancient approach to living, which Western medicine has begun to recognize as a powerful tool for dealing with stress, illness and other medical or psychological conditions. It can help soldiers in any circumstance,' said Maj. Victor Won, deputy assistant chief of staff of Intelligence, general staff section, 1st Armored Division. 'It would be more effective for soldiers to learn and train mindfulness prior to deployment since the practice will offer soldiers [a means] to cope with their mental stress before getting into a high-stress environment,' Won said. 'However, practicing the meditation on a regular basis will help anyone no matter where they are.'" Daniel Schneider, "Mindfulness Helps Soldiers Cope," http://www.army.mil/article/43269/Mindfulness_helps_Soldiers_cope.

The use of meditation in the army has been criticized by some Buddhist teachers as "abuse" and as contradicting the Buddhist principle of nonviolence (See, for instance, Michael Stone, "Abusing the Buddha: How the U.S. Army and Google Co-opt Mindfulness," *Salon*, March 17, 2014, http://www.salon.com/2014/03/17/abusing_the_buddha_how_the_u_s_army_and_google_co_opt_mindfulness.) However, I believe that mindfulness meditation can improve absolutely anybody's life and that there is no reason to exclude any particular group from practicing it.

23. Emma M. Seppälä et al., "Breathing-Based Meditation Decreases Posttraumatic Stress Disorder Symptoms in U.S. Military Veterans: A Randomized Controlled Longitudinal Study," *Journal of Traumatic Stress* 27 (2014): 397–405. The army has given a $1.72 million grant to Amishi Jha, a neuroscientist who directs the University of Miami's Mindfulness Research and Practice Initiative, to further study the effects of mindfulness. See http://www.amishi.com/lab/strongproject.

24. Douglas C. Johnson et al., "Modifying Resilience Mechanisms in At-Risk Individuals: A Controlled Study of Mindfulness Training in Marines Preparing for Deployment," *American Journal of Psychiatry* 171 (2014): 844–53, doi:10.1176/appi.ajp.2014.13040502.

25. Hedy Kober, "Lo que podemos lograr con conciencia plena (mindfulness)." TEDx video, 19:17, published April 9, 2013, http://www.youtube.com/watch?v=mzEh5nE-tNU&feature=youtu.be; Judson A. Brewer et al., "Meditation Experience Is Associated with Differences in Default Mode Network Activity and Connectivity," *Proceedings of the National Academy of Sciences* (*PNAS*) 108 (2011): 20254–259.

26. As the army concedes in its Tech Report 4 from April 2013, "The results of the evaluation indicate that the effects of training upon the outcomes under consideration were relatively small, meaning that resilience training will likely result in only a slight reduction in the odds of a Soldier experiencing one of these negative outcomes as a result of the training. However, when a small reduction in the odds of such outcomes is considered in light of the fact that the army has over one million Soldiers, it is possible to see the potentially far-reaching impact that resilience training might have on the psychological health of the entire army and those who serve in it." P. D. Harms et al., "The Comprehensive Soldier and Family Fitness Program Evaluation Report #4" (2013), http://csf2.army.mil/support docs/TR4.pdf.

27. The support received from significant others and military peers is particularly important as it has proven to lower levels of PTSD in combat veterans. The results suggest that social support may have a protective effect on the level of PTSD. Sherrie Wilcox, "Social Relationships and PTSD Symptomatology in Combat Veterans," *Psychological Trauma: Theory, Research, Practice, and Policy* 2 (2010): 175–82.

28. *Goliath*, 161–62.

29. Jennifer Percy, "The Wake of Grief," *New York Times*, February 22, 2015.

4. PLAY

1. I first met Coco Schumann in 1996 when I interviewed him for the *Süddeutsche Zeitung*. He mentioned his wish to write his autobiography and I helped him realize this vision by finding a publisher and cowriting *Der Ghetto-Swinger*. We have kept in touch ever since, and I met him in Berlin in 2014 to update his biography for this book.
2. In his foreword to Viktor E. Frankl. *Man's Search for Meaning*, x.
3. Coco Schumann, Max Christian Graeff, Michaela Haas, *Der Ghetto-Swinger* (Munich: DTV, 1997), 86.
4. Ibid., 164–65.
5. Ibid., 90.
6. Ibid., 90.
7. Ibid., 133.
8. Ibid., 9.
9. *Man's Search*, 66–67.
10. Ibid. He is referring to Dostojewski's statement "There is only one thing I dread: not to be worthy of my sufferings."
11. William B. Helmreich, *Against All Odds* (Piscataway, NJ: Transaction Publishers, 1995), 276.
12. *Man's Search*, 65–66.
13. In an extensive meta-analysis that surveyed studies with 12,749 participants, the researchers concluded that Holocaust survivors "showed substantially more posttraumatic stress symptoms. They did not lag, however, much behind their comparisons in several other domains of functioning (i.e., physical health, stress-related physical measures, and cognitive functioning) and showed remarkable resilience. Alongside the profound and disturbing pain, the researchers also found "room for growth." Holocaust survivors were dedicated to rebuilding their lives by raising families, becoming involved in social activities, and showing achievement in various domains of social functioning, thus "establishing protective mechanisms in the form of social acceptance and support." Efrat Barel et al., "Surviving the Holocaust: A Meta-Analysis of the Long-Term Sequelae of a Genocide," *Psychological Bulletin* 136 (2010): 677–98. See also Devora Carmil and Rafael S. Carel, "Emotional Distress and Satisfaction

in Life among Holocaust Survivors: A Community Study of Survivors and Controls," *Psychological Medicine* 16 (1986): 141–49.

14. When psychologists interviewed Holocaust child survivors, they found that symptoms of PTSD and posttraumatic growth existed simultaneously. Rachel Lev-Wiesel and Marianne Amir, "Posttraumatic Growth among Holocaust Child Survivors," *Journal of Loss and Trauma* 8 (2003): 229–37.

    "Other new studies have found that the biochemical changes characteristic of post-traumatic stress syndrome persist in survivors even half a century later. . . . Though many survivors are in general tight-lipped about what happened to them, several studies have found that being able to talk over wartime experiences with others who understood them was strongly related to a better adjustment. . . . 'We needn't look at survivors as pathological specimens,' said Dr. Eva Kahana. 'They are normal people who have endured something horrible, human beings who are responding in surprisingly positive ways. Yes, they may have nightmares and psychosomatic problems; they have been traumatized. But at the same time they have lifted themselves.'" Daniel Goleman, "Holocaust Survivors Had Skills to Prosper," *New York Times*, October 6, 1992, http://www.nytimes.com/1992/10/06/science/holocaust-survivors-had-skills-to-prosper.html.

15. *Against All Odds*, 14.
16. Ibid., 265.
17. Ibid., 264–66.
18. Ibid., 15.
19. Ibid., 267–68.
20. Ibid., 268.
21. Devora Carmil and Shlomo Breznitz interviewed a nationwide sample of 533 Israelis, including 125 Holocaust survivors. They wanted to see how the Holocaust experience had affected their political attitudes, religious identity, and outlook. According to the results, the Holocaust survivors were more likely to hold moderate political opinions (90 versus 71 percent), were more religious (14 versus 7 percent), and significantly more optimistic about the future (42 percent believed in a better future compared to 23 percent). Devora Carmil and Shlomo Breznitz,

"Personal Trauma and World View: Are Extremely Stressful Experiences Related to Political Attitudes, Religious Beliefs, and Future Orientation?" *Journal of Traumatic Stress* 4 (1991): 393–405, doi:10.1002/jts.2490040307. Quoted after Joseph, *What Doesn't Kill Us*, 225–26, Kindle edition.

22. *Against All Odds*, 276.
23. *Ghetto-Swinger*, 212.
24. Ibid., 212.
25. Ibid., 213–14.
26. Ibid., 165.

5. ACCEPT

1. At the Second Global Conference on World's Religions, organized by Montreal's McGill University, September 7, 2011.
2. *When Things Fall Apart*, 5.
3. I wrote about her more extensively in *Dakini Power* (Boston: Shambhala, 2013).
4. *When Things Fall Apart*, 5.
5. Quoted after *Dakini Power*, 125. From an interview with Bill Moyers for "Bill Moyers on Faith and Reason," PBS, August 4, 2006.
6. For a translation of the full prayer, see *Masters of Meditation and Miracles*, 126, translated by Tulku Thondup, or http://www.shambhala.org/karuna/jigme-lingpa-poem-about-sickness.html.
7. *Man's Search*, 138.
8. Iris B. Mauss, Maya Tamir, Craig L. Anderson, and Nicole S. Savino, "Can Seeking Happiness Make People Unhappy? Paradoxical Effects of Valuing Happiness," *Emotion* 11 (2011): 807–15.
9. *Man's Search*, 114.
10. "An Update on Thay's Health," Plum Village, November 30, 2014.
11. *Man's Search*, 44.
12. Psychologists Krzysztof Kaniasty of Georgia State University and Fran Norris of Indiana University of Pennsylvania distinguish between the "heroic phase" with its initial outpouring

of empathy and help, and the long-term perspective with its inevitable deterioration of material and emotional sustenance when supporters readjust their focus to their own lives or other people in need. See, for instance, Krzysztof Kaniasty and Fran H. Norris, "Mobilization and Deterioration of Social Support following Natural Disasters," *Current Directions in Psychological Science* 4 (1995): 94–98.

13. Roy Baumeister, a Francis Eppes Professor of Social Psychology at Florida State University, and colleagues found that happiness is more associated with positive events, getting what one wants, and being a taker, while meaning is associated with being a "giver" and less immediate gratification, but more long-term satisfaction. Negative life events tend to decrease happiness but increase meaning. Roy F. Baumeister et al., "Some Key Differences between a Happy Life and a Meaningful Life," *Journal of Positive Psychology* 8 (2013): 505–16, doi:10.1080/17439760.2013.830764.

14. According to the 2008 survey of the Centers for Disease Control and Prevention (CDC). Rosemarie Kobau et al., "Well-Being Assessment: An Evaluation of Well-Being Scales for Public Health and Population Estimates of Well-Being among US Adults," *Applied Psychology: Health and Well-Being* 2 (2010): 272–97.

15. A life purpose seems to serve as a buffer against stress and even decreases mortality risk. People with a purpose outlive their peers in significant numbers (15 percent). For the protective effect it did not really matter how the subjects defined their life purpose, whether it was making their family happy, creating art, or contributing to social change. Patrick L. Hill and Nicholas A. Turiano, "Purpose in Life as a Predictor of Mortality Across Adulthood," *Psychological Science* 25 (2014): 1482–86.

16. "The search for meaning is considered to be central to psychological adaptation and is assumed to be associated with the perception of posttraumatic growth," Zöllner and Maercker have found. A study of college students indicates that "those who reported searching for a way to make sense of a distressing experience and were currently distressed by PTSD symptoms

were more likely to also report PTG compared to those who were not trying to make sense of anything." Zöllner and Maercker, "Posttraumatic Growth in Clinical Psychology," 648.

17. *Man's Search*, 113.

18. The episode is quoted after William J. Winslade, in the afterword to Frankl's *Man's Search*, 164–65.

19. Quoted after *Dakini Power*, 234.

20. Thich Nhat Hanh, "Happy Teachers Will Change the World," Mahachulalungkornrajavidyalaya University in Bangkok, Thailand, April 5, 2013, podcast, MP3, 1:59:06, http://plum village.org/audio/happy-teachers-will-change-the-world.

21. *Unspoken Voice*, 15.

22. "Demystifying Meditation—Brain Imaging Illustrates How Meditation Reduces Pain," Wake Forest Baptist Medical Center, April 5, 2011, http://www.wakehealth.edu/News-Releases /2011/Demystifying_Meditation_Brain_Imaging_Illustrates _How_Meditation_Reduces_Pain.htm. Fadel Zeidan et al., "Brain Mechanisms Supporting the Modulation of Pain by Mindfulness Meditation," *Journal of Neuroscience* 31 (2011): 5540–48.

23. Joshua A. Grant et al., "Cortical Thickness and Pain Sensitivity in Zen Meditators," *Emotion* 10 (2010): 43–53; Joshua A. Grant and Pierre Rainville, "Pain Sensitivity and Analgesic Effects of Mindful States in Zen Meditators: A Cross-Sectional Study," *Psychosomatic Medicine* 71 (2009): 106–14.

24. David Spiegel, "The Mind Prepared: Hypnosis in Surgery," *Journal of the National Cancer Institute* 99 (2007): 1280–81, doi:10.1093/jnci/djm131.

25. Guy H. Montgomery et al., "A Randomized Clinical Trial of a Brief Hypnosis Intervention to Control Side Effects in Breast Surgery Patients," *Journal of the National Cancer Institute* 99 (2007): 1304–12.

26. David Spiegel, "The Mind Prepared."

27. Ibid.

28. "Transforming Suffering and Happiness," trans. Adam Pearcey, Lotsawa House, www.lotsawahouse.org/tibetan-masters/do drupchen-III/transforming-suffering-and-happiness.

29. For an overview of different versions, see "The Story of the Taoist Farmer," last updated November 18, 2006, http://www.noogenesis.com/pineapple/Taoist_Farmer.html.

30. *Goliath*, 134–35.

31. "In the last 15 years or so, academics have spent an increasing amount of time studying the affluent and what can ail them, and there is an emerging consensus that their children often have higher rates of depression and anxiety and elevated levels of substance abuse and certain delinquent behaviors." Ron Lieber, "Growing Up on Easy Street Has Its Own Dangers," *New York Times*, January 9, 2015.

32. Dean Keith Simonton, "Genius and Giftedness: Parallels and Discrepancies," in *Talent Development: Proceedings from the 1993 Henry B. and Jocelyn Wallace National Research Symposium on Talent Development*, ed. Nicholas Colangelo, Susan G. Adouline, and Deann L. Ambroson (Tucson, AZ: Great Potential Press, 1996): 39–82. Quoted after Gladwell, *David and Goliath*, 142.

33. Adam Alter et al., "Overcoming Intuition: Metacognitive Difficulty Activates Analytic Reasoning," *Journal of Experimental Psychology: General* 136 (2007): 569–76. I discovered this research through *David and Goliath*, 102–5.

34. Vladimir Konieczny, *Glenn Gould: A Musical Force* (Toronto: Dundurn Press, 2009), 31.

35. Norbert Schwarz, "Warmer and More Social: Recent Developments in Cognitive Social Psychology," *Annual Review of Sociology* 24 (1998): 239–64. Quoted after *Other Side of Sadness*, 31.

36. It is important to clarify that these functions can be highly specific. Of course, extreme emotional stress can have the opposite effect and impair memory, but moderate emotional stress has proven to improve learning in certain areas, for instance in navigating a maze. Positive moods can enhance verbal creativity, while negative moods tend to enhance performance on spatial tasks. Justin Storbeck and Gerald L. Clore, "With Sadness Comes Accuracy; With Happiness, False Memory: Mood and the False Memory Effect," *Psychological Science* 16 (2005): 758–91. See also Bonanno, *Other Side of Sadness*, 31.

37. Galen V. Bodenhausen, Lori A. Sheppard, and Geoffrey P.

Kramer, "Negative Affect and Social Judgement: The Differential Impact of Anger and Sadness," *European Journal of Social Psychology* 24 (1994): 45–62.

38. *Other Side of Sadness*, 32.

39. Ibid., 31.

40. "In light of the hardships reported by study participants, the low levels of psychological distress are particularly striking. Average symptom severity ratings typically fell between *not at all* and *a little* on standardized measures, with only 10 percent (n =77) of the sample demonstrating clinically significant depression or anxiety. Among torture survivors, anxiety and depression were more common, but still occurred in only 12 percent (for anxiety) and 9.6 percent (for depression) of this subgroup. Perhaps most surprisingly, only one study participant (0.1 percent) had clinically significant PTSD symptoms. In short, this study suggests an unusual degree of resilience among Tibetans refugees, even those who have survived torture." Emily Sachs et al., "Entering Exile: Trauma, Mental Health, and Coping among Tibetan Refugees Arriving in Dharamsala, India," *Journal of Traumatic Stress* 21 (2008): 199–208. See also Sara E. Lewis, "Trauma and the Making of Flexible Minds in the Tibetan Exile Community," *Ethos* 41 (2013): 313–36.

41. Padmal De Silva, "The Tsunami in Sri Lanka and Its Aftermath: The Explorations of a Buddhist Perspective," *International Review of Psychiatry* 18 (2006): 281–87.

42. "It is noteworthy that participants (including torture survivors) typically reported that they had suffered less than most Tibetans. . . . Significantly, when asked to rank their most upsetting experiences in order of severity, the majority of participants named religious persecution as the most upsetting experience, even in the presence of torture experiences." Sachs et al., "Entering Exile," 207.

43. See, for instance, Jamgon Kongtrul Lodro Tayé, trans. Ken McLeod, *The Great Path of Awakening: The Classic Guide to Lojong, a Tibetan Buddhist Practice for Cultivating the Heart of Compassion* (Boston: Shambhala, 2005).

6. THRIVE

1. According to congressional testimony from the American Society of Interventional Pain, May 24, 2011, asipp.org/documents /TESTIMONY-FROMEXECUTIVECOMMITTEE-RESPONDING TOTHEPRESCRIPTIONDRUGEPIDEMIC-STRATEGIESFOR REDUCI.pdf.

2. "Prescription Painkiller Overdoses in the US," Centers for Disease Control and Prevention, last modified November 1, 2011, http://www.cdc.gov/vitalsigns/PainkillerOverdoses/index.html.

3. Recent studies show that even over-the-counter painkillers such as Tylenol numb patients' sensitivity so that they not only perceive negative stimuli as less painful, but also positive stimuli as less positive. Geoffrey R. O. Durso, Andrew Luttrell, and Baldwin M. Way, "Over-the-Counter Relief from Pains and Pleasures Alike: Acetaminophen Blunts Evaluation Sensitivity to Both Negative and Positive Stimuli," *Psychological Science* 2 (2015): 750–8, doi:10.1177/0956797615570366.

4. The leprosy specialist Paul Brand examined thousands of patients who suffered from the inability to feel pain as a result of nerve damage from leprosy or diabetes. He was the doctor who first discovered that leprosy patients did not lose their limbs due to the leprosy bacilli, but due to injury from not noticing pain. Much like Meggie, leprosy patients would pick up burning objects or walk around with a nail in their foot, oblivious. He gives striking examples in his book *The Gift of Pain* of the dangers of bigger and smaller injuries. For instance, he noticed that a jogger will shift his stride innumerable times during a run, whereas painless people never change their gait and thus continue to put pressure on the same spots until they develop sores so severe that limbs might have to be amputated. Even an ill-fitting shoe can lead to the loss of feet. "Soon I found painlessness to be the single most destructive aspect of this dread disease," he writes about leprosy. *The Gift of Pain*, 117.

5. Justin Heckert, "The Hazards of Growing Up Painlessly," *New York Times Magazine*, November 15, 2012, 30.

6. "IASP Taxonomy," updated from "Part III: Pain Terms, A Cur-

rent List with Definitions and Notes on Usage," *Classification of Chronic Pain*, Second Edition, IASP Task Force on Taxonomy, ed. H. Merskey and N. Bogduk (IASP Press: Seattle, 1994): 209–14, http://www.iasp-pain.org/Taxonomy.

7. From the documentary *A Life Without Pain* by Melody Gilbert, Frozen Feet Films, 1:13:27, 2005.

8. In 2013, the Israeli company Teva was the first to obtain permission in America to test an orphan drug called XEN402 that inhibits the SCN9A sodium channel. "Teva and Xenon Announce FDA Orphan Drug Designation for Pain Drug XEN402," April 13, 2013, http://www.xenon-pharma.com/2013/04/xen402-orphan. It has also been discovered that nature occasionally employs a similar principle. The toxin of a bark scorpion, for instance, is deadly for most small animals, but grasshopper mice are able to use the toxin as an analgesic by binding it to sodium channels in the mouse pain neurons, and this blocks the neuron from firing a pain signal to the brain. "Grasshopper Mice Are Numb to the Pain of the Bark Scorpion Sting," *UT News*, October 24, 2013, https://www.utexas.edu/news/2013/10/24/grasshopper-mice-bark-scorpion.

9. Jonas Tesarz et al., "Pain Perception in Athletes Compared to Normally Active Controls: A Systematic Review with Meta-analysis," *PAIN* 153 (2012): 1253–62.

10. "Studies have shown that writing about oneself and personal experiences can improve mood disorders, help reduce symptoms among cancer patients, improve a person's health after a heart attack, and even boost memory." Tara Parker-Pope, "Writing Your Way to Happiness," *New York Times*, January 19, 2015. See also *Power of Resilience*, 4–12 and 23–48.

11. *Power of Resilience*, 3.

12. I first learned about Karen Cann from Heckert, "The Hazards of Growing Up Painlessly." This paragraph is based on my interview with Tara Blocker and the *New York Times*.

7. PRAY

1. This quote has been attributed to the eighth-century Buddhist scholar Shantideva.

2. Dr. Paul Brand has identified factors he calls "pain intensifiers" such as fear, anger, guilt, loneliness, and helplessness. He thinks that these intensifiers "may have more impact on the overall experience of pain than any prescription drug" a patient might take. "Research studies in the laboratory and in the hospital confirm that fear is the strongest intensifier of pain. Newcomers in laboratory tests report a lower pain threshold until they learn they can control the experiment and have nothing to fear. In measure-able physiological ways, fear increases pain. When an injured person is afraid, muscles tense and contract, increasing the pressure on damaged nerves and causing even more pain." *Gift of Pain*, 262–63.

3. Ram Dass, "Suffering as Transformation," *Huffington Post*, October 27, 2014.

4. "We found that psychological distress was most likely to be found in those who blamed themselves in some way." *What Doesn't Kill Us*, 4.

5. James C. Coyne, Michael Stefanek, Steven C. Palmer, "Psychotherapy and Survival in Cancer: The Conflict Between Hope and Evidence," *Psychological Bulletin* 133 (2007): 367–94, http://dx.doi.org/10.1037/0033-2909.133.3.367.

6. David Spiegel, "Mind Matters in Cancer Survival," *Journal of the American Medical Association* 305 (2011): 502–3, doi:10.1001 /jama.2011.69; David Spiegel, Joan R. Bloom, and Irvin D. Yalom, "Group Support for Patients with Metastatic Cancer: A Randomized Outcome Study," *Archives of General Psychiatry* 38 (1981): 527–33; David Spiegel and Joan R. Bloom, "Group Therapy and Hypnosis Reduce Metastatic Breast Carcinoma Pain," *Psychosomatic Medicine* 45 (1983): 333–39; David Spiegel, Joan R. Bloom, Helena C. Kraemer, Ellen Gottheil, "Effect of Psychosocial Treatment on Survival of Patients with Metastatic Breast Cancer," *Lancet* 2 (1989): 888–91; David Spiegel and Michael C. Glafkides, "Effect of Group Confrontation with Death and Dying," *International Journal of Group Psychotherapy* 33 (1983): 433–47.

7. "Remembering and telling the truth about terrible events are prerequisites both for the restoration of the social order and for the healing of individual victims," writes trauma specialist Judith Herman. *Trauma and Recovery*, 1.

8. "The kind of response that people receive when they do articulate their experience of growth may also play a role in the process. Our guiding assumption is that when self-disclosures about posttraumatic growth are met with social acceptance or support, they are more likely to lead to a clearer sense that growth has indeed occurred. Overall, social groups that support the kind of self-disclosure about their situation that trauma survivors want to make, and that support appropriate disclosures about growth themes, are more likely to encourage not only effective coping, but posttraumatic growth as well." *Posttraumatic Growth in Clinical Practice*, Kindle locations 1111–15.

9. Tzipi Weiss, "Correlates of Posttraumatic Growth in Married Breast Cancer Survivors," *Journal of Social and Clinical Psychology* 23 (2004): 733–46; Tzipi Weiss, "Correlates of Posttraumatic Growth in Husbands of Breast Cancer Survivors," *Psycho-Oncology* 13 (2004): 260–68. Other studies have shown posttraumatic growth in psychotherapists, funeral directors, and spouses of former prisoners of war. See *What Doesn't Kill Us*, 76.

10. Because *tonglen* is a powerful, advanced practice, I urge you to seek the guidance of a qualified instructor before attempting it. Before we can practice for others, we need to open the heart of compassion for ourselves. If you are interested in learning more, I recommend the instructions by the American Buddhist teacher Pema Chödrön, "The Practice of Tonglen," http://www.shambhala.org/teachers/pema/tonglen1.php.

11. Pema shared this simplified version of *tonglen* practice in an interview with Oprah Winfrey, *Super Soul Sunday*, OWN, broadcasted on October 19, 2014, http://www.oprah.com/own-super-soul-sunday/Pema-Chodron.

12. Gail Ironson, Rick Stuetzle, Mary Ann Fletcher, "An Increase in Religiousness/Spirituality Occurs after HIV Diagnosis and Predicts Slower Disease Progression over 4 Years in People with HIV," *Journal of General Internal Medicine* 21 (Suppl 5)(2006): S62–S68.

13. "Numerous studies have shown a clear relationship between a sense of control and the level of perceived pain. In laboratory experiments, rats that have some control over a mild electric shock—they can turn off the lever—respond very differently than rats that have no access to such control. The 'helpless'

rats experience actual harm: their immune system radically weakens and they become much more vulnerable to disease. [McGill University Professor Emeritus and pain expert] Ronald Melzack says, 'It is also possible to change the level of pain by giving people the *feeling* that they have control over it even though, in fact, they do not. When burn patients are allowed to participate in the debridement of their burned tissues, they claim that the process is more bearable. . . . Patients with terminal cancer tend to use less pain medication when given some control over the dosage.' [When patients are put in charge of their morphine drip, they] 'experience less pain, use less analgesia, and have shorter hospital stays.'" *Gift of Pain*, 280–81.

14. *Head First*, 2.
15. *Gift of Pain*, 286.
16. "Several recent studies found that as many as 60 percent of patients who sought a second opinion received a major change in their diagnosis or treatment. Yet according to a 2010 Gallup Poll, 70 percent of Americans don't feel the need to ask for one—most said they feel confident in their doctor's advice and saw no need to gather additional information." Lisa Zamosky, "A Second Opinion Could Save Your Life," *Los Angeles Times*, May 25, 2015, http://www.latimes.com/business/la-fi-health-care-watch-20150525-story.html.
17. *Other Side of Sadness*, 76.
18. Ibid., 78; George A. Bonanno et al., "The Importance of Being Flexible: The Ability to Both Enhance and Suppress Emotional Expression Predicts Long-Term Adjustment," *Psychological Science* 15 (2004): 482–87.
19. *Head First*, 25.

8. EVOLVE

1. The primary sources for this chapter are three interviews I conducted with Temple Grandin between 2009 and 2014. Additional information came from her own writings, especially *The Autistic Brain* and *Animals in Translation*, as well as some of her scholarly articles that she directed me to read.

2. "Savant syndrome is a rare, but extraordinary, condition in which persons with serious mental disabilities, including autistic disorder, have some 'island of genius' which stands in marked, incongruous contrast to overall handicap. As many as one in ten persons with autistic disorder have such remarkable abilities in varying degrees, although savant syndrome occurs in other developmental disabilities or in other types of central nervous system injury or disease as well. Whatever the particular savant skill, it is always linked to massive memory." Darold A. Treffert, "The Savant Syndrome: An Extraordinary Condition," *Philosophical Transactions of the Royal Society B: Biological Sciences* 364 (2009): 1351–57, doi:10.1098/rstb.2008.0326. Wisconsin psychiatrist Darold Treffert is the eminent authority on savants, and has been studying savants for four decades. He also diagnosed Jason Padgett.

3. See also *Thinking in Pictures*, 27.

4. Even bullying has a silver lining. Alongside many negative effects, researchers found increased sympathy and respect for victims, greater toughness of mind and an increased willingness to enter a helping profession such as social work as positive outcomes of being bullied. See Kanako Taku, "Posttraumatic Growth in Japan," in *Posttraumatic Growth and Culturally Competent Practice*, chapter 10.

5. See also *Animals in Translation*, 10.

6. Michelle Dawson et al., "The Level and Nature of Autistic Intelligence," *Psychological Science* 18 (2007): 647–62.

7. In 2014, the British Psychological Society published a new report that effectively redefines mental illness and posits that "there is no clear dividing line between psychosis and other feelings"; "Hearing voices or feeling paranoid are common experiences which can often be a reaction to trauma, abuse or deprivation. Calling them symptoms of mental illness, psychosis or schizophrenia is only one way of thinking about them, with advantages and disadvantages. . . . Some people find it useful to think of themselves as having an illness. Others prefer to think of their problems as, for example, an aspect of their personality which sometimes gets them into trouble but which they would not want to be without." Anne Cooke (ed.),

"Understanding Psychosis and Schizophrenia," British Psychological Society, 2014, http://www.bps.org.uk/networks-and-communities/member-microsite/division-clinical-psychology/understanding-psychosis-and-schizophrenia.

8. Temple Grandin and Richard Panek, *The Autistic Brain: Thinking across the Spectrum* (New York: Houghton Mifflin Harcourt, 2013, Kindle edition), Kindle locations 1625–27.

9. I was first alerted to Specialisterne through Gareth Cook, "The Autism Advantage," *New York Times Magazine*, November 29, 2012, http://www.nytimes.com/2012/12/02/magazine/the-autism-advantage.html.

10. Patricia Howlin, Susan Goode, Jane Hutton, Michael Rutter, "Savant Skills in Autism: Psychometric Approaches and Parental Reports," *Philosophical Transactions of the Royal Society of London Series B: Biological Sciences* 364 (2009): 1359–67.

11. "Savant syndrome, both in the congenital and acquired types, provides compelling evidence of remarkable brain plasticity. Indeed, brain plasticity will be a central aspect of all neuroscience research in the decades ahead." Treffert, "The Savant Syndrome."

12. The longer they worked as cabbies, the greater the difference. When they retired, the hippocampus that sustained their "inner GPS" shrank to its normal size. Eleanor A. Maguire et al., "Navigation-related Structural Change in the Hippocampi of Taxi Drivers," *Proceedings of the National Academy of Sciences* 97 (2000): 4398–4400.

13. Temple talks in detail about her brain scans in *The Autistic Brain*, Kindle location 422.

14. Watch an interview with him on the Science Channel, "Ingenious Minds," https://www.youtube.com/watch?v-dxRBxK9xlyI. Amato also gave an interesting TEDx talk: Derek Amato, "My Beautiful Disaster: Derek Amato at TEDxMiddlebury." TEDx video, 18:01, published August 18, 2013, https://www.youtube.com/watch?v=k3zrJ70iB1w.

15. "About Orlando Serrell," http://www.orlandoserrell.com/about.htm.

16. Jason Padgett wrote a fascinating book about his experience (with Ann Maureen Seaberg), *Struck by Genius* (New York: Houghton Mifflin Harcourt, 2014), 41.

17. A synesthete mixes sense impressions. For instance, synesthetes might smell color or taste forms. A surprising number of famous artists and musicians are synesthetes. Tilda Swinton, for instance, tastes words, and Jimi Hendrix saw melodies as colors.

18. Daniel Simons, "The Monkey Business Illusion," YouTube video, 1:41, uploaded April, 28, 2010, https://www.youtube .com/watch?v=IGQmdoK_ZfY.

19. I have greatly simplified these complex studies, mainly from Virginia Hughes, "Stress: The Roots of Resilience," *Nature*, October 10, 2012, http://www.nature.com/news/stress-the -roots-of-resilience-1.11570.

20. Ibid.

21. Jennifer S. Stevens et al., "Disrupted Amygdala-Prefrontal Functional Connectivity in Civilian Women with Posttraumatic Stress Disorder," *Journal of Psychiatric Research* 47 (2013): 1469–78, http://dx.doi.org/10.1016/j.jpsychires.2013.05.031; quoted after Hughes, *Nature*.

22. Quoted after Hughes, *Nature*.

23. Thus it is not surprising that meditation has also proven effective in calming autistic people, e.g., Nirbhay N. Singh et al., "A Mindfulness-Based Strategy for Self-Management of Aggressive Behavior in Adolescents with Autism," *Research in Autism Spectrum Disorders* 5 (2011): 1153–58.

24. Sara Lazar, "How Meditation Can Reshape Our Brains: Sara Lazar at TEDxCambridge 2011." TEDx video, 8:33, published January 23, 2012, https://www.youtube.com/watch?v =m8rRzTtP7Tc; Britta K. Hölzel et al., "Mindfulness Practice Leads to Increases in Regional Brain Gray Matter Density," *Psychiatry Research* 191 (2011): 36–43.

25. Eileen Luders et al., "Enhanced Brain Connectivity in Long-term Meditation Practitioners," *Neuroimage* 57 (2011): 1308–16, doi:10.1016/j.neuroimage.2011.05.075; Sara Lazar et al., "Meditation Experience Is Associated with Increased Cortical Thickness," *Neuroreport* 16 (2005): 1893–97.

26. Richard Davidson and Antoine Lutz, "Buddha's Brain: Neuroplasticity and Meditation," *IEEE Signal Process Magazine* 25 (2008): 172–74.

27. Fadel Zeidan et al., "Neural Correlates of Mindfulness Meditation-Related Anxiety Relief," *Social Cognitive and Affective Neuroscience* 9 (2013): 751–59, doi:10.1093/scan/nst041.

28. Antoine Lutz et al., "Long-Term Meditators Self-Induce High-Amplitude Gamma Synchrony during Mental Practice," *PNAS* 101 (2004): 16369–73, doi:10.1073/pnas.0407401101.

29. I first learned about Mingyur Rinpoche's experience when I met him in France in 2007, and he has since written a powerful book about his journey, *The Joy of Living* (New York: Harmony, 2008).

30. The US Department of Veterans Affairs is currently undertaking the first full-fledged three-year study of the effects of service dogs. "The Psychiatric Service Dog Society (PSDS) has been developing the concept of using service dogs with a variety of mental health disabilities, including PTSD for the past thirteen years. In a 2005 survey of Psychiatric Service Dog (PSD) handlers, 82 percent of the respondents with PTSD who are using a Psychiatric Service Dog reported a decline in symptom manifestation." Craig Love, "The Use of Psychiatric Service Dogs in the Treatment of Veterans with PTSD," Report for the U.S. Army Medical Research and Materiel Command, Fort Detrick, 2009.

31. Cindy Meehl, "Buck," 2011.

32. Lawrence G. Calhoun and Richard G. Tedeschi, *Posttraumatic Growth in Clinical Practice*, Kindle locations 609–12.

33. *Animals in Translation*, 184.

34. A.V. Apkarian et al., "Prefrontal Cortical Hyperactivity in Patients with Sympathetically Mediated Chronic Pain," *Journal of Neuroscience Letters* 311 (2001): 193–97. Quoted after *Animals in Translation*, 185.

35. See also her detailed description in *Animals in Translation*, 186.

36. See also Antonio Damasio, *Descartes' Error* (New York: Penguin, 1994), 264.

37. See also *Animals in Translation*, 188.

38. See also her more elaborate explanation in *Animals in Translation*, 186.

9. BREATHE

1. The main source for this chapter is an in-depth interview with Roshi Bernie Glassman in Los Angeles in July 2014 and his teachings I attended in Los Angeles between 2012 and 2014. Additional insights and quotes came from his own writings, especially his blogs and his books *Instructions to the Cook* and *Bearing Witness*, in which he describes his visits to Auschwitz in great detail.

2. Excerpted from Leonard Cohen, *Stranger Music: Selected Poems and Songs.* Copyright ©1993 Leonard Cohen. Reprinted by permission of McClelland & Stewart, a division of Random House of Canada Limited, a Penguin Random House Company.

3. At a press conference during the New York Film Festival 2014, as reported by Bernie Glassman, "Richard Gere Talks About Wandering New York Streets as a Homeless Man," published September 27, 2014, http://zenpeacemakers.org/2014/09/richard-gere-talks-about-wandering-new-york-streets-as-a-homeless-man.

4. Ellen Burstyn, *Lessons in Becoming Myself* (New York: Penguin, 2007), Kindle locations 6957–58.

5. David Fear, "Life on the Streets: Richard Gere on Going Homeless," *Rolling Stone*, September 15, 2014.

6. "From moment to moment, we perceive objects in the world as continuous despite fluctuations in their image properties due to factors like occlusion, visual noise, and eye movements. The mechanism by which the visual system accomplishes this object continuity remains elusive." Alina Liberman, Jason Fischer, and David Whitney, "Serial Dependence in the Perception of Faces," *Current Biology* 24 (2014): 2569–74.

7. www.Greyston.com.

8. The quotes in this paragraph are from Bernie's blog, "Why Do I Keep Going Back to Auschwitz-Birkenau?" http://zenpeacemakers.org/events/bearing-witness-retreat-at-auschwitzbirkenau. Quoted with Bernie's kind permission.

9. Ibid.

10. Ibid.

11. Ibid.

12. *Long Walk to Freedom* (New York: Hachette, 2008).
13. Jon Stewart, "Daily Show," Comedy Central, October 8, 2013.

10. ADRENALIZE

1. I met Rick Allen and Lauren Monroe at their drum circle in Woodland Hills in 2014 where they presented their work and I had the opportunity to speak with them briefly. At the time, Rick was enthusiastic about the book, but then his tour schedule did not allow for a longer interview. Nevertheless, I was so impacted by participating in the drum circle and the incredible work Rick and Lauren do that I decided to keep his chapter in the book. Their Resiliency Radio project with its in-depth interviews about trauma and recovery provided additional insights.
2. http://project-resiliency.org.
3. Rick Allen and Lauren Monroe, "Resiliency and Risk Taking," Resiliency Radio, 50:26, September 27, 2013, http://www .blogtalkradio.com/resiliency-radio/2013/09/27/resiliency-and -risk-taking.
4. "The central significance of close relationships for resilience has been noted in virtually every review on resilience in development over the past half-century." Ann Masten, *Ordinary Magic*, 150.
5. Studies of neglected Romanian orphans showed that the brains of the children remained physically smaller if they did not receive adequate attention in the early years of their lives. For instance, their hippocampus was smaller while parts of their amygdala were enlarged. Margaret A. Sheridan et al., "Variation in Neural Development as a Result of Exposure to Institutionalization Early in Childhood," *PNAS* 109 (2012): 12927–32, www.pnas.org/cgi/doi/10.1073/pnas.1200041109; Ross E. Vanderwert et al., "Timing of Intervention Affects Brain Electrical Activity in Children Exposed to Severe Psychosocial Neglect," *PLoS ONE* 5 (2010): e11415, doi:10.1371/journal .pone.0011415.
6. *Trauma and Recovery*, 51–52.
7. "The more friends and the more love in your life, the less illness. George Vaillant found that people who have one per-

son whom they would be comfortable calling at three in the morning to tell their troubles were healthier. John Cacioppo found that lonely people are markedly less healthy than sociable people. . . . Happy people have richer social networks than unhappy people, and social connectedness contributes to a lack of disability as we age. Misery may love company, but company does not love misery, and the ensuing loneliness of pessimists may be a path to illness." *Flourish*, 206.

8. "2014 PTSD Awareness Day Message From A Rockstar and A Warrior," Wounded Warrior Project, 1:56, published June 27, 2014, https://www.youtube.com/watch?v =3N9TqbnxDKA.

9. "Resiliency and Risk Taking," Resiliency Radio.

10. *Trauma and Recovery*, 56. There might even be physical triggers. In Part II we discussed how we can reshape our brain with meditation and other techniques, and we mentioned the possibility of brain trauma leading to new capabilities, but unfortunately brain trauma can also set the brain on a trajectory to disintegration and violence. There is mounting evidence that there might be a physical link between brain injury and impulse control.

11. "Resiliency and Risk Taking," Resiliency Radio.

12. Bob Woodruff, "Def Leppard Drummer Rick Allen, Marine Help Injured Vets with PTSD," ABC News, December 26, 2012, http://abcnews.go.com/US/def-leppard-drummer-rick-allen -marine-injured-vets/story?id=18056193.

13. Rick Allen and Lauren Monroe, "Giving the Gift of Resiliency," Resiliency Radio, February 26, 2010, http://www.blogtalkradio .com/resiliency-radio/2010/02/26/giving-the-gift-of-resiliency.

14. Julius Segal, *Winning Life's Toughest Battles* (New York: Ivy Books, 1987), 100.

15. Theme Time Radio Hour 2012.

16. He was awarded the Humanitarian Award by Maria Shriver's Best Buddies of CA in 2002 and was the recipient of a Carry Forward Award from the Wounded Warrior Project in 2012. See more information on his website Stikrick.com.

17. "Def Leppard Drummer Rick Allen, Marine Help Injured Vets with PTSD," ABC News.

18. Ibid.
19. "Giving the Gift of Resiliency," Resiliency Radio.

11. SHINE

1. The primary sources for this chapter are interviews with Jesse Billauer and his friends and family. I spoke with his father George Billauer, his grandparents Engelina and Richard Billauer, his wife Samanta, his friends Brett Sanson, and Matt Diamond. The moving documentary *Jesse's Story*, directed by Mark Jacobs and produced by Jesse Billauer, provided additional insights, and with Jesse's permissions I quote from the documentary in this chapter.
2. Aimee Mullins, "The Opportunity of Adversity," TED video, October 2009.
3. *Jesse's Story*.
4. Ibid.
5. The following quotes in this paragraph are from Christopher Reeve, *Still Me*, 28.
6. *Jesse's Story*.
7. Ibid.
8. Ibid.
9. Ibid.
10. http://www.diananyad.com/blog/jesse-billauer.
11. "The ability to accept situations that cannot be changed is assumed to be crucial for adaptation to uncontrollable or unchangeable life-events. Therefore, accepting that the traumatic event happened is proposed to be one important factor within the process that can lead to personal growth (Calhoun et al., 2000). The link between acceptance coping and posttraumatic growth has been demonstrated in several studies: In the study by Park et al. (1996), acceptance coping was a significant predictor of personal growth cross-sectionally." Zöllner and Maercker, "Posttraumatic Growth in Clinical Psychology."
12. *Power of Resilience*, 17.
13. *Jesse's Story*.
14. Ibid.

12. FORGIVE

1. The primary source for this chapter is my three-day visit with Cindi Lamb and her family in Cecil County, Maryland. At her request I left out some personal information about family members. With her permission, I also quote from the draft of her memoir, of which she published excerpts on her website under the title "I'm Not MADD Anymore." Additional information came from the *Frederick News-Post*, which published several in-depth articles about the accident, Russell Willows, and Cindi. I tried to contact Russell Willows, the drunk driver, but was unable to get a response. Though I know his real name, I changed his name in this chapter because I could not confirm his perspective of events.

2. Marge Neal and Ron Cassie, "Laura's Legacy: The Road to MADD," *Frederick News-Post*, November 8, 2009.

3. Barron H. Lerner's *One for the Road* (Baltimore: The Johns Hopkins University Press, 2011), a chronicle of drunk driving, reminds us how cavalierly police treated drunk drivers in the late seventies and early eighties. Even after causing deadly accidents, intoxicated drivers were routinely slapped with small fines of ten or twenty dollars, and routine offenders rarely suffered severe legal consequences. Lerner's book's cover is a black-and-white photo of Cindi's crash.

4. Later the name was changed to the less controversial Mothers Against Drunk Driving.

5. *One for the Road*, 84.

6. Ibid., 85.

7. Others set the estimate lower, quoting better safety standards in cars, airbags, etc., as additional reasons for lower death rates, but while the exact numbers are hard to determine, there is no question that MADD's initiative saved many thousands.

8. *One for the Road*, 84–85.

9. "At the State University of New York, Lynn Videka-Sherman studied nearly 200 patients after they had lost a child. Her results showed significantly less depression among parents who reinvested their energies in another person or activity." *Winning Life's Toughest Battles*, 115. This is true for other traumas

as well. Trauma therapist Judith Herman writes about rape victims, "But we do know that the women who recover most successfully are those who discover some meaning in their experience that transcends the limits of personal tragedy. Most commonly women find this meaning by joining with others in social action." *Trauma and Recovery*, 73.

10. *Tiny Beautiful Things*, 22.

11. Ron Cassie, "Jail, Tragedy, Death," *Frederick News-Post*, November 8, 2009.

12. The description of their first meeting is largely quoted from Cindi Lamb's own memoir, a work in progress. She has made the chapter about her meeting with Russell Willows available on her website and kindly gave permission to let me quote from it here.

13. Many psychologists believe that alcohol and tranquilizers relieve the pain short-term, but "lead to greater difficulties" in the long run. *What Doesn't Kill Us*, 5.

14. This and the following paragraphs describing the meetings are largely quoted from Cindi's memoir, with her permission.

15. Erick Messias, Anil Saini, Philip Sinato, and Stephen Welch, "Bearing Grudges and Physical Health: Relationship to Smoking, Cardiovascular Health and Ulcers," *Social Psychiatry and Psychiatric Epidemiology* 45 (2010): 183–87.

16. Kathleen A. Lawler et al., "The Unique Effects of Forgiveness on Health: An Exploration of Pathways," *Journal of Behavioral Medicine* 28 (2005): 157–67, doi:10.1007/s10865-005-3665-2.

17. The Forgiveness Project (theforgivenessproject.com) was started by fellow journalist Marina Cantacuzino after she observed atrocities in Iraq to explore pathways beyond the dogma of vengeance. The nonprofit operates independently of any religious or political affiliations.

18. "We found that the more widows and widowers laughed and smiled during the early months after their spouse's death, the better their mental health was over the first two years of bereavement. In other words, people who showed genuine smiling or laughter when they talked about their loss coped better over time. Part of the reason for this health bonus is that laughing and smiling give us a break, a temporary respite from the

pain of loss; they allow us to come up for air, to breathe." *Other Side of Sadness*, 39.

19. Stanley A. Tan, Linda G. Tan, and Lee S. Berk, "Humor, as an Adjunct Therapy in Cardiac Rehabilitation, Attenuates Catecholamines and Myocardial Infarction Recurrence," *Advances in Mind-Body Medicine* 22 (2007): 8–12.

20. *Man's Search*, 43–44.

13. LOVE

1. The primary source for this chapter is an interview I conducted with Dr. Maya Angelou in November 2013. Her collected autobiographies and poems have been invaluable sources in understanding her childhood, her life, and her accomplishments. Dolly A. McPherson's *Order Out of Chaos* (New York: Peter Lang Publishing, 1990) provided additional insights. I also quote from two extensive interviews Oprah Winfrey conducted with her mentor Maya Angelou, specifically Oprah's "Master Class" from January 16, 2011, OWN (http://www.oprah.com/own -master-class/Oprah-Presents-Master-Class-with-Maya-Ange lou) and *O Magazine*, December 2000 (http://www.oprah.com /omagazine/Oprah-Interviews-Maya-Angelou) as well as a tribute by Bill Moyers.

2. From his speech at the 11th Convention of the Southern Christian Leadership Conference, August 16, 1967, in Atlanta, GA.

3. *Caged Bird*, 5.

4. Bill Moyers, "Maya Angelou on Facing Evil," Public Affairs Television, August 14, 2014.

5. "Master Class."

6. Ibid.

7. Maya Angelou, *The Collected Autobiographies of Maya Angelou* (New York: Random House, Modern Library), 49, Kindle edition.

8. "Master Class."

9. Azzam, "Handle with Care."

10. Ibid.

11. Michael Meaney, professor at McGill University in Montreal, pioneered the study of epigenetics, showing long-term genetic changes after neglect. He first showed that the level of care rats

received from their mothers altered the chemistry of the DNA in genes involved in stress response. Rats that were neglected as babies produced more stress hormones and were more fearful when encountering challenging situations as adults. He was later able to show a similar relationship between early childhood neglect and stress response in humans. See Patrick O. McGowan, Michael J. Meaney, et al., "Epigenetic Regulation of the Glucocorticoid Receptor in Human Brain Associates with Childhood Abuse," *Nature Neuroscience* 12 (2009): 342–48, doi:10.1038/nn.2270.

12. "Child abuse is a pervasive societal problem, with nearly one million substantiated reports of child maltreatment each year, many reported cases of actual abuse that are not verified, and countless other cases that never come to the attention of authorities. Although not all abused children develop difficulties, many experience a chronic course of psychopathology, with depression as one of the most common psychiatric sequelae reported in maltreated children." Kaufman et al., "Social Supports and Serotonin Transporter Gene Moderate Depression in Maltreated Children."

13. "Master Class."

14. Ibid.

15. *Ordinary Magic*, 7. Developmental psychologist Emmy Werner acknowledges, "For many years mental health professionals tended to focus almost exclusively on the negative effects of biological and psychosocial risk factors by reconstructing the life histories of individuals with persistent behavior disorders or serious emotional problems. . . . This retrospective approach created the impression that a poor developmental outcome is inevitable if a child is exposed to trauma, parental mental illness, alcoholism, or chronic family discord, since it examined only the lives of the 'casualties,' not the lives of the successful 'survivors.'" Emmy Werner, "Resilience and Recovery: Findings from the Kauai Longitudinal Study," *Focal Point Research, Policy, and Practice in Children's Mental Health* 19 (2005): 11–14.

16. Bazelon, "A Question of Resilience."

17. The effect of childhood poverty and physical abuse on resilience has been studied extensively by Norman Garmezy, "Children

in Poverty: Resilience Despite Risk," *Psychiatry* 56 (1993): 127–36; Suniya S. Luthar, "Vulnerability and Resilience: A Study of High-Risk Adolescents," *Child Development* 62 (1991): 600–16.

18. Studies that demonstrate the effect of intelligence on resilience in children include Ann S. Masten et al., "Competence in the Context of Adversity: Pathways to Resilience and Maladaptation from Childhood to Late Adolescence," *Development and Psychopathology* 11 (1999): 143–69; Ann Masten, Norman Garmezy, et al., "Competence and Stress in School Children: The Moderating Effects of Individual and Family Qualities," *Journal of Child Psychiatry* 29 (1988): 754–64.

    However, "resilience does not appear to require extraordinary intelligence." *Ordinary Magic*, 155.

19. Quoted from Brooks and Goldstein, *Power of Resilience*, 152.

20. Numerous studies evidenced that at-risk children with a history of abuse, neglect, and school failure "had risen above the hardship they encountered. . . . One of the most important factors these resilient individuals cited as helping them to become successful was having at least one adult who cared about and loved them when they were children." *Power of Resilience*, 152–53.

21. Azzam, "Handle with Care."

22. *Caged Bird*, 42. Quoted after *Order Out of Chaos*, 27.

23. "Master Class."

24. *Caged Bird, The Collected Autobiographies of Maya Angelou*, 74, Kindle edition.

25. *Caged Bird*, 236.

26. *O Magazine*.

27. "Master Class."

28. *O Magazine*.

29. Bill Moyers, "Maya Angelou on Facing Evil," Public Affairs Television, August 14, 2014.

30. Ibid.

31. "When we examined the links between individual dispositions and external sources of support, we discovered that the resilient men and women were not passively reacting to the constraints of negative circumstances. Instead, they actively sought out the people and opportunities that led to a positive

turnaround in their lives." Werner, "Resilience and Recovery." German psychologists came to near-identical conclusions in the Bielefelder Invulnerabilitätsstudie. They, too, found resilient children to be more extroverted, motivated, and active in confronting everyday problems. The resilient people impressed on them how to solve problems and learned early on to take responsibility for themselves and others. Doris Bender and Friedrich Lösel, "Protektive Faktoren der psychisch gesunden Entwicklung junger Menschen: Ein Beitrag zur Kontroverse um saluto- und pathogenetische Ansätze," in ed. Jürgen Margraf, Johannes Siegrist, and Simon Neumer, *Gesundheits—oder Krankheitstheorie?* (Berlin: Springer, 1998).

32. Werner, "Resilience and Recovery."
33. Ibid.
34. Ibid.
35. Bazelon, "A Question of Resilience."
36. Werner, "Resilience and Recovery."
37. "Planfulness, autonomy, and adult support outside the family appeared to play a role. Individual case data showed a variety of pathways toward resilience in these individuals, including moving away from troubled friends and families, formation of healthy romantic relationships, and a new job or educational opportunity.

    "Most of these cases were women, as observed also by Werner and Smith (1992) in the late bloomers among the children of Kauai." Ann S. Masten and Auke Tellegen, "Resilience in Developmental Psychopathology: Contributions of the Project Competence Longitudinal Study," *Development and Psychopathology* 24 (2012): 356.
38. "Master Class."
39. *Miss Calypso* was the title of her 1957 album. Shortly afterward and at the advice of her managers, she changed her formal name from Marguerite Johnson to Maya Angelou. Maya had been the nickname her brother Bailey had given her, and the last name was inspired by her first husband, Tosh Angelos.
40. Joan Kaufman and Edward Zigler, "Do Abused Children Become Abusive Parents?" *American Journal of Orthopsychiatry* 57 (1987): 186–92.

41. Buck Brannaman with William Reynolds. *The Faraway Horses* (Guilford, CT: Lyons Press, 2001), 228.

42. *Collected Autobiographies*, 672.

43. Ibid., 674.

44. *Order Out of Chaos*, 10–11.

45. *O Magazine*.

46. "On the Pulse of Morning" from *On the Pulse of Morning* by Maya Angelou, copyright © 1993 by Maya Angelou. Used by permission of Random House, an imprint and division of Penguin Random House LLC. All rights reserved.

47. "A Brave and Startling Truth" from *A Brave and Startling Truth* by Maya Angelou, copyright © 1995 by Maya Angelou. Used by permission of Random House, an imprint and division of Penguin Random House LLC. All rights reserved.

EPILOGUE

1. Jon Kabat-Zinn, "Meeting Pain with Awareness," *Mindful Magazine* 2011, http://www.mindful.org/in-body-and-mind/mindfulness-based-stress-reduction/meeting-pain-with-awareness.

2. "The Phoenix Again" from *The Silence Now: New and Uncollected Earlier Poems* by May Sarton, copyright © 1988 by May Sarton. Used by permission of W. W. Norton & Company, Inc.

GUIDE

1. Steve Paulson, Richard Davidson, Amishi Jha, and Jon Kabat-Zinn, "Becoming Conscious: The Science of Mindfulness," *Annals of the New York Academy of Sciences* 1303 (2013): 87–104, doi:10.1111/nyas.12203.

2. Zeidan et al., "Neural Correlates of Mindfulness Meditation-Related Anxiety Relief."

3. Richard J. Davidson et al., "Alterations in Brain and Immune Function Produced by Mindfulness Meditation," *Psychosomatic Medicine* 65 (2003), 564–70; Perla Kaliman et al., "Rapid Changes in Histone Deacetylases and Inflammatory Gene Expression in Expert Meditators," *Psychoneuroendocrinology* 40 (2014): 96–107; Linda Witek-Janusek et al., "Effect of Mind-

fulness Based Stress Reduction on Immune Function, Quality of Life and Coping in Women Newly Diagnosed with Early Stage Breast Cancer," *Brain, Behavior, and Immunity* 22 (2008): 969–81, doi:10.1016/j.bbi.2008.01.012.

4. Melissa A. Rosenkranz et al., "A Comparison of Mindfulness-Based Stress Reduction and an Active Control in Modulation of Neurogenic Inflammation," *Brain, Behavior, and Immunity* 27 (2013): 174–84.

5. Teresa I. Sivilli and Thaddeus W. W. Pace, "The Human Dimensions of Resilience," The Garrison Institute, 2014, http://www.academia.edu/8451583/The_Human_Dimensions_of_Resilience.

6. John D. Teasdale, "Metacognitive Awareness and Prevention of Relapse in Depression: Empirical Evidence," *Journal of Consulting and Clinical Psychology* 70 (2002): 275–87, doi:10.1037/0022-006X.70.2.275; Jacob Piet and Esben Hougaard, "The Effect of Mindfulness-based Cognitive Therapy for Prevention of Relapse in Recurrent Major Depressive Disorder: A Systematic Review and Meta-Analysis," *Clinical Psychology Review* 31 (2011): 1032–40, doi:10.1016/j.cpr.2011.05.002.

7. Paulson, Davidson, Jha, and Kabat-Zinn, "Becoming Conscious: The Science of Mindfulness."

8. I am primarily recommending MBSR because it is widely available in many cities and online and has been proven to be effective, but there are other renowned programs, such as Mindfulness-Based Cognitive Therapy (MBCT), Cognitively Based Compassion Training (CBCT), professional training programs rooted in contemplative practices (e.g., Cultivating Awareness and Resilience in Education [CARE]), Contemplative-Based Resilience Training (CBRT) by the Garrison Institute, and many more.

9. Robert A. Emmons and Michael E. McCullough, "Counting Blessings Versus Burdens: An Experimental Investigation of Gratitude and Subjective Well-Being in Daily Life," *Journal of Personality and Social Psychology* 84 (2003): 377–89, doi:10.1037/0022-3514.84.2.377. Emmons's website offers additional exercises and research: www.greatergood.berkeley.edu/author/Robert_Emmons.

10. Alex M. Wood, Stephen Joseph, Joanna Lloyd, and Samuel Atkins, "Gratitude Influences Sleep through the Mechanism of Pre-sleep Cognitions," *Journal of Psychosomatic Research* 66 (2009): 43–48.

11. Philip C. Watkins, Kathrane Woodward, Tamara Stone, and Russell L. Kolts, "Gratitude and Happiness: Development of a Measure of Gratitude, and Relationships with Subjective Well-Being," *Social Behavior and Personality* 31 (2003): 431–51; Alex M. Wood, Jeffrey J. Froh, and Adam W. A. Geraghty, "Gratitude and Well-Being: A Review and Theoretical Integration," *Clinical Psychology Review* 30 (2010): 890–905; Kennon M. Sheldon and Sonja Lyubomirsky, "How to Increase and Sustain Positive Emotion: The Effects of Expressing Gratitude and Visualizing Best Possible Selves," *Journal of Positive Psychology* 1 (2006): 73–82; Ursula Nuber, "Wieder schätzen lernen, was man hat," *Psychologie Heute Compact* 32 (2012): 44.

12. Seligman gives a concise description in *Flourish*, 33ff.

13. www.gratefulness.org.

14. For inspiration, watch the gratitude video: www.youtube.com /watch?v=oHv6vTKD6lg.

15. Martin E. P. Seligman, Tracy A. Steen, Nansook Park, and Christopher Peterson. "Positive Psychology Progress: Empirical Validation of Interventions," *American Psychologist* 60 (2005): 410-421; Sonja Lyubomirsky and Kristin Layous, "How Do Simple Positive Activities Increase Well-Being?" *Current Directions in Psychological Science* 22 (2013): 57–62.

16. Kristin D. Neff and Katie A. Dahm, "Self-Compassion: What It Is, What It Does, and How It Relates to Mindfulness," in *Handbook of Mindfulness and Self-Regulation*, ed. Brian D. Ostafin, Brian P. Meier, and Michael D. Robinson (New York: Springer, 2015).

17. Ibid.

18. Sharon Salzberg and Tenzin Robert Thurman, *Love Your Enemies* (Carlsbad: Hay House, 2013), xiii.

19. I thank Emma Seppälä, the associate director of the Stanford University Center for Compassion and Altruism Research and Education, for alerting me to this research in her illuminating writings, for instance her overview "18 Science-Based Reasons

to Try Loving-Kindness Meditation," *Huffington Post*, September 17, 2014.

20. Barbara Fredrickson et al., "Open Hearts Build Lives: Positive Emotions, Induced through Loving-Kindness Meditation, Build Consequential Personal Resources," *Journal of Personality and Social Psychology* 95 (2008): 1045–1462, doi:10.1037 /a0013262.

21. David J. Kearney et al., "Loving-Kindness Meditation for Posttraumatic Stress Disorder: A Pilot Study," *Journal of Traumatic Stress* 26 (2013): 426–34, doi:10.1002/jts.21832.

22. Olga Klimecki, Susanne Leiberg, Matthieu Ricard, and Tania Singer, "Differential Pattern of Functional Brain Plasticity after Compassion and Empathy Training," *Social Cognitive and Affective Neuroscience* 9 (2014): 873–79.

23. Yoona Kang, Jeremy R. Gray, and John F. Dovidio, "The Nondiscriminating Heart: Lovingkindness Meditation Training Decreases Implicit Intergroup Bias," *Journal of Experimental Psychology* 143 (2014): 1306–13, doi:10.1037/a0034150.

24. Cendri A. Hutcherson, Emma M. Seppälä, and James J. Gross, "Loving-Kindness Meditation Increases Social Connectedness," *Emotion* 8 (2008): 720–24, doi:10.1037/a0013237.

25. Michael A. Cohn and Barbara L. Fredrickson, "In Search of Durable Positive Psychology Interventions: Predictors and Consequences of Long-Term Positive Behavior Change," *Journal of Positive Psychology* 5 (2010): 355–66, doi:10.1080 /17439760.2010.508883.

26. Antoine Lutz et al., "Regulation of the Neural Circuitry of Emotion by Compassion Meditation: Effects of Meditative Expertise," *PLoS ONE* 3 (2008): e1897.

27. This exercise is inspired by Brooks and Goldstein's advice. See *Power of Resilience*, chapter 7.

28. In their meta-analysis, Prati and Petrantoni speak of "social support as a key environmental resource . . . for understanding positive outcomes of life crises and transitions. In addition, Tedeschi and Calhoun's . . . revised model of posttraumatic growth includes social support as a predictor of positive change in the aftermath of traumatic events." Prati and Pietrantoni, "Optimism, Social Support, and Coping Strategies."

29. James A. Coan, Hillary S. Schaefer, and Richard J. Davidson, "Lending a Hand: Social Regulation of the Neural Response to Threat," *Psychological Science* 17 (2006): 1032–39.

30. Marta Scrignaro, Sandro Barni, and Maria E. Magrin, "The Combined Contribution of Social Support and Coping Strategies in Predicting Post-Traumatic Growth: a Longitudinal Study on Cancer Patients," *Psycho-Oncology* 20 (2011): 823–31, doi:10.1002/pon.1782.

31. "A great deal of correlational research has shown that individuals with more social support experience less cancer pain (Zaza & Baine, 2002), are less at risk for back pain (Hoogendoorn, van Poppel, Bongers, Koes, & Bouter, 2000), take less pain medication, are less likely to suffer from chest pain following coronary artery bypass surgery (King, Reis, Porter, & Norsen, 1993; Kulik & Mahler, 1989), report less labor pain, and are less likely to use epidural anesthesia during childbirth (Chalmers, Wolman, Nikodem, Gulmezoglu, & Hofmeyer, 1995; Kennell, Klaus, McGrath, Robertson, & Hinkley, 1991)." Naomi I. Eisenberger and Matthew D. Lieberman, "Why It Hurts to Be Left Out: The Neurocognitive Overlap Between Physical and Social Pain," in *The Social Outcast: Ostracism, Social Exclusion, Rejection, and Bullying*, ed. Kipling D. Williams, Joseph P. Forgas, and William von Hippel (New York: Cambridge University Press, 2005), 109–27.

32. James S. House, Karl R. Landis, and Debra Umberson, "Social Relationships and Health," *Science* 241 (1988): 540–45, doi:10.1126/science.3399889.

33. Coan, Schaefer, and Davidson, "Lending a Hand."

34. George E. Vaillant, "What Are the Secrets to a Happy Life?" *Greater Good*, October 23, 2013.

35. Craig Lambert, "The Talent for Aging Well," *Harvard Magazine*, March–April 2001, http://harvardmagazine.com/2001/03/the-talent-for-aging-wel-html.

36. *Power of Resilience*, 165.

37. Sara Konrath, Andrea Fuhrel-Forbis, Alina Lou, and Stephanie Brown, "Motives for Volunteering Are Associated with Mortality Risk in Older Adults," *Health Psychology* 31 (2012): 87–96.

38. Elizabeth W. Dunn, Lara B. Aknin, and Michael I. Norton, "Prosocial Spending and Happiness: Using Money to Benefit Others Pays Off," *Current Directions in Psychological Science* 13 (2014): 347–55.

39. Lara B. Aknin, J. Kiley Hamlin, and Elizabeth W. Dunn, "Giving Leads to Happiness in Young Children," *PLoS ONE* 7 (2012): e39211, doi:10.1371/journal.pone.0039211.

40. *Flourish*, 20.

Bibliography

Angelou, Maya. *The Collected Autobiographies of Maya Angelou*. New York: Random House, 2012. Kindle edition.

———. *I Know Why the Caged Bird Sings*. New York: Ballantine Books, 2009.

Bonanno, George A. *The Other Side of Sadness*. New York: Basic Books, 2009.

Brand, Paul, and Philip Yancey. *The Gift of Pain*. Grand Rapids, MI: Zondervan, 1997.

Brannaman, Buck, with William Reynolds. *The Faraway Horses*. Guilford, CT: Lyons Press, 2001.

Brooks, Robert, and Sam Goldstein. *The Power of Resilience: Achieving Balance, Confidence, and Personal Strength in Your Life*. New York: McGraw-Hill, 2004.

———. *Raising Resilient Children: Fostering Strength, Hope, and Optimism in Your Child*. New York: McGraw-Hill, 2001.

Burstyn, Ellen. *Lessons in Becoming Myself*. New York: Penguin, 2007. Kindle edition.

Calhoun, Lawrence G., and Richard G. Tedeschi. *Posttraumatic Growth in Clinical Practice*. New York: Routledge, 2013. Kindle edition.

Chödrön, Pema. *When Things Fall Apart*. Boston: Shambhala Publications, 2002.

Cornum, Rhonda, and Peter Copeland. *She Went to War*. Novato: Presidio, 1992.

Cousins, Norman. *Head First: The Biology of Hope and the Healing Power of the Human Spirit*. New York: Penguin, 1989.

Damasio, Antonio. *Descartes' Error: Emotion, Reason, and the Human Brain*. New York: Penguin, 1994.

Dweck, Carol. *Mindset: The New Psychology of Success*. New York: Random House, 2006.

Emmons, Robert. *Gratitude Works! A 21-Day Program for Creating Emotional Prosperity*. San Francisco: Jossey-Bass, 2013.

Frankl, Viktor E. *Man's Search for Meaning*. Boston: Beacon Press, 1959.

Fredrickson, Barbara. *Positivity: Top-Notch Research Reveals the 3-to-1 Ratio That Will Change Your Life*. New York: Harmony, 2009.

Giffords, Gabrielle, and Mark Kelly (with Jeffrey Zaslow). *Gabby: A Story of Courage and Hope*. New York: Scribner, 2011. Kindle edition.

Gladwell, Malcolm. *David and Goliath: Underdogs, Misfits, and the Art of Battling Giants*. New York: Little, Brown and Company, 2013.

Glassman, Bernie. *Bearing Witness: A Zen Master's Lessons in Making Peace*. New York: Blue Rider Press, 1998. Kindle edition.

Glassman, Bernie, and Rick Fields. *Instructions to the Cook: A Zen Master's Lessons in Living a Life That Matters*. Boston: Shambhala, 2013.

Graham, Linda. *Bouncing Back: Rewiring Your Brain for Maximum Resilience and Well-Being*. Novato: New World Library, 2013.

Grandin, Temple. *Thinking in Pictures*. New York: Vintage Books, 1995.

Grandin, Temple, and Catherine Johnson. *Animals in Translation*. New York: Houghton Mifflin Harcourt, 2005.

Grandin, Temple, and Richard Panek. *The Autistic Brain: Thinking Across the Spectrum*. New York: Houghton Mifflin Harcourt, 2013. Kindle edition.

Helmreich, William B. *Against All Odds: Holocaust Survivors and the Successful Lives They Made in America*. Piscataway, NJ: Transaction Publishers, 1995.

Herman, Judith L. *Trauma and Recovery: The Aftermath of Violence—from Domestic Abuse to Political Terror*. New York: Basic Books, 1997.

Joseph, Stephen. *What Doesn't Kill Us: The New Psychology of Posttraumatic Growth*. New York: Basic Books, 2011. Kindle edition.

Kabat-Zinn, Jon. *Full Catastrophe Living: Using the Wisdom of Your Body and Mind to Face Stress, Pain, and Illness*. New York: Bantam Books, 2013.

Kahneman, Daniel. *Thinking, Fast and Slow*. New York: Farrar, Straus and Giroux, 2013.

Konieczny, Vladimir. *Glenn Gould: A Musical Force.* Toronto: Dundurn Press, 2009.

Lamott, Anne. *Stitches. A Handbook on Meaning, Hope and Repair.* New York: Riverhead Books, 2013.

Lerner, Barron H. *One for the Road: Drunk Driving Since 1900.* Baltimore: The Johns Hopkins University Press, 2011.

Levine, Peter A. *In an Unspoken Voice: How the Body Releases Trauma and Restores Goodness.* Berkeley: North Atlantic Books, 2010.

Mandela, Nelson. *Long Walk to Freedom.* New York: Hachette, 2008. Kindle edition.

Masten, Ann S. *Ordinary Magic: Resilience in Development.* New York: Guilford Press, 2014.

McPherson, Dolly A. *Order Out Of Chaos: The Autobiographical Works of Maya Angelou.* New York: Virago Press, 1990.

Merton, Thomas. *The Seven Storey Mountain.* San Diego: Harcourt Brace, 1999.

Padgett, Jason, and Maureen Ann Seaberg. *Struck by Genius: How a Brain Injury Made Me a Mathematical Marvel.* New York: Houghton Mifflin Harcourt, 2014.

Reeve, Christopher. *Still Me.* New York: Random House, 1998.

Reivich, Karen, and Andrew Shatté. *The Resilience Factor: 7 Keys to Finding Your Inner Strength and Overcoming Life's Hurdles.* New York: Broadway Books, 2002. Kindle edition.

Rinpoche, Yongey Mingyur, and Eric Swanson. *Joyful Wisdom: Embracing Change and Finding Freedom.* New York: Harmony, 2009.

Salzberg, Sharon. *Lovingkindness: The Revolutionary Art of Happiness.* Boston: Shambhala, 2002.

Salzberg, Sharon, and Robert Thurman. *Love Your Enemies: How to Break the Anger Habit and Be a Whole Lot Happier.* Carlsbad, CA: Hay House, 2013.

Sarton, May. *The Silence Now: New and Uncollected Earlier Poems.* New York: W. W. Norton, 1988.

Schumann, Coco, Max Christian Graeff, and Michaela Haas (eds). *Der Ghetto-Swinger: Eine Jazzlegende erzahlt.* Munich: DTV, 1997.

Segal, Julius. *Winning Life's Toughest Battles.* New York: Ivy Books, 1987.

Seligman, Martin E. P. *Flourish: A Visionary New Understanding of Happiness and Well-being.* New York: Atria, 2013.

Strayed, Cheryl. *Tiny Beautiful Things: Advice on Love and Life from Dear Sugar.* New York: Vintage Books, 2012.

Weiss, Tzipi, and Roni Berger. *Posttraumatic Growth and Culturally Competent Practice: Lessons Learned from Around the Globe.* Hoboken, NJ: John Wiley & Sons, 2010.

Zolli, Andrew, and Ann Marie Healy. *Resilience: Why Things Bounce Back.* New York: Free Press, 2012.

Permissions

The following are the captions and permissions for the photographs used in this book.

1. Survive: Rhonda Cornum with her Gordon setter puppy on her farm in Kentucky. © Michaela Haas.
2. Grow: Psychologist Richard Tedeschi at the University of North Carolina at Charlotte. © Michaela Haas.
3. Dig Deep: Resilience expert Karen Reivich tries to instill positive thinking in the army. © Michaela Haas.
4. Play: Jazz legend Coco Schumann decided he either could live the rest of his life being broken by Auschwitz or be joyful that he survived. © Archiv Coco Schumann.
5. Accept: Author Michaela Haas finds mindfulness meditation to be a powerful method for facing pain with awareness. © Gayle M. Landes.
6. Thrive: Meggie Zahneis is the Cincinnati Reds' "most valuable player." © Michaela Haas.
7. Pray: Alain Beauregard enjoys the sun at Hermosa Beach, California. © Michaela Haas.
8. Evolve: Animal behaviorist Temple Grandin at her ranch in Colorado. © Rosalie Winard.
9. Breathe: Roshi Bernie Glassman realizes that healing can arise from bearing witness. © Peter Cunningham.
10. Adrenalize: Rick Allen's life changed after he started reaching out to fellow amputees. © Damian Dovarganes/AP/Corbis.
11. Shine: "Life Rolls On" for Jesse Billauer at Surfrider Beach in Malibu, California. © Catherine Gregory.

12. Forgive: Cindi Lamb in front of the house at Chesapeake Bay, where she spent the last months with her daughter Laura. © Michaela Haas.

13. Love: The biography of "phenomenal woman" Maya Angelou reads like a course book for posttraumatic growth. © Rob DeLorenzo/ZUMA Press/Corbis.

A Conversation with
Michaela Haas

How did you come up with the title *Bouncing Forward*?

The title is a nod to civil rights icon Dr. Maya Angelou. She defines defying hardships as "bouncing forward, going beyond what the naysayers say." I had the privilege of interviewing her for this book. Hearing her tell her story of overcoming such deep childhood trauma to become an international voice in effectuating positive change touched me deeply.

What does this term "posttraumatic growth" actually mean?

Posttraumatic growth refers to the benefit we can derive from experiencing a crisis. Almost every trauma survivor I spoke with thought, at first, that they could never lead a happy life again. But the science of posttraumatic growth offers an entirely new perspective of trauma and plenty of healing strategies. This perspective of the growth mindset makes a tremendous difference: if you show people how they can grow, you increase the chance that they will.

According to Richard Tedeschi, posttraumatic growth's leading researcher, as many as 90 percent of survivors report at least *one* aspect of posttraumatic growth, such as a renewed appreciation for life or a deeper connection to their heart's purpose. This does not happen immediately or easily, and rarely does it happen by itself.

It is crucial for people to know that a trauma does not have to be a life sentence, and that it can be a catalyst for positive growth. People might at first believe talking about growth in this context means whitewashing trauma, but in researching this book, I have learned that trauma can transform us in positive ways when we acknowledge it and face the pain.

What are the five main areas of growth that trauma survivors experience?

1. A majority of trauma survivors report finding a new appreciation for life.
2. Relationships deepen, we find out who our true friends are, and we become more compassionate to the suffering of others.
3. A third area of change is our own strength, knowing our resilience.
4. Many people find new opportunities and meaning that they wouldn't otherwise have explored.
5. Spiritual progress and a new spiritual connection.

"We are stronger than we think"—what do you mean by that?

When I first began the research, I thought resilience was rare and that only a few really strong people thrive after trauma. But, actually, posttraumatic growth is much more common than PTSD. The research surprised me, too! We are so vulnerable, and yet so strong at the same time. Posttraumatic growth does not mean that there is no pain. It is the struggle that acts as a force to find a new meaning and build a resilient life.

Can you tell us a bit about Rhonda Cornum and her story?

Rhonda was an army flight surgeon serving in Iraq when her helicopter was shot down. She was badly injured, with two broken arms. She was taken hostage by the Iraqis, sexually assaulted, and detained for seven days. When asked about her experience and how traumatized she was, Rhonda responded that she was not traumatized. This, of course, astounded questioners. She said her experience of being totally helpless had helped her to understand what other people are going through, and that it made her a better doctor, a better soldier, a better person. This is a stunning example of post-traumatic growth, but it wasn't until about a decade later that she realized there were actually proven methods and scientific research to help train people to grow from such harrowing experiences. Therefore, she started a comprehensive program that teaches resilience to every soldier in the US Army. Rather than just treat soldiers for trauma *after* they return from war, she reasoned, wouldn't it be so much better to prepare them *before* they deploy?

What can we as civilians learn from this training?

The strategies that work in a military crisis situation are really not that different from those we can apply to civilian life. In fact, many of the soldiers I spoke with told me the resilience training helps them every day at home. It teaches skills such as:

- Honest and skillful communication
- Learning to keep calm under stress
- Realistic optimism instead of catastrophizing
- Asking for help
- Mindfulness and meditation

Who else is in the book?

I only included people in the book I deeply admire—for instance, autistic pioneer Temple Grandin, who turned a so-called handicap into an advantage; Def Leppard's "Thunder God" Rick Allen, who devotes much of his time to helping other amputees; Zen master Roshi Bernie Glassman, who takes people to the places they fear; MADD founder Cindi Lamb, who found forgiveness for the man who killed her daughter; and business consultant Alain Beauregard, who was diagnosed with terminal cancer. There are twelve inspiring stories of people who emerged from these experiences stronger, wiser, and more compassionate. I also spoke with the psychologists and pioneers of posttraumatic growth to highlight what those of us who aren't naturally resilient can learn in order to face tough situations well and what exactly it is that makes some people grow in the midst of adversity.

Can you talk about Jesse Billauer a little bit?

Everyone loves Jesse! Jesse is an exceptional athlete who was about to become a pro surfer. When he was seventeen a wave threw him headfirst into a sandbank in Malibu. He is paralyzed from the chest down, but that does not stop him from going back into the ocean. He now surfs with the help of a motorized surfboard. He surfs big waves in Fiji, dives with sharks, goes skydiving. Through his nonprofit organization, Life Rolls On, he helps other paralyzed surf and skate enthusiasts get back into the game.

Hardly anything irks trauma survivors more than statements such as, "Maybe something good will come out of it." How is the science of posttraumatic growth different?

One thing that has become very clear is that glossing over trauma is counterproductive. Posttraumatic growth requires us to face the struggle and tend to the wounds. The pain is the catalyst for the growth. We need to integrate what happened into our life story. The good only comes from what we decide to do with it—from our *struggle*, which unveils what needs to change in us and in our society; from honing our ability to make meaning out of events that seem senseless; from not trying to rebuild an exact replica of what was lost, but to engineer a stronger, sturdier foundation for our life.

One of the best things we can do is to connect with other people who have been through something tough. This is, in fact, what I am offering with *Bouncing Forward*. Here we meet people who are not afraid to talk honestly about their struggles along with their insights. The book is to help people see the possibilities of growth.

What was the personal motivation for you to write this book?

My grandfather contracted polio when he was only six months old. He was physically handicapped, but he was one of the most dynamic, loving, and lovable people you could ever meet. He made a big imprint on my life. As a reporter, I often interviewed people who had been through something hard, and I always wondered why some people break down while others not only survive, but thrive. For instance, the Tibetan refugees I studied with in Nepal had lost everything—their homeland, their families, their health—and yet they were some of the most content, cheerful people I have ever met. What makes the difference? This question became deeply personal when I got quite ill in my twenties. I had thought of myself as resilient, but when I was bedridden for eight months, I was shocked by how badly I coped with it. So I started researching what others had found helpful.

Can you share a bit about your story?

When I was studying in Nepal in my twenties, I got so ill I could hardly get out of bed or keep any food down. I went back to France, where my husband lived at the time, and the doctors there tested me for brain tumors, multiple sclerosis, everything under the sun. I got increasingly scared. I was so weak that I couldn't even go to the mailbox. And then I found out that my husband was cheating on me, at a time when I needed him the most. I call the years that followed "my years in hell," because everything just went downhill from there. I was perpetually at the wrong place at the wrong time. Eventually I moved back to Germany, where I'm from, and slowly reassembled the pieces of my life. But I never reclaimed my health completely, and I had to readjust my priorities and make big changes.

How did you put your life back together?

Step by step. Not being able to do a lot physically, I had to tune into the internal resilience of my mind. That is where Buddhist meditation really helped me to be present with what is and to work through the pain with compassion. I couldn't change many of the external conditions, but I could change my attitude and how I dealt with it. The illness forced me to readjust my priorities and to rewrite the script of my life in major ways.

What is the main takeaway for readers of this book?

Don't give up! For this book I have interviewed people who have experienced things that I don't think I could survive. But they did survive, and emerged with tremendous insight and wisdom. Maybe heroes such as Nelson Mandela and Malala Yousafzai were born with an extra dose of courage, but we must not underestimate how we are all hardwired for survival and resilience. It is my hope that readers of *Bouncing Forward* will learn that many of our common notions about trauma are simply not true. We belittle survivors if we predict that they will fail. The purpose of *Bouncing Forward* is to show how we can support them and help them heal. *Bouncing Forward* highlights more than sixty strategies survivors have found helpful, from reconnecting with our bodies to finding forgiveness.

What would you say is the recipe to overcome trauma?

Every person is different, and we all have to find our own recipe. But the ingredients turn out to be surprisingly similar. The number one thing is to acknowledge the trauma and to connect with others instead of isolating ourselves. Nobody can do it alone. We often think no one else can comprehend our pain, but the truth is that there is always someone we can reach out to. Scouting for allies, deepening our compassion, and helping others emerge as common threads.

What are some exercises that can help?

Meditation has proven to counteract the effects of trauma. With mindfulness meditation and breathing exercises, we can reduce anxiety and handle stress better. We can literally rewire our brains and heal our hearts. Shame and guilt are among the most common feelings after trauma, so the healing process has to start with love toward ourselves. This book contains a brief guide with effective meditation exercises that anyone can do, including loving-kindness for ourselves and a gratitude practice. It sounds deceptively simple, but it truly makes a difference.

About the Author

Michaela Haas is a reporter, lecturer, and consultant. With a PhD in Asian studies, she has taught at the University of California, Santa Barbara; the University of the West; and study centers in America and Europe. Since the age of sixteen, she has worked as a writer and interviewer for major European newspapers, magazines, and TV stations, including hosting numerous successful live talk shows. She is the owner of HAAS live!, an international coaching company that specializes in media and mindfulness training. She has been practicing Buddhist meditation for twenty years and combines powerful storytelling with scientific research and spiritual depth. Michaela divides her time between Malibu, California, and Munich, Germany. Visit MichaelaHaas.com.

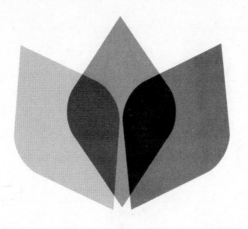

ENLIVEN™

About Our Books: We are the world's first holistic publisher for mission-driven authors. We curate, create, collaborate on, and commission sophisticated, fresh titles and voices to enhance your spiritual development, success, and wellness pursuits.

About Our Vision: Our authors are the voice of empowerment, creativity, and spirituality in the twenty-first century. You, our readers, are brilliant seekers of adventure, unexpected stories, and tools to transform yourselves and your world. Together, we are change-makers on a mission to increase literacy, uplift humanity, ignite genius, and create reasons to gather around books. We think of ourselves as instigators of soulful exchange.

Welcome to the wondrous world of Enliven Books, a new imprint from Zhena Muzyka, author of *Life by the Cup: Inspiration for a Purpose-Filled Life*, and Atria, an imprint of Simon & Schuster, Inc.

To explore our list of books and learn about fresh new voices in the realm of Mind-Body-Spirit, please visit us at

EnlivenBooks.com | **/EnlivenBooks**